ANTI-AGING CURES

ANTI-AGING CURES

LIFE CHANGING SECRETS TO REVERSE THE EFFECTS OF AGING

Your Key to the REAL Fountain of Youth

BY JAMES W. FORSYTHE, MD, HMD

FOREWORD BY SUZANNE SOMERS

Vanguard Press
A Member of the Perseus Books Group

Published by Vanguard Press,

A Member of the Perseus Books Group

Books published by Vanguard Press are available at special discounts for bulk purchases in the United States by corporations, institutions, and other organizations. For more information, please contact the Special Markets Department at the Perseus Books Group, 2300 Chestnut Street, Suite 200, Philadelphia, PA 19103, or call (800) 810-4145, extension 5000, or e-mail special.markets@perseusbooks.com.

Editorial production by Lori Hobkirk at the Book Factory.

Designed by Anita Koury.

Cataloging-in-Publication Data is available at the Library of Congress

ISBN-13: 978-0-984-430-734

The information in this book is intended for educational purposes only. The content of this book should not be considered medical advice or counsel. If you have questions about your health, then please consult your physician. This book should not be used as a substitute for medical help. Opinions provided here are those of the author and do not necessarily represent the opinions of the medical societies of which he is a member.

10 9 8 7 6 5 4 3 2 1

From James and Earlene Forsythe:
To our children Marc, Michele, Lisa, Pompeo, and Sarah,
and their children—our grandchildren—
Kiley, Clayton, Teson, Previn, Sebastian, and Luke.
May their lives be enhanced by our work.

Contents

Foreword

by Suzanne Somers

JAMES FORSYTHE IS MY DEAR FRIEND. HE IS A KIND, SOFT-SPOKEN MAN with a profound understanding of true cutting-edge health and wellness.

We met a few years ago when I interviewed him for my book, *Knockout: Doctors Who Are Curing Cancer*. From the beginning, he had always been at the top of my list of Western doctors I wanted to interview. He is one of the brave ones, a doctor who has chosen to integrate orthodox Western medicine with alternative approaches. In other words, he combines the best of both worlds, showing how it all can work together to create true health, disease management, and anti-aging.

I had long heard of patients making miraculous turnarounds in their health under the care of Dr. Forsythe, whether their health issue was cancer or the normal ravages of aging. I asked him why he got his homeopathic license when he was already one of the country's leading oncologists. He said, "So I could build up my patients nutritionally and stimulate their immune systems to work at optimum."

Over the years in treating cancer patients, Dr. Forsythe recognized the amazing anti-aging benefits of hormonal, nutritional, and other biochemical protocols. Now he wants to share his discoveries with the world.

I believe in Dr. James Forsythe's approach to health and aging. It is very much in sync with my philosophy and message. I am proud to present his pivotal book, which is destined to serve as an essential anti-aging health guide for many generations to come.

As you will read, Dr. Forsythe is widely respected as a medical professional who has won well-deserved praise for his courageous and cutting-edge work, ensuring that the public can have access to the advantages and health benefits of injectable human growth hormone and other natural cures for aging.

He explains and demystifies in this step-by-step, easy to understand, informative, and readable guide that human growth hormone, along with other natural biostimulators, can delay or even stop the impacts of the aging process while also improving your health. This book is the ultimate user's guide, showing how to use legally prescribed human growth hormone and related products in a natural and safe anti-aging regimen.

You will also read the shocking and documented true-life saga of Dr. Forsythe's battle against bogus criminal charges by the federal government. His story makes his determination in bringing this life-saving, anti-aging information to the public even more compelling.

What happened to Dr. Forsythe is not only unfair and shocking, but if it were a novel by, say, best-selling author John Grisham, it would certainly fly off bookshelves. This book chronicles those details firsthand, straight from the one who endured our government's horrific prosecution attempt.

Throughout our nation's history, pivotal leaders have fought tough and diligent battles to preserve our rights and freedoms. Everyone from presidents Washington and Lincoln to women such as Betsy Ross, Clara Barton, and Abigail Smith Adams, has played integral roles in protecting the lifestyles we can enjoy today, many working behind the scenes.

Dr. Forsythe's work has always interested me. For the last fifteen years, I have been an outspoken advocate of bioidentical hormone replacement therapy. My twenty books sing the praises of restoration through replacement of declining or missing vital hormones. Without question, Dr. Forsythe is one of my teachers and reigns among the medical professionals who have played an important role in understanding that replacement is vital for optimal health and vitality.

Dr. Forsythe and his wife, Earlene, rank as courageous pioneers in the field of medicine. They are fearless. They believe in true health and that aging can be a happy and quality-filled experience. Even if you have never heard of them until now, their positive legacy is likely to endure for reasons you'll soon discover in the pages that follow.

Suzanne Somers is the voice and face of anti-aging medicine. Her twenty books—most of which are New York Times *best sellers—are focused on achieving and maintaining peak health by utilizing integrative and alternative protocols. Ms. Somers is the recipient of many prestigious awards in the fields of medicine and science. She lectures extensively in the United States and abroad.*

Acknowledgments

THIS BOOK BECAME POSSIBLE THANKS TO THE DEDICATED ASSISTANCE and encouragement of our entire office medical staff at Century Wellness.

Reno R. Rollé envisioned and developed this publication with the invaluable assistance of publishing expert William Gladstone and editor Randall Fitzgerald.

For their support and dedication, credit also goes to Dr. Burton Goldberg, the "voice of alternative medicine"; Joseph E. Brown of Perfect Balance; and Albert Sanchez, PhD, of AMARC. Wayne Rollan Melton and Nancy Padron helped put this project together in a cohesive form in order to ensure that readers learn essential aspects of our personal story and vital medical information integral to this book. Patty Atcheson-Melton, along with her partner, Margie Enlow, contributed exceptional creativity, patience, and persistence. Transcriptionist Diane Comstock became crucial, thanks to her keen ability at fact-checking while reviewing integral medical terminology.

Professional guidance and endorsement credit is given to the American Academy of Anti-Aging Medicine. Special thanks also go to "rock stars" in A4M, including Robert Goldman, MD, Ronald Klatz, MD, Ronald Rothenberg, MD, and Mark Gordon, MD.

INTRODUCTION

We All Need
Anti-Aging Cures

YOU'VE PROBABLY HEARD THE OLD EXPRESSION "NOTHING IS CERTAIN but death and taxes." We all grow old. We develop health problems. Then we die. That's the certainty we've been taught to expect. We're told that aging and all of the painful and unsightly symptoms associated with aging are unavoidable conditions that must simply be endured.

But I am here to tell you that from my own personal and professional experience, what you've been told about aging and what you may believe are no longer true! For the first time in human history, thanks to a series of recent breakthrough discoveries by medical science that uncovered the biochemical key to aging, you can virtually stop and even reverse the aging process.

You can do this naturally! You can do it quickly! You can do it without spending money like a millionaire! You can do it in the privacy of your own home! The key is to stimulate production or replacement of the "Master Hormone" in your body. I will tell you all about that natural hormone and how to supplement it in ways that achieve the greatest possible positive effects for your body.

There is another old saying, "Youth is wasted on the young." We've all wished that we could go back to a younger time with all of the wisdom we have accumulated with advancing age. Medical science is showing us how to actually begin to make that dream possible through the science of age deceleration using bioidentical blueprinting. It works with the biochemistry of your body.

Aging and most of the medical conditions resulting from it occur because of declining amounts of human growth hormone, a life force substance naturally generated by the human body but in rapidly declining amounts as you get older. It's manufactured by your pituitary gland, which is about the size of your thumbnail and can be found in your head, right between your eyes.

There exists an arsenal of previously secret bioidentical blueprinting weapons that are now at your disposal to combat the ravages of aging caused by this hormone decline. I call this protective arsenal the biostimulators—the natural products proven to enhance your biological response to the aging process. Bioidentical chemistry enables you to match in present time the blueprint of how your body was programmed to work when you were twenty-five years of age.

Some of these natural cures for aging involve making a few simple lifestyle choices if you are in your twenties, thirties, and forties, which I will detail in these pages. They involve the use of ancient health remedies, such as deer antler velvet and royal jelly, whose effectiveness and wide range of uses have been rediscovered by medical science. I will also tell you about new innovations using proprietary formulas that take advantage of the latest anti-aging research. And I will describe for you the important role of sleep in slowing down the aging process, an overlooked factor that when combined with changes in your beliefs and attitudes about aging, can dramatically influence the entire aging process.

A second approach, what I refer to as the "silver bullet," involves getting a prescription for this miracle growth hormone, with its special delivery system, that will revitalize you once you reach your fifties and beyond. I will provide you with all of the details about how to use it and acquire it, and answer all of your questions, when you are ready to introduce this natural cure into your life.

Through publication of this book, I am launching a worldwide crusade to tell health care consumers the truth about the many benefits of these amazing, natural biostimulator substances. I feel motivated by an urgent sense of responsibility to tell everyone that human growth hormone—particularly the injectable kind, used under proper medical supervision—can treat numerous medical conditions and increase the quality of your life during your mature years, while making you look and feel younger.

Despite government attempts to prevent you from discovering the many revolutionary benefits of this natural hormone, including an attempt to silence me and prevent me from sharing its secrets, these scientifically proven miracles of anti-aging can no longer be hidden from you. Many standard-medicine physicians undoubtedly will become upset that we're divulging the truth here, because in some instances consumers might actually find themselves needing the services of these physicians less and less as they use biostimulators more and more.

Big Pharma would also love to suppress the information you're receiving. The reason is simple. It's all about money. How much money will the mainstream medical industry lose as an anti-aging lifestyle and the use of legally prescribed human growth hormone and related biostimulators increase in popularity? If you're no longer suffering from memory loss, if you're enjoying greater vitality, improved organ functions, and a heightened libido, you're not going to need all of those pharmaceutical drugs and physician visits and care that you might ordinarily need. That translates into billions of dollars in lost income for the vested interests. This is one of the reasons that the giant pharmaceutical companies and the conventional medical industry tried—with government help—to close my clinic, put me in prison, and ruin my reputation.

But with this book, Big Pharma's loss is your gain because access to this natural hormone is an opportunity for you to experience greater health and vitality—and in the process, lower your health care costs—during all stages of your life.

What This Book Gives You

Anti-Aging Cures will reveal the natural and affordable substances that you can utilize to biostimulate your biological blueprint to look and feel young again. You'll learn in these pages the basics of growth hormone and its use in easy-to-understand terms. You'll learn where, in nature, this vital substance is found, how it is produced, and why we need it to grow as children and later as adults to maintain youthful vigor.

You'll discover how to readily make some lifestyle choices to facilitate your control over the aging process. These are simple yet powerful, natural techniques. Some are ancient and have been proven safe through generations of use, while others are relatively recent discoveries with clinical evidence to support their use.

You'll find out how to determine if you are a candidate to use injectable growth hormone. Once you know, it's important to find a qualified physician who can give you a proper and reliable diagnosis that will help to determine whether your treatment or therapy should include bioidentical growth hormone. This book will help you to do that with a step-by-step approach to biologically transforming yourself at the molecular level. Keep in mind that this is pure science, but it's presented here in an understandable and accessible way.

Information is provided so that you will know the potential costs of treatment, whether insurance companies will help to pay, and how-to basics on the usual course of therapy. I also address many of the usual questions raised by patients. What specific results should you expect or hope for when receiving these treatments? How much younger will you look and feel? What about your energy levels, memory, overall organ functions, and life expectancy?

You'll get to know all of the pros and cons of using this growth hormone. I'll warn you of what fearmongers or a traditional medicine doctor will likely try to tell you in an attempt to dissuade you with myths and fearmongering. You'll learn how my own research can shoot down many or all of these bogus arguments.

Other questions I'll raise and answer include, Is there a point in life when it's too late to start receiving injectable bioidentical human growth hormone? Why do humans produce less of this natural substance as we grow older, resulting in the signs of aging—from increased body fat to wrinkles, brittle bones, memory loss, chronic fatigue, and graying hair?

Why do some people seem to age more rapidly than others? What uniform criteria for biostimulators should be enacted nationwide? How can a person naturally increase his or her growth hormone levels without having the substance administered? At what point is it appropriate to issue prescriptions?

As baby boomers push through their middle-age years and into senior status, it's essential for them and everyone in the aging generations behind them to gain a greater understanding of these and related issues. As you find out more about growth hormone and related biostimulators, you'll discover the intricacies of how such biological mechanisms work in the miracle of life. Imagine the exhilarating feeling of having your quick memory return as your body regains its youthful strength. Think of how you'll feel when people tell you, "Wow, you look so young. How do you do that?"

We Use It Ourselves

Friends and patients that my wife and I come into contact with on a daily basis view us as at least ten to fifteen years younger than our actual ages. That's because, since we are both well past the age of fifty, we use injectable human growth hormone ourselves under the care of another physician. We have never for a moment regretted our decision.

We can honestly say that our zest for life, our productivity, and our overall vitality rival the levels that we enjoyed three or four decades ago. That's when we worked nonstop as students and budding medical industry professionals. Every day we express gratitude for the many benefits our enhancement of the Master Hormone provides to us.

The word is getting out about the miraculous effects. At our alternative medical office—the Century Wellness Clinic in Reno, Nevada—our parking lot is usually jammed with vehicles, many with license plates from as far away as New England, Alaska, and the Deep South.

"Don't thank us," we often tell these appreciative patients. "Thank Mother Nature." We simply allow each patient's physical response to growth hormone to do all of the explaining for us, though, as with almost any type of treatment, specific results vary among patients.

As you'll discover in this book, laws vary widely nationwide on who can prescribe the injectable form of growth hormone. For instance, a physical fitness trainer in a certain state might be committing a felony if he or she gives or administers the injectable form to a client. Yet in the same state a doctor of homeopathic medicine can prescribe the substance without raising an eyebrow. There are few, if any, restrictions, however, on your use of the natural anti-aging remedies I describe in Part One of this book.

To her credit, my wife, Earlene, stood tall throughout the horrible ordeal that our government put us through over our advocacy of these anti-aging miracle substances. Much of the credit for spreading the positive message about this natural hormone must go to this vibrant woman, who is blessed with the most infectious laugh that you've ever heard. My gratitude also goes to our attorney, Kevin Mirch, who successfully defended me against baseless charges and in the process became a close friend. You will learn more about their role in defending your health care rights in the last section of this book.

Make This Book a Personal Journey

It's no exaggeration to say that I truly do believe that the information in this book provides you with access to a fountain of youth that will make you look and feel decades younger. These biostimulators work. They're safe. They're legal. They're becoming more widely available.

These were anti-aging secrets long known to a select few wealthy people and Hollywood celebrities, especially actors who played action roles. They're now finally accessible to ordinary people. And it's about time! You are just as deserving as any rich person or any celebrity to have all of the benefits of health and youthfulness that growth hormone and its natural biostimulators can offer.

Think of this book as pulling back the curtain of the great and powerful Oz and revealing what's behind the cloak of silence and secrecy when it comes to anti-aging. I felt compelled to write this book to give you the complete and truthful story about a remarkable scientific medical breakthrough. I am doing it because I couldn't remain silent any longer while the government, the media, Big Pharma, and certain segments of the medical establishment were spreading so much misinformation about this antidote to aging.

The claims that I make for the benefits of growth hormone and its biostimulators are all based on case studies and a wealth of medical science data that I collected when I wrote the protocol (the standards of use) for human growth hormone at the request of the U.S. government. (This protocol is reproduced in Appendix A.) Hormone therapy and biostimulators rejuvenate your DNA and biochemistry, slowing down and even reversing the aging process, which will revolutionize the health of millions of people. It's going to change attitudes and beliefs about what it means to grow old. It's going to shatter all of the limitations and stereotypes about what people past the age of fifty can and cannot do with their bodies, their minds, and their lives.

Living a long life and doing so with dignity and optimal good health should be everyone's birthright. Now you have the tools in hand to make the ancient human quest for the fountain of youth your own personal discovery. Think of this as more than just a book. It's a roadmap for a proven system and a revolutionary approach to age deceleration that will rejuvenate you and transform how you look and how you feel.

As you begin your exciting journey of self-discovery by reading this book, I would like to congratulate you. In taking this step, you are opening your eyes to Mother Nature's endless possibilities. The fountain of youth is not a myth. It exists as potential within each and every one of us.

PART I

CREATE YOUR ANTI-AGING LIFESTYLE

Chapter 1

Meet Your Master Hormone

WE ALL KNOW FIRSTHAND WHAT THE AGING PROCESS LOOKS LIKE AND feels like. We've seen it wreak havoc on the people who we know and love. We've seen it on display when the people in our life seem to literally age before our eyes. We've seen its effects in photographs taken of others and us over the years.

You may even see the ravages of aging every day when you look in the mirror and wonder "what happened to that vital and youthful-looking person who used to be me?"

Maybe you wake up most mornings without the energy, drive, and determination that you once had. You no longer act or feel youthful. Maybe you've even convinced yourself that feeling old is "normal" and "natural."

How many of the following conditions apply to you?

- You no longer get full nights of restful, undisturbed sleep.
- You can't seem to shed those extra pounds no matter how hard you exercise or how closely you monitor your diet.
- Your skin is wrinkling and becoming discolored with what you call liver spots or sunspots, but which are really aging spots.
- Your hair is thinning and turning gray.

- Your sexual appetite and ability to perform sexually have diminished.
- You have developed stiff joints, arthritis, or weak and brittle bones.
- Your mental clarity and sharpness are beginning to decline.
- Your immune system is weaker, making you more vulnerable to colds, the flu, and other ailments.
- You no longer feel optimistic or enthusiastic about life.
- When you go for annual physical exams, the test results show that your body is degenerating with age. Your heart function declines as that organ becomes more inefficient at pumping blood. Your cholesterol levels go haywire. Your metabolism slows down. Your reflexes are slower.

These are all among the classic effects of aging. Why does it happen? Is this cascade of negative effects and conditions inevitable?

Do you remember how you looked and felt at age twenty-five? Yes, you may have physically aged since then, but what actually changed in the biochemistry and hormone levels of your body that now has you looking and feeling older? Recent breakthroughs in science have identified exactly what happens.

Your Body's Orchestra Conductor

Aging and most of the medical conditions resulting from it develop as a result of declining amounts of human growth hormone (HGH), a substance naturally produced in the human body by your pituitary gland. Think of it as the master hormone that's like a band or orchestra leader. It orchestrates all of the other endocrine hormone functions in the body, such as your sex hormones. It has been described by the American Academy of Anti-Aging Medicine and the International Hormone Society as the prime factor controlling the aging process.

If human growth hormone is like an orchestra conductor for the body, then the instruments that are played to support the conductor to make inspiring music are the range of biostimulators discussed in the following chapters, with injectable growth hormone being the featured performer. Together they produce the harmony of a healthy body and mind producing youthful vigor.

All of us, from the day we're born up to about age twenty-five, produce huge amounts of growth hormone, and that is what has kept us young. It is the key to youth and anti-aging. Think about how you were in your early twenties. You could stay up all night and cram for exams. Or you could party all night, if that was your inclination. You could drive across the country in a few days. Your sexual appetite and sexual performance level was always high. You recovered quickly from injuries. You felt like you had boundless energy and enthusiasm for life.

But as we all know, this youthful energy feeling doesn't last. Our bodies produce less growth hormone year by year, and that sets in motion the aging process.

Our natural levels of HGH decline by about 10 to 15 percent per decade, starting around our mid-twenties, our peak years. By the time we are in our forties and fifties, our diminished levels have become obvious because the symptoms of aging are there for everyone to see. With less of this hormone in our bodies, we become more vulnerable to serious medical conditions, and that further hastens the effects of aging.

People also contribute to accelerating the aging process with unhealthy lifestyles and the absorption of toxins from our environment. Some people eat at fast-food restaurants three times a week. They take nonprescription and prescription drugs every day. They don't exercise. They smoke. They don't eat any, or enough, organic produce. All of these things combine to have a negative effect on the human body and contribute to less growth hormone being produced.

Who Wins the Genetic Lottery?

There are certain fortunate people who, thanks to their genetic programming, coupled with heavy exercise and great dietary habits, are able to maintain their growth hormone levels higher for longer than most other people. But even in these individuals, its production still diminishes with age, just more slowly.

An estimated one in five people worldwide won this genetic lottery and will live longer and stay in better health than everyone else because they carry a "centenarian gene." That's according to a January 2010 study published in the *Journal of the American Medical Association*. They got lucky. Their bodies are programmed to produce a lot of growth hormone for a long time. They will stay the healthiest. They will look the youngest. They will live the longest.

But what about the rest of us ordinary people? Are we doomed to age faster, get sicker more often, and die younger simply because we didn't get a winning ticket in the genetic lottery?

The answer is no! Let me tell you why. The rules of the game have changed. All of the rules of aging have changed because the Master Hormone needn't be in short supply in your body any longer. Production of it can be stimulated using biostimulators. Levels of the Master Hormone can be replaced. I am going to tell you and show you how.

You cannot only stop the decline in your growth hormone, but you can also put its levels back to where they were when you were in your twenties. And guess what? When you do, you'll start feeling like you're back in your roaring twenties again!

You can slow down the aging clock. You can even stop it, in my opinion. I will provide you with a strategy, a game plan, for living a long life with optimum good health. Science has finally figured out a way for you to look and feel years younger than you really are.

Congratulations! With this book you've won the information lottery!

CHAPTER 2

How This "Life Force" Rejuvenates You

MOST OF US GREW UP BELIEVING THAT GROWING OLD IS LIKE A DISEASE with no cure, a disease that will eventually kill every one of us. That is a mindset that actually contributes to aging. While immortality may not yet be available to humans, solutions to the aging mystery are within our grasp, and they involve alterations in your biology to bioidentically match what you were like when you were younger.

Many people these days are scrambling around in desperate attempts to deal with the visible symptoms of aging. Once over the age of fifty, many of them rush to get liposuctions, tummy tucks, breast implants, face lifts, hair implants, eyebrow lifts, nose reconstruction, Botox cosmetic injections, facial fillers, and more—all procedures and terms absent from the overall public mindset as recently as the mid-1960s. With wider use of growth hormone biostimulators, I guarantee that a lot of these cosmetic attempts to preserve youthfulness will become obsolete.

Have you ever given any serious thought to why or how we age? What makes us youthful, vibrant, and pleasant to look at? Gaining some understanding of the basic biological mechanisms goes a long way in explaining the many benefits and uses of biostimulators and injectable growth hormone.

The scientific search for answers to the aging question goes back to at least 1908, when Russian microbiologist Ilya Ilyich Mechnikov won the Nobel Prize in Medicine for a groundbreaking study on cells, the immune system, and aging. He developed a theory that aging was caused "by a build-up of toxins from the intestinal tract, which over a period of a lifespan contributed to aging and ultimately death."

During the ensuing century, other scientists, physicians, and home-opaths developed a maze of vastly different theories. In my view, the actual biological factors that cause aging might involve a handful or even a large number of these various ideas.

Mother Nature has apparently programmed each person with an internal biological clock that tells our cells when to wind down and cease functioning. You might call this a nature-mandated planned obsolescence for humans—something like cars built by auto manufacturers so that they'll break down after a certain number of miles. In humans, physicians have pinpointed a program that sets predesignated times when milestone events occur.

Medical professionals and just about every parent knows the time-frame after birth when infants will get those first teeth, crawl, walk, learn initial words, and start talking in cohesive sentences. Growth spurts and sexual maturity evolve during puberty. Within a few short decades, the degenerative phase cruelly starts to kick into gear.

Current theories of aging on the cellular molecular level say that besides the preset clock, we also age due to a random series of adverse events. Each individual sits within a designated slot on a proverbial roulette wheel. Whether the odds are in your favor or not, if the "ball" of fate lands in your slot, it's time to start aging faster than your peers of the same age.

Perhaps you've known people who have aged rapidly after sudden, severe injury or the rapid onset of illness. Many of these individuals, including some of our favorite celebrities, could have been helped by a biostimulator-oriented lifestyle or the use of injectable growth hormone.

Without getting into too much medical jargon, you might want to know that in scientific terms the random theories of aging rely on chance coupled with the notion that organisms get older because of a random series of events. Wear and tear on one vital organ might cause a domino effect, sparking a series of organ failures as aging accelerates faster than nature originally intended.

———

When we're young, the neuroendocrine system enables hormones to regulate vital body functions, everything from reactions to stress and sexual activity to determining the individual's ultimate height, weight, and organ growth.

Under the neuroendocrine theory of aging, these systems malfunction as we age. During our mature years, the hypothalamus, located within the brain above the pituitary gland, starts to regulate the release of various hormones without the great efficiency that it once achieved during youth. Thus, the signs of aging begin to emerge.

Should You Fear "Free Radicals?"

These days the term "free radicals" takes on a much different connotation than it might have during the rebellious, anti-establishment 1960s. Within the medical profession, the free radical theory of aging (FRTA) has gained some degree of acceptance along with the "Wear-and-Tear" and "Random Events" theories.

Many of you might remember high school chemistry class where you learned that a radical—also called a free radical—is an atom, molecule, or ion, each with an unpaired electron that results in an open-shell configuration. The result is an imbalanced electrical energy that forces free radicals to attach to other molecules.

Negative environmental factors such as carcinogens or excessive radiation can cause the cells to generate free radicals, creating havoc in the structure of vital proteins, body chemistry, and metabolism—thereby creating extensive bodily damage. Worsening matters, free radicals attack cell membranes and create metabolic waste products, including lipofuscins.

Although the word *lipofuscin* might sound like an evil character from the top-selling Harry Potter book series, in real-life biology these substances are wicked metabolic waste products that darken the skin of mature Caucasians—commonly known as those dreaded age spots or liver spots. Even worse, these pigments interfere with our cells' abilities to repair and reproduce themselves, while disturbing RNA and DNA syntheses and destroying vital cellular enzymes necessary for our body's vital chemical processes.

We know that far more mature people suffer damage from free radicals than young adults and children. Could the body's natural decrease in growth hormone among older people increase the likelihood that free radicals will occur in such individuals? I am not alone among experts who think the answer is "yes."

The vast majority of patients who use the injectable form of growth hormone are in their sixties, seventies, and eighties. These people are overjoyed when they discover that their liver spots or age spots have disappeared. Such reversals are among primary factors that lead me to the belief that this hormone can cease or at least curtail the horrific biological damages that free radicals inflict.

How Your Body Yearns to Make This Hormone

Let's go over some information about how and why human growth hormone gets generated by the body. It's important for you to know these things because you should never put anything into your body that you haven't properly researched.

Some of this may sound technical. But read on. The payoff is worth it.

The pituitary gland, which is the size of a large kidney bean at the base of the brain, produces the growth hormone that keeps people healthy and vital—giving the ability to grow, heal fast, and maintain a youthful appearance.

Adding to its importance, the Master Hormone also mobilizes fat stored for fuel and enhances protein synthesis. Thanks to this function, mature patients who receive the injectable form in replacement therapy lose body fat and gain muscle, even when treated for a short period of time.

That part of the brain called the hypothalamus, lying above the pituitary, sends out a variety of signals, including one called growth hormone releasing hormone (sometimes called GHRH). At times, the hypothalamus generates somatostatin, a hormone that temporarily inhibits the production of HGH. On command, in order to regulate the body's growth, healing, and youthful characteristics, the hypothalamus shuts down somatostatin production, while also sending signals to the pituitary—commanding that it send bursts of active growth hormone into the body.

It surges into the blood stream for brief, intermittent periods, mostly during our deepest sleep, a limited time of rapid-eye movement, characterized by our most vivid dreams. Meantime, the pituitary also secretes a variety of other hormones, including prolactin, a thyroid stimulating hormone, a luteinizing hormone, a follicle-stimulating hormone, and an adrenal corticotropic hormone.

Once released into the bloodstream, the Master Hormone lasts only a very short period of time, usually a half hour at most. During this period, the liver plays a vital role in transforming the initial growth hormone that it receives via the blood into another hormone-related substance, commonly known as insulin-like growth factor one, or IGF-1.

As the primary and active metabolite of human growth hormone, IGF-1 works on primary endocrine organs such as the thyroid gland, the adrenal glands, and the gonads in both males and females.

How the Master Hormone Works Its "Magic"

From the liver, IGF-1 travels to the body's various tissues, giving organs, muscles, and bones the ability to grow from infancy through the young adult years. These same growth-oriented factors enable the body to heal from wounds, while also keeping the muscles and skin firm and healthy looking.

To keep the body from growing too much, the pituitary gland senses when maximum amounts of growth hormone are in the bloodstream, and at that point this vital gland shuts down production of the hormone. This also signals to the hypothalamus to stop making GHRH.

Physicians consider the injectable type of human growth hormone as natural rather than synthetic, because the body produces the same hormone. The recombinant form of this hormone, produced in pharmaceutical laboratories, also gets a natural designation because pharmaceutical production companies make it from genetic engineering. At times, some physicians refer to such produced human growth hormone as rGH, the first letter designating "recombinant."

To fully understand the power of the Master Hormone, it's essential to know how the body's endocrine or glandular system communicates between cells and organs. The endocrine system serves as an immensely complicated process that encompasses complex biochemical, physiologic, and cellular biological applications. Keep in mind that the endocrine system takes orders from both the central nervous system and the immune system. These dual functions make understanding the endocrine system's full and comprehensive functions a formidable challenge. The word "endocrine" means "the internal secretion of biological active substances into the blood stream, in order to regulate the function of a target organ." Medical professionals and laymen alike refer to these biological substances as hormones.

At this point, you should also know that the Master Hormone is not a steroid. Unlike human growth hormone, steroids are heralded, and rightly so, as potentially harmful substances—especially when injected without proper supervision from a medical professional.

Nature's Ingenious Hormone Triggers

Three different mechanisms or triggers play a significant role in the pituitary's release of growth hormone and other hormones:

1. **Daily brain interactions.** These functions, sometimes called "circadian rhythms," hinge on essential, daily sleep-wake cycles.
2. **Negative feedback interaction.** After a target organ gets an amount of hormone that satisfies its needs, the pituitary stops production of those hormones—temporarily.
3. **Other intervening influences.** Factors such as stress, emotional trauma, nutritional illnesses, infections, and other activities in hormonal glands influence the secretion of the Master Hormone.

Doctors call the normal physiologic decrease in growth hormone as we age "somatopause," the equivalent of menopause in women and andropause in men. While scientists have yet to proclaim a specific reason for this decline, I suspect that various factors might contribute, such as a drop in available amino acid precursors necessary for the actual production within the pituitary gland.

In addition, the hypothalamus might sustain a decrease in its release of stimulatory hormones that generate growth hormone, while the hormone that inhibits its production—somatostatin—might increase.

Natural Decreases Remain Inevitable

The body's ability to absorb, digest, and assimilate proteins diminishes as people age, losing the ability to absorb protein and proper amounts of hydrochloric acids through digestive enzymes. Called hypochlorhydria, this condition becomes evident in many digestive diseases, including diabetes mellitus, hypothyroidism, chronis hepatitis, osteoporosis, and chronic autoimmune malfunctions.

The frequent or chronic use of antacid drug therapy or anti-inflammatory drugs might influence these digestive problems. Also, mature patients sometimes exacerbate these difficulties by reducing their body's production of hydrochloric acid by eating or drinking foods or drinks high in carbohydrates, sugars, alcohol, caffeine, and refined meals.

The aging process occasionally results in increased stress or trauma, potentially causing the hypothalamus to lose its ability to manufacture and release growth hormone releasing hormone—GHRH. Adding to the problem, a lack of certain nutrients in the diet might contribute to the downturn in production. In diabetics, high blood sugar levels reduce growth hormone—releasing activity. Scientists have discovered that in a natural reaction to stress, the body generates glucocorticoid hormones that inhibit the effect of growth hormone production. And high levels of blood sugars and glucocorticoids stimulate the inhibitory hormone, somatostatin.

Your Master Hormone Levels from Birth to Death

Let me tell you a story about a man named David Cartwright. You probably don't know him, but you don't really need to know him personally because his story is also your story. It's your story, too, because we all go through the same stages of the hormonal dance with life. As you read along, just imagine that you are the person being talked about.

Just like you did when you were conceived, David's body began producing growth hormone while still in his mother's womb. This process began at the onset of the embryonic stage within three weeks after his parents conceived him in July 1933.

In the womb and following birth, the same growth process happens to all healthy individuals. Like David's body did within his mother, your pituitary gland near the base of the brain began broadcasting to the rest of your tiny body when you were in your mother. Ever since, your brain has pumped out the Master Hormone.

When in his mother's womb, tiny David's entire immature body needed and craved these growth hormone signals from his pituitary gland in order to grow enough to live after birth. Without appropriate amounts of these hormones within the womb, he would have died, resulting in a miscarriage. To handle this chore, nature provides the hypothalamus just above the pituitary gland. Think of the hypothalamus as your body's expert in giving each organ and cell all the appropriate hormones that each craves and needs. From the day he was born, little David's hypothalamus preferred to blare out 75 percent of his body's essential growth signals during the wee hours of the morning.

Amplifying the Internal Vibration Station

David's hypothalamus pumped out vital growth hormone chemicals, mostly during REM sleep, a normal stage of sleep characterized by rapid eye movements. Most of us reach our deepest sleep during late-night hours or the early hours of the morning, or within a few hours after we begin our longest period of daily sleep.

Scientists have yet to determine why our internal broadcasting system prefers to pump out its most intense growth hormone signals during periods of heavy sleep and the remaining 25 percent through the rest of the day. The strength increases steadily, month-to-month and year-to-year, until it peaks in our mid-twenties.

After initially being produced by the pituitary and released into the blood system, the Master Hormone enters the liver—which transforms this substance into the amazing insulin growth factor-1, also known as IGF-1, as previously described. You might want to think of IGF-1 as the speakers that amplify, strengthen, or target the vital signals or songs that each cell of the body craves.

Just like all newborns, at birth soft spots riddled the top of David's skull, spaces where the bones had not yet grown together, so that his mother could squeeze him through the birth canal.

Regulating and Growing Cells and Tissues

Just three months after David's birth, his father, Carl, boasted to a neighbor, "Our new little guy is growing like a weed. Only God could understand how this happens, but I'm proud."

Herein comes proof of the miracle of the Master Hormone. Without proper amounts of the hormone little David would have died a painful death during his first year, and the same horrible fate would have happened to you had your signals during infancy gone haywire.

Proper growth hormone signals, as mandated by the hypothalamus, cause regulation and growth of nearly every cell and tissue, from childhood through adolescence. Overly rapid growth of any single organ or insufficient growth of some areas of the body could cause fatal organ dysfunction.

By the end of infancy at his first birthday, David's skull bones had begun to fuse together, lessening the danger of a fatal injury or accidental fall that might cause horrific trauma to the head. As with the vast majority of children, the Master Hormone had done its job well.

Making the Emergence of Self-Identity Possible

The growth hormone—regulating area of the brain—the hypothalamus— knows exactly what hormonal signals to send, at what intensity, and when. During the toddler stage from ages one through three, David learned to walk, talk, and go to the bathroom on demand.

Thanks to the natural miracle of the Master Hormone, coupled with guidance or examples set by his parents, like most toddlers at thirty-six months he began to speak in cohesive sentences, play different games, know the difference between genders, anticipate routines, play with toys in imaginative ways, and attempt to sing songs. The growth process enabled David's brain to develop on schedule.

As we know, sadly or at least as biology intended, David already was pre-programmed to slow down during middle age, show signs of aging, and eventually die—preferably well after age fifty. But before that all could happen, he first needed to grow at the predictable schedule, largely because humans are programmed to achieve physical and sexual maturity in order to repopulate the earth.

David evolved through early childhood as predicted from ages four through six. An only child, he entered the first grade in the fall of 1940.

Seemingly as if in a science fiction movie, each night during David's deepest sleep the mysterious and life-giving growth hormone signals continued to course through his body, more than at any other time of day. By preadolescence from ages nine through twelve, for the first time David developed an attitude of self-identity and independence, plus a sense of responsibility such as handling chores and envisioning a future career. The Master Hormone helped make all this possible.

Keeping the Teenage Growth Years on Track

Just as yours did, David's hypothalamus and pituitary gland conducted a symphony of work behind the scenes from the beginning of his elementary school days through high school. Like cymbals conducted to clang at an exact, precise second during a symphony, his final baby teeth popped out during reading time in first grade.

The many wonders of the Master Hormone worked magic for him, pushing in his adult teeth straight and true, and hard enough—hopefully—to last a lifetime. At age nine, David suffered a fractured right leg when he stupidly drove his bicycle in front of a cruising Buick Roadmaster. Right away, the hypothalamus and pituitary put David's internal growth hormone production and distribution into a crescendo mode, and just less than six weeks later the fracture had fully healed.

Those mystical internal signals skipped at a natural and predictable offbeat mode at ages thirteen through fifteen, when some of David's limbs and physical characteristics seemed either too big or too small for the rest of his burgeoning body. A keen observer might conclude that the confounding hypothalamus was off kilter, a vital gland's natural skills had gone awry. Yet all went well, just as the case with other young teens thanks to the great powers of this vital hormone.

David's voice cracked on occasion during this period as his body transformed from that of a boy into the frame of a strong, young man. He never told his parents this, but starting at age fourteen, about a year after pubic hair spouted around his testicles, his body began confusing him, displaying the sexual characteristics of adulthood. Without even consulting with David's external thought process, growth hormone had started to play a supposed trick on him, right on schedule.

Helping to Repair the Body

Just as they do for many young guys, David's internal hormones forced him to reach his most active sexual capacity well before he ever enjoyed intimate relations for the first time. At David's eighteenth birthday in his family's backyard in April 1952, all he could think about were the women his own age and the sensual things he would like to do with them. Typically mischievous, the hypothalamus played this signal about every thirty seconds, driving David wild with desire—as Mother Nature demands.

This continued the following June, on the day David scurried to the local Marine Corps recruiting office without first consulting his parents. He joined on the spot, incurring the wrath of his folks. By midsummer David got shipped off to boot camp. In mid-November, he began serving on the frontlines in the Korean War.

Thanks to the Master Hormone, David's body was already pulsating with boundless energy and strapping muscles by the time he reached basic training. His V-shaped frame and strength adapted well to vigorous, regimentary routines. This put him in perfect physical condition in time for the Battle for Pork Chop Hill in 1953, when a sniper's bullet cruelly ripped through a fleshy area just below his right shoulder. On the spot, medics worked feverishly to stop his profuse bleeding.

Since David's hypothalamus didn't want to die, either, this amazing gland feverishly worked overtime. The vital talents of this organ paid off, rejuvenating vital muscles, blood vessels, and even some significant nerve endings.

The hypothalamus is an expert at growth, enabling cells to differentiate, rejuvenate, and repair. David's wound undoubtedly would have killed a much older man who lacks the maximum amounts of naturally produced growth hormone.

Sparking Passion and Romance

Like it does for many young men on the cusp of their third decade, the hypothalamus also continued pumping anabolic hormones into David at age nineteen when he returned home to his worried family. At exactly six feet, he was a full two inches taller than he was on high school graduation day. And by age twenty, the Master Hormone added on another inch for good measure.

Following an early honorable military discharge due to his war wound, at his parents' urging, David entered New York University in the fall semester. There he joined the wrestling team and promptly suffered a broken nose, which the hypothalamus soon repaired to its original, prominent stature. The Master Hormone continues to exert its effect on the repair of bone and supporting tissues throughout life, particularly during the first two and a half decades.

Amid his engineering studies, a plethora of growth hormone gave young David the energy and seemingly endless zest to hit the books, work a part-time job, and party around the clock. Thanks to this hormone, sleep didn't seem to matter. Do you remember when your internal growth hormone—band broadcast station gave you similar pep and vigor—seemingly enough spunk to tackle just about any challenge?

Somehow the hormone enabled him to find the time to amass bonds or friendships with numerous young women. Finally, David lost his virginity. That night, the hypothalamus went into overdrive, as if he and this gland had worked their entire lives to prepare David's body for this moment—and indeed, that was the very case.

Since the sexual urge reigns as one of the most powerful internal and natural drives, the hypothalamus had paid lots of attention to this aspect of David's physical make-up. Each time, always excited and eager, David responded the way nature told him to, culminating in a blast off that would have made the then-burgeoning NASA program proud.

David and Pamela Galloway fell in love within one week after they met for the first time at NYU in April 1957, the day after his twenty-third birthday. At age nineteen, thanks to her own hypothalamus's focus on the female gender, Pamela's hips were firm and round, accenting her taut, muscular waist. Her internal hormone mechanisms created full, firm breasts, and the sight of him ignited her passion.

Par for customs dictated by the times, the couple started dating that summer when their hormone glands did everything possible to motivate them to mate. Morals and personal preferences enabled them to overcome natural urges as they gyrated that summer away, often dancing to popular current tunes from Elvis and Buddy Holly to the Big Bopper.

David's hypothalamus made him fantasize about Pamela night and day. His naturally high and persistent growth hormone gave no relief, pumping appropriate amounts of hormones.

Pamela broke into tears and said "yes" right away, as soon as David proposed to her in October 1957 in Central Park after they enjoyed chocolate shakes at a nearby malt shop. Pamela's hormones sent sparks of anticipation roaring through her body. Unlike her fiancé, at the time she was a virgin, and the Master Hormone made her libido soar.

Enjoying the Hormonal Wave

Four weeks after David earned a bachelor's degree in civil engineering, he and Pamela were married at Saint Patrick's Cathedral in New York City in June 1958. Like many young people, their bodies responded the way nature commands that night while making love until sunrise.

Do you remember your young adult years when you were able to share such nonstop joy and passion? Just like you have, in the years and decades that followed, Pamela and David showed a significant decrease in both their desire and ability for such intense lovemaking, largely because their internal growth hormone production tapered off to a small percentage of its former maximum levels.

Shortly after their wedding, though, in denial of their pending old age and eventual death, this hormone enabled Pamela and David to tackle many of life's most formidable challenges. You see, eight days after the newlyweds returned from their honeymoon, David's father died of a sudden cardiac arrest while working at his accounting firm, exactly twenty-five years to the day after David was conceived.

Back in 1933 when David was conceived, his father reigned as a vibrant stud, thanks to his own hypothalamus and pituitary gland. Yet par for the course as dictated by Mother Nature, Carl's growth hormone levels dropped off dramatically in his thirties, forties, and early fifties, contributing to his deteriorating heart function and leading to his eventual demise.

Peaking and Falling Hormones

By our estimates, David's internal growth hormone levels reached their maximum amounts on or about August 1959, when the measurable amounts of the hormone pulsated through his bloodstream at a predictable and high level of 347. Average men attain maximum IGF-1 levels of 300 to 350 while in their mid-twenties, while the level of IGF-1 for women peaks at 250 to 300.

Just as yours did in your thirties, this relationship among the body's internal systems begins to function with much less efficiency than just a decade earlier. Once these automatic "on" and "off" switches start going haywire, many vital organs throughout the body begin receiving less of this vital hormone than necessary, sometimes getting the hormone at the wrong times or failing to receive adequate supplies when needed most.

For both David and his late father, these steadily decreasing efficiencies lowered good cholesterol, worsened cardiac function, put blood pressure off kilter, and weakened their abilities to ward off coronary artery disease. Exacerbating the problem, the efficiency of growth hormone depends largely on the complex endocrine or glandular system of the body—which, during good health, communicates complex and important information among cells and organs.

At age thirty-nine, David suffered a mild heart attack while at his job as a civil engineer. An ambulance crew rushed him to a hospital, where physicians blamed coronary artery disease rather than pinpointing the underlying reason, the decreased efficiency of his Master Hormone distribution.

When in good health, complex interactions occur between the glandular, nervous and immune systems. Various compounds within the body generate hormones from essential proteins, polypeptides, fatty acids, amino acids, steroids, and vitamins. All these integral systems had started going off kilter within David's body—which just twenty years earlier had been at the peak of efficiency, saving him from potential death from his war wound.

By the time David reached sixty-one and Pamela was fifty-seven, the couple had not made love for a full three years, due largely to their natural decrease in HGH, each having lost enough significant interest to "give it a try." Tests would have shown that by this point David's growth hormone distribution had lost more than 50 percent of its former peak efficiency. Pamela's growth hormone levels had slid way downhill as well.

On Labor Day that year, this couple's thirty-five-year-old sons, Carl and Kevin, each visited David and Pamela's home. By this point the twins sported similar-size potbellies, each more than a decade past his hormonal prime. The family enjoyed a lavish summer barbecue, while David and Pamela's seven grandchildren—ages five through twelve—scurried about the backyard, all of their young bloodstreams overflowing with the Master Hormone.

That was David's story . . . and a version of it was yours, too! Now let's look at how things could have turned out differently for him—and will turn out differently for you—by adopting a biostimulator lifestyle.

Chapter 3

Natural Anti-Aging Biostimulators

You have available to you a roster of anti-aging players in the game of life. Which players you choose to be part of your anti-aging team depends largely on your needs and your lifestyle preferences. What they have in common is their ability to change your biochemistry through the new science of bioidentical blueprinting.

When you replace or supplement your missing human growth hormone using the miraculous, natural anti-aging biostimulators revealed here, virtually everyone who does so experiences some or most of the following age-reversal effects.

- For many people, within a matter of months, if not weeks, their skin tightens, gets thicker and more elastic, and those unsightly wrinkles begin to go away.
- Both men and women, but especially women who have experienced bone thinning, will notice a steady improvement in bone density. That should help to prevent fractures and osteoporosis.
- Energy levels improve. Chronic fatigue goes away. With the newfound physical vitality comes an improvement in motivation and outlook on life. Optimism goes up; depression goes down.
- Mental clarity and sharpness return. Memory improves.

- Quality of sleep becomes more consistent. Things like obstructive sleep apnea—common in men over the age of fifty, where they stop breathing at night—becomes less severe and may disappear completely.
- Immune system functions strengthen. Natural killer cell activity—a key to resisting viruses and infections—intensifies. The body is able to heal itself faster. People get sick less often.
- Metabolism goes up, muscle reappears and gets stronger, and fat begins to disappear.
- Hair thinning stops and hair color can even return to its natural shade.
- Heart function strengthens. The heart muscle gets stronger, beats with more force, which is important to cardiovascular health.
- Libido goes up dramatically, as does sexual performance, and with it, your pleasure and sexual satisfaction.

People who are now in their forties, fifties, sixties, and beyond, will start looking younger and feeling younger as a result of using these natural substances. That's why we call the Master Hormone and related biostimulator products true anti-aging miracles, a veritable fountain of youth. The overall quality of life for users goes up dramatically. They use fewer pharmaceutical drugs. They experience fewer illnesses. They're hospitalized less.

All of this together makes taking these anti-aging miracles a cost-saving medical procedure that will not only save you money in the long term, but will lower the overall medical bills for society as a whole. That should count for a lot in this day and age when Medicare and Medicaid costs are out of control.

Also consider this: Many of us see our parents, grandparents, and other relatives who are in their seventies, eighties, and nineties languishing in nursing homes. These are human warehouses, for the most part. The folks inside exist on a steady diet of pharmaceutical drugs and possess little or no hope about the future. These are some of the very people for whom biostimulatory growth factors would provide the most dramatic new lease on life.

My wife, Earlene, and I have been taking the injectable form of growth hormone for a number of years, and that's one reason why we can speak from firsthand experience about the wondrous effects of this substance on the human body. We are also familiar with all of the biostimulator techniques and products that comprise a range of legal, inexpensive, and natural substances to help to stimulate the body's rejuvenation process.

Again, there are two ways to increase human growth hormone and related growth factor levels in your body: natural, anti-aging biostimulator miracle substances such as royal jelly, deer antler velvet, and supplements that I will recommend for you. These will safely stimulate your body to produce more HGH, or will provide you with growth factors and biological stimulation that are important to counteracting the symptoms of aging. Taken together, with proper nutrition and super foods, enhanced sleep, an exercise regimen, and keeping a youthful state of mind, you will have the ingredients for a complete anti-aging lifestyle.

After a while, when the biostimulator growth factors stop working as effectively as they once did, which could be as early as forty years of age, or as late as your sixties, it's time to switch to the injectable form of the Master Hormone to keep raising your levels. That's considered the Rolls-Royce treatment because it's the fastest way to see and feel profound effects. I will tell you more about that in a later chapter.

Keep in mind that many of these over-the-counter and relatively inexpensive remedies either help your body to naturally release more human growth hormone, or they supplement the effects of the Master Hormone in your body. They are most effective for people in their twenties, thirties, and forties to slow down the aging process before its symptoms become too obvious. But you can safely continue to use these precursors and related biostimulator anti-aging miracle products throughout your life, if you so choose, to provide added benefits if and when you begin using the injectable form in your fifties and beyond.

There is also a newly developed category of stimulators called "secretagogues," which I will also tell you about.

So here they are, a group of affordable and yet effective biostimulator products and substances for addressing the symptoms of aging.

Oral Growth Hormone Secretagogue

Thanks to an expanding understanding of how hormone production is regulated in the human body, researchers and clinical medical professionals, such as the widely acclaimed anti-aging physician and Interventional Endocrinologist, Mark L. Gordon, MD, director of the Millennium Health Center in Los Angeles, have developed an amino acid complex that is available as a spray. This oral growth hormone is called a "secretagogue."

The term "secretagogue" refers to any chemical substance, whether natural or synthetic, that causes another substance to be secreted in the body. The use of nanotechnology (engineering particles down to ultra-tiny sizes) allows for the amino acid complex to be delivered into the blood without being destroyed by the stomach acid.

In the past, tens of thousands of milligrams of amino acids had to be ingested in order to get the same increase in growth hormone that Dr. Gordon's product, called Secretropin, produces with only 1200 mg. Additionally, such large amounts of amino acids were also associated with gastric and intestinal distress (diarrhea). Dr. Gordon's product avoids triggering these reactions.

Based on nine years of clinical research, Dr. Gordon's findings support the effectiveness of Secretropin (see www.raisemygh.com). Over the course of the product's clinical testing starting early in this century, Secretropin has been found to increase the body's production of IGF-1 and IGFBP-3—two important markers of growth hormone production. In two separate yearlong clinical trials of Secretropin's effects on one hundred patients conducted by Dr. Gordon's medical team, an average increase in IGF-1 of 50 to 200 percent was documented in up to 92 percent of participants. That's pretty impressive!

When administering injectable rhGH, it is the relative increase in IGF-1 that relates to the beneficial effects of the hormone. Therefore, an elevation in IGF-1 corresponds to the use of biologically active GH. The body's ability to produce or increase IGF-1 levels when using a growth hormone secretagogue relates to the biological activity of the product.

Among the ingredients in Dr. Gordon's Secretropin oral spray are L-arginine and L-ornithine, both of which are amino acids that have been found to increase the body's levels of growth hormones. At least one independent study indicated that prescribed doses of ornithine and arginine, when taken together and combined with a strength-training program, might also help to increase the body's growth hormone and IGF-1 levels.

COMMONLY ASKED QUESTIONS
ABOUT SECRETROPIN
When should it be used and who should use it?

It has been found to be as effective as a nighttime only product. Anyone at any age can find benefit from its use, but it is not intended for anyone under eighteen years of age, or if a woman is pregnant or nursing.

Are there any serious side effects from using it?

No serious side effects have been reported. A few people complain of having too much energy after absorbing it, but even that is uncommon. Because the level of growth hormone induced by the product is significant, it is distributed primarily through physicians or pharmacies as a precautionary measure.

How does it affect the libido?

Men particularly find their libido enhanced from using the product. The growth hormone stimulates the body's receptor for testosterone, and that in turn benefits the libido and sexual stamina and performance.

Grow Young Oral Spray

Nick Delgado, who is certified by the American Board of Anti-Aging Health Practitioners, developed Grow Young Oral Spray. It contains growth factors and vitamin B_{12} to stimulate body cells and organs. The specific ingredients in this oral spray are vitamin B_{12}, L-Lysine, Lysine, Sodium Citrate, and pure acidulated water.

Anti-Aging master Delgado has experimented with himself using various HGH products and precursors and has documented the results in various publications, including the summer-fall 2002 issue of *Anti-Aging Medical News*. Using what he calls the Delgado Protocol, he supplements his growth hormone precursor use by consuming a mostly vegetarian diet, rarely eating meat or dairy products, and engaging in resistance weight training five days a week (see www.DelgadoProtocol.com).

Seconds after using the oral growth hormone spray, says Delgado, the substance sends an electronic vibration to receptor cells in the body that instructs the pituitary gland to produce more growth hormone. It then travels to the liver to produce IGF-1, which, among its many functions, does the work of helping the body's DNA to repair itself prior to cell division, one key to combating aging.

Delgado shares his own experience from using oral replacement human growth hormone: "Within eight weeks, my report blood tests revealed my IGF-1 levels had climbed to a level you would find in a twenty-five-year-old! I noticed an increase in strength, an increase in muscle density, an improvement in sexual activity, and the rate at which my fingernails and hair grew. Obviously, I was extremely happy to get the same physical and emotional benefits from oral HGH as I did with injections. As I continued with my research, I began taking oral HGH analog (somatotropin). I noticed that I slept deeper, my skin looked healthier, and my wrinkles decreased. Also, my muscular density increased by five pounds and I lost over 5 percent body fat. That was quite an improvement after only twelve weeks of using the oral spray!"

"We know absorption of the oral growth hormone is taking place," notes Delgado, "because IGF-1 levels increase an average of 18 percent and as much as 99 percent after frequent daily use of the oral spray over a period of eight to fourteen weeks." He points to clinical outcome-based studies reported in 2001 in which sixty-three patients using oral growth hormone and oral growth factors were monitored for up to three years; 90 percent of them experienced positive results that included higher energy and fitness levels, enhanced sexual activity, immune and mental function, and improved skin and hair quality. In still another study that Delgado reviewed, involving 194 patients using oral human growth hormone, there were also significant improvements in LDL and HDL cholesterol for both men and women aged thirty-five to eighty years.

COMMONLY ASKED QUESTIONS ABOUT GROW YOUNG ORAL SPRAY
Can it treat health conditions other than aging?

A range of chronic, debilitating health problems have been treated using the oral human growth hormone spray. Arthritis pain and inflammation are two; multiple sclerosis and fibromyalgia are two more. There is even evidence that restoring growth factors in the body can improve circulation and elasticity in the arteries, lowering blood pressure and reducing LDL (bad) cholesterol. As Delgado points out, being able to dissolve the plaque in arteries and restore them to a more youthful condition can help to reduce the incidence of strokes and heart attacks.

What is its safety record?

It's virtually impossible to overdose using the oral spray. Even if you were to absorb the entire contents of a bottle at one time, it could be easily excreted from the body because the body can use only small amounts at any one time during daily intervals.

No harmful side effects have been reported from its use. Delgado recommends that people under the age of twenty, along with pregnant or nursing women, not use the product unless it is prescribed by a physician, though he isn't aware of any negative side effects from the product's use among those groups.

Rumors that growth hormone might increase the risk for cancer have also proven unfounded. "There is no evidence to indicate either an increased incidence or progression of cancer during or after HGH replacement therapy," states Dr. Cass Terry, chairman of Neurology, professor of Neurology and Physiology at the Medical College of Wisconsin.

How is the oral spray created?

A genetic engineering process creates ingredients for the product. Its maker insists the substance isn't synthetic and is identical in structure to the human growth hormone naturally produced by the human body. Genetic engineering simply involves taking the blueprint from the actual growth hormone molecule and letting it replicate itself inside a safe bacterial culture.

Deer Antler Velvet

You may have heard of Deer Antler Velvet in connection with traditional Chinese medicine, which has used it for several thousand years as a health, energy, and sexual tonic. Deer antler velvet is now recognized as a source of the important insulin-like growth factors IGF-1 and IGF-2, isolated after the velvet is scraped off the antlers, and then dried and crushed.

Other growth factors identified in antler velvet that work together synergistically for enhanced health and anti-aging include growth factor alpha, growth factor beta, erythropoietin (a stimulant for red blood cell growth), nerve growth factors, three types of fibroblast growth factors, hepatocyte growth factor, epidermal growth factor, and numerous other cofactors. Though deer antler velvet isn't a growth hormone precursor, the IGF-1 growth factor found in it is also secreted by the human liver as a result of stimulation by human growth hormone.

Royal Velvet from the www.beeyoungnow.com website is a favorite of ours among deer antler products because it's more potent than other products. That is because it has a more effective delivery system and the source of this product is from a select herd of six hundred thousand red deer stags in New Zealand. Deer antler velvet from this herd contains hundreds of nutrients that are up to 97 percent absorbed by your body within a minute of use.

While other products purporting to be deer antler velvet are administered as either a liquid alcohol extract, as a solution for injections, or in powdered tablet form, Royal Velvet has a patented liposomal delivery system. It sprays directly into your mouth for rapid absorption into the bloodstream, giving it ten times the absorption rate of powders, capsules, tablets, or liquid forms of antler velvet in which the nutrients are destroyed by the digestive system.

Various peptides isolated from the velvet have been shown in medical science studies to be anti-inflammatory and stimulate wound healing and skin growth. Other study trials have shown that extracts of velvet stimulate the immune system. A 2006 study published in the *Journal of Anatomy* even found stem cells in the velvet that are responsible for antler regeneration. Deer with their antlers provide the only known example of mammals able to regrow large complex body organs.

Among the dozen or so growth factors found naturally in parts of deer antler velvet are nerve growth factors, which are important players along with the two insulin-like growth factors IGF-1 and IGF-2. Nerve growth factors are essential for neuron maintenance and survival (neurons are the cells that make up your brain and nervous system) and supplementation with nerve growth factors may help to treat diseases of the nervous system.

The 1986 Nobel Prize in Medicine winner, Professor Rita Levi-Montalcini of Italy, a neurologist and biologist who reached the age of one hundred in 2009, attributes her mental sharpness and vigor to regular doses of nerve growth factor, a research area that she helped to pioneer and for which she received the Nobel Prize. She takes the nerve growth factor in the form of eye drops to enable her brain neurons to survive longer.

Royal Velvet, which first became available in the United States just a dozen years ago, guarantees its users that 90 percent of them will experience at least seven of twenty-five typical benefits within the first month of using the product. These benefits range from dramatic increases in energy and stamina, improved mental clarity and more restful sleep, to quicker wound healing, increased immune system function, and a heightened libido.

While there are many products claiming to be deer antler velvet, one must be wary of the scams and ineffective products out there! For example, there are synthetic IGF-1 products that claim to be antler velvet but are really just genetically modified synthetics. Some come from a genetically engineered e.coli bacteria. Other products place their antler velvet material in a solution of ethanol, which is unwise because ethanol has been shown to inhibit the development of growth factors in the human fetus.

COMMONLY ASKED QUESTIONS ABOUT
DEER ANTLER VELVET
Isn't it just an aphrodisiac?

This is a widespread misconception. While deer antler velvet does enhance virility and staying power for many men who try it, that is just one of numerous benefits reported from its use. Aphrodisiac powers have been ascribed to it for several thousand years in China, starting with stories about Chinese emperors who consumed it to keep up with the sexual demands from having large harems of concubines.

Are the deer killed for their antler velvet?

No deer are killed or harmed to extract their antler velvet. Doing so wouldn't make financial sense. The animals must be kept alive and in good health to grow another antler rack each season. Additionally, the red deer herd in New Zealand is a special population whose numbers are kept as high as possible. Care is taken to keep them in the best health possible.

Why should this product be effective when others aren't?

Some consumers try products labeled as deer antler velvet a few times, and when they don't feel or see any benefits, they assume it is the fault of deer antler rather than just the particular product they tried. One of the big differences between this Royal Velvet product and others is in the delivery system. Most antler products are powders that must be swallowed and, as a result, are barely absorbed by the human body because the nutrients are destroyed by acids in the stomach. Royal Velvet's patented delivery system uses microscopic liposomes to "encase" the delicate nutrients from antler velvet so when they are sprayed into the mouth, they can be quickly assimilated into the bloodstream for delivery throughout the body.

Is this product safe to use?

Some consumers have expressed only two types of concerns after using Royal Velvet, according to Blake Sawyer of Austin, Texas, who is the exclusive distributor for North America. Women who have gone through menopause may start menstruating again, which some find disconcerting. They weren't counting on becoming fertile once more with the use of this product. A second concern expressed is that some people have their libidos rekindled to the point that they may feel too much sexual energy. Lowering the dosage levels usually helps to counteract those effects. Otherwise, there have been no negative side effects reported, largely because Royal Velvet is recognized by the body as a nutrient dense food.

Live Cell Therapy

Live Cell Therapy uses organ cells from sheep placenta to create either an injectable or oral supplement to counteract the symptoms of aging. MFIII of Switzerland (www.ableyounger.com) comes in capsule form. This oral supplement is designed to bypass the stomach and its acids so it can dissolve in the small intestine for maximum absorption by the body.

Cell therapy revitalizes the body's immune system, reinvigorates old and degenerating cells, promotes sexual satisfaction, and stimulates overall vitality. It improves alertness and concentration, improves skin elasticity, and reduces wrinkles. MFIII isn't a drug and contains no hormones or proteins.

If you're a vegetarian and oppose the ingestion of an animal product in any form, there is also a plant-based anti-aging substitute made by the same company called Dermacenta (vegetal placenta, or VP). It's extracted from the cell cultures of a rare species of a nongenetically modified plant. It's rich in amino acids and the manufacturer promises that it, like the nonvegetarian version, produces no noticeable side effects.

Here are some of the bodily effects from MFIII that many users report:

- a strengthened immune system
- improved alertness and concentration
- escalated stamina and energy levels
- more elastic skin and reduced wrinkling
- deeper and more restful sleep
- enhanced sex drive and sexual potency
- delayed menopause with symptoms lessened

COMMONLY ASKED QUESTIONS ABOUT MFIII
Is MFIII a drug?

It's not a medicine or a drug, nor is it a genetically modified substance, nor does it contain any chemicals. It's a natural nutritional supplement that can be taken along with your other vitamin and nutritional supplements.

Has it been adequately tested?

This product has been approved by the U.S. Food and Drug Administration, according to the product's website. It was researched, developed, and manufactured in Switzerland after clinical trials conducted by Bio-HC, a research center in Pessac, France. It has also been analyzed by three other Swiss research labs including Laboratoire Dr. Matt.

Are there any side effects to be concerned about?

No side effects have been reported with either short- or long-term usage. One reason may be that the bio-molecules in the product are metabolized and excreted via the same pathways as other orally taken supplements.

What is the history of live cell use?

During the early part of the twentieth century the injectable live cell therapy was used by celebrities such as actor and comedian Charlie Chaplin, who attributed his use to enabling him to father children after he turned seventy years of age. By mid-century it was being taken by Winston Churchill, Dwight Eisenhower, and other heads of state who valued the higher energy levels it gave them. Now, after seventy years of use by the rich, the famous, and the powerful, this cell therapy is available in soft gel capsule form, a much more inexpensive option for public use.

How is it produced?

Using a biotechnology process starting with sheep placental cells, the active substances in MFIII are extracted, with molecular fat and hormones removed, making the ingredients highly pure and 99 percent water soluble. The human body, without any loss of regenerative function, readily absorbs the tiny molecular peptides in the product.

Royal Jelly

Royal Jelly is the stuff secreted from glands in the heads of worker bees and used as nutrition inside bee colonies by adult queen bees. It's a rich source of B-complex vitamins and contains seventeen different amino acids, aspartic acid, fatty acids, trace minerals, and enzymes. It can be obtained only from nature because it cannot currently be duplicated in a laboratory.

Many different cultures for thousands of years valued honey and Royal Jelly for their healing powers, especially wound healing. Medical science studies have recently affirmed a wide range of these health benefits from the use of Royal Jelly. It stimulates the growth of neural stem cells in the brain. It lowers cholesterol, fights inflammation and tumor formation, speeds wound healing, and acts as an antibiotic, an anti-allergic, and anti-cholesterol agent. (Source: C. Erem, O. Deger, E. Ovali, and Y. Barlak, *Endocrine* 2 [Oct 30, 2006]: 175–183.)

If you want more evidence for its health benefits and anti-aging properties, consider just a few of these findings:

- **It has the potential to rejuvenate your pituitary gland to produce more HGH.** A 2009 study by Japanese researchers, published in the journal, *Bioscience Biotechnology Biochemistry*, showed that Royal Jelly "compensated for age-associated declines in pituitary functions" among lab animals.
- **It may facilitate the restoration of cognitive ability.** Another 2009 study, in the *Evidence Based Complementary Alternative Medicine* journal, found Royal Jelly reverses cognitive impairment in lab animals by regenerating hippocampal cells in the brain.
- **It could delay or reverse many autoimmune diseases.** In the journal *Lupus,* a 2009 study determined that oral administration of Royal Jelly not only "significantly delayed" onset of lupus in lab animals, it "significantly" improved kidney function and extended the lifespan of these animals.
- **It holds the promise of regenerating fertility.** A 2010 study in *Animal Reproductive Science* uncovered strong evidence that Royal Jelly reverses infertility in male rabbits, increasing sperm output and motility, while decreasing cholesterol levels. This finding, like all of the others that used animal test subjects, might soon be replicated in human clinical trials.

Side effects such as hives from consuming Royal Jelly may occur in persons who already have been diagnosed with other known allergies.

For recommendations on the highest quality Royal Jelly, visit www.beeyoungnow.com.

Two New Anti-Aging Cures Coming Your Way

Within months you might have access to several new biostimulator products that are being hailed as an "elixir of life" formula and a "fountain of youth" pill.

The "elixir" consists of three amino acids—isoleucine, leucine, and valine—that are already used in some formulations taken by bodybuilders to enhance muscle development. Scientists in Italy at Pavia University tested the concoction on mice and found that it extended their lifespans by 12 percent, while giving the rodents higher exercise endurance and better motor coordination.

In their study, published in an October 2010 issue of the journal, *Cell Metabolism,* the researchers theorized that the amino acid cocktail increases production of mitochondria in the muscles, which are the cell compartments producing energy for the body. Mice fed the formula also measured increases in expression of the gene SIRT1, a gene that may be a key to longevity. They additionally experienced a reduction in Reactive Oxygen Species (ROS) production, which is thought to be helpful in slowing down aging symptoms.

Though these effects and others—such as improving cognitive function—have been demonstrated only in lab animals, the scientists are hopeful that clinical trials in humans will produce similar anti-aging benefits from ingesting this amino acid combination, some of which individually are already available for purchase in health food stores.

A second and even more promising anti-aging research development, nicknamed the "fountain of youth" pill by the news media, has been created by a prominent Russian scientist after forty years of research. It, too, involves mitochondria and lowering the ROS level to slow down the aging process but uses a specially formulated antioxidant.

Moscow State University professor Vladimir Skulachev, dean of the school of bioengineering, developed an antioxidant much stronger and longer lasting than any known natural antioxidant to halt the damaging effects that oxygen often has on cells in the human body. Most of the oxygen that enters our bodies is converted to water, but a small percentage evolves into harmful forms of oxygen that accumulate over a lifetime and damage the body to trigger symptoms of aging.

Professort Skulachev's innovation was to find a combination of chemical antioxidants that worked together to neutralize the dangerous form of oxygen inside body cells. In lab experiments, he doubled the lifespan of mice and kept them healthier far longer than normal using these antioxidants in their diet. Equally remarkable, the professor used himself as a guinea pig and successfully removed a cataract from one of his eyes with the antioxidant formula in eye drops. (The antioxidant compound he synthesized is called SkQ1, its chemical name being *plastoquinonyl decyltriphenylphosphonium*.)

No less an authority, Dr. Gunter Blobel—a Nobel Prize winner in Physiology and Medicine, and a professor at Rockefeller University in New York—told me in an email exchange how Professor Skulachev's anti-aging work could turn out to be historic: "It has been shown that oxidative damage is huge (as a contributor to aging), but we do not have an antioxidant of the type that Professor Skulachev has developed. He is one of the world's best biochemists and bioenergists."

In a May 2010 presentation to anti-aging scientists gathered at Moscow State University, Professor Skulachev and his son, M. V. Skulachev, who is a biologist at the university, revealed the following results they uncovered from testing SkQ1 on a variety of animal species: Both males and females increased their lifespan due to prevention of age-linked declines of immunity; there were decelerations in the declines usually associated with osteoporosis, wound healing, balding, cataracts, changes in appearance and skin health, even the appearance of cancers. All that remains is for these scientists to conduct clinical trials of SkQ1 in human subjects.

And Finally . . . A Fix For The Cellular Clock of Aging

One last biostimulator deserves your attention and consideration. It's known as TA-65, a rare naturally occurring single molecule that's found in small amounts in the ancient Chinese medicinal herb Astragalus.

T.A. Sciences is a company based in New York City, founded by Noel Thomas Patton, which secured nutraceutical manufacturing rights to a discovery by the California biotech company Geron demonstrating that TA-65 has cellular rejuvenation properties.

Here is how the molecule works to repair the cellular clock of aging. Within each of the trillions of cells in your body are 23 pairs of chromosomes, which are long sequences of DNA, the code of life. At both ends of each chromosome are telomeres, tiny bits of DNA critical to cell function. Think of telomeres as being like the plastic tips at the ends of shoelaces. These plastic tips help prevent shoelaces from fraying just as the telomere tips protect the chromosomes from fraying and mutating, which happens with aging. Each time a cell divides, telomeres become shorter, and over time that shortening process facilitates emergence of the conditions we associate with advancing age. In fact a recent peer reviewed paper written by Harvard scientists published in the scientific journal *Nature*, claims that telomere shortening is the *root cause* of aging. What TA-65 does is to activate telomerase, a naturally-occurring enzyme in your body that has the unique capacity to elongate short telomeres thereby rejuvenating the cell and extending its lifespan.

TA-65, the rare molecule from Astragalus (see more about this herb in Chapter 4) is a capsule supplement that is the centerpiece of an anti-aging program called the *Patton Protocol*, named after the company founder. Though the supplement can be taken by itself, the accompanying protocol includes bloodwork to assess immune function and mean telomere lengths, along with other aging biomarker testing. A user of TA-65 for the past several years has been Dr. Frederic Vagnini, a renowned New York heart, lung and blood vessel surgeon and book author, who told me the following, "Telomerase Activation with TA-65 for preventing telomere shortening is one of the most exciting aspects of Anti-Aging Medicine. I recommend TA-65 to my clients and have been on the program for over three years. A proven area of benefit for me has been immune system enhancement." Dr. Vagnini was so enthused about its anti-aging benefits that he became a consultant to the company manufacturing TA-65.

Results from two medical studies lend support to the potential effectiveness of TA-65 in boosting the immune system, lengthening short telomeres, and improving vision and skin appearance.

• A February 2011 study in the journal, *Rejuvenation Research,* examined the first year of data from the *Patton Protocol* health maintenance program using TA-65 and determined that "a significant reduction in the percent of short telomeres" had occurred with a positive effect on the immune system.

• Just a month later, in March 2011, a report appeared in the journal *Aging Cell* in which the six study scientists concluded: "these results indicate that TA-65 treatment results in telomerase-dependent elongation of short telomeres and rescue of associated DNA damage." An improvement in lab animals was also noted in their glucose tolerance, osteoporosis and skin fitness.

For more information or to purchase TA-65, visit: www.tasciences.com. To learn details about the science behind telomeres, telomerase, and aging, go to The Telomere Science Library at: www.telomerescience.com.

CHAPTER 4

Miraculous Nutrients to Keep You Youthful

LET'S TELL IT LIKE IT IS ABOUT OUR FOOD. MOST OF WHAT CONSTITUTES the typical diet today is toxic! It's not fit to eat. It's not giving us the nutrients that we need and that our bodies crave.

It's a diet guaranteed to shorten your lifespan by inflicting harm to your body, even if you're using biostimulators. Add to that a sedentary lifestyle in which the only consistent exercise is the movement of your jaw muscles, and you've got a recipe for faster physical and mental degeneration.

Are you one of those people who roll their eyes and space out when the suggestion of a healthy diet and regular exercise comes up? If you are, then it's time to snap out of it! You're not only harming yourself with that complacent attitude, you're helping to bankrupt the country with all of your unnecessary medical bills.

If you do want to change your life for the better, if you do want to be healthier and live longer while lowering the costs of your medical care, then following the guidelines in this chapter will make your use of human growth hormone and its biostimulators that much more effective.

One place to start is with the word *synergy*. It needs to be in your awareness and in your vocabulary because synergy is a force of nature that can help you to keep the effects of aging in check! Here is a simple definition. Synergy means combining two or more things so they interact to create something much more powerful than any one thing can be on its own.

To remain healthy and youthful as you advance in age, you can harness a powerful synergy to your advantage by combining a few lifestyle choices. With the injectable form of the Master Hormone and biostimulators at the core of your health regimen, surround this dynamic duo with a powerful synergy-producing supporting cast—a proper diet, good sleep, regular exercise, and activities that promote vitality and a positive frame of mind.

Let's look at the healthy nutrients you need to be absorbing.

Two Dietary Anti-Aging Strategies

There are two surefire ways to get anti-aging benefits from your dietary habits: (1) you can severely restrict the number of calories you consume; (2) you can consume high-nutrient super foods or supplements based on their nutrient content. A third option would be to fast for one day, once a week, and limit your calorie intake by consuming only, or mostly, a super foods diet when you do eat.

Those people who engage in fasting for a day every week, or for longer periods of time, are wise to something, whether they realize it or not. Plenty of science studies done on both animals and humans have uncovered evidence that a restriction of calorie intake far below the calories consumed in most diets today can delay cardiac aging and prevent cardiovascular disease, certain types of cancer and other diseases, along with having other anti-aging effects on various organs. An unexpected benefit that some fasters discover is the purging of parasites they never suspected they had colonizing in their colon.

Periodic fasting, or the adoption of the Mediterranean or Okinawan diets that drastically limit calorie consumption, are all good dietary strategies for living a longer life. Hundreds of medical science studies demonstrating the benefits of caloric restrictive diets and fasting emerged over the past decade, though the first evidence appeared as far back as 1935, when scientists at Cornell University discovered that rats placed on a very low calorie diet extended their lifespans by 33 percent and suffered fewer late-in-life diseases than other rats that were fed normal diets.

Here is a summary of just a few pieces of the medical evidence.

- A July 1996 study in the journal *Science* concluded that "restriction of caloric intake lowers steady-state levels of oxidative stress and damage, retards age-associated changes, and extends the maximum life-span in mammals."
- In a May 2003 study published by the *Proceedings of the National Academy of Sciences* it was found that intermittent fasting in lab animals regulated glucose and neuronal resistance to injury in ways that could extend their lives.
- The *Journal of the American Medical Association* featured an April 2006 study in which a group of men and women were placed on a calorie-restricted diet for six months at the end of which the study authors concluded that "our findings suggest that two biomarkers of longevity (fasting insulin level and body temperature) are decreased by prolonged calorie restriction in humans."
- A twenty-year-long study of aging in rhesus monkeys conducted at the University of Wisconsin, and published in a July 2009 issue of *Science,* found that those monkeys eating a third less food than control study monkeys aged much more slowly.
- An *Archives of Neurology* study in February 2009 determined that adherence to the Mediterranean diet with its emphasis on low calorie foods and olive oil resulted in study participants having a reduced risk of mild cognitive impairment and a lower risk of developing Alzheimer's disease.
- The January 2009 issue of the *Proceedings of the National Academy of Sciences* carried a study article titled "Caloric restriction improves memory in elderly humans," which detailed "significant increases in verbal memory scores after caloric restriction," an effect that was also correlated with decreases in fasting plasma levels of insulin showing a protective effect against several diseases.

Before undertaking any sort of fasting regimen, you might want to visit www.fasting.com to take advantage of this site's wealth of information about how to safely go about periodic fasting and get the most out of the experience.

Many of you probably don't want to fast like a monk to achieve these anti-aging results. So what can you do with your diet that's effective instead? The answer is to choose the nutrients in the foods you consume very carefully and wisely. The following are some good choices. Try them in combination to increase their effects.

Quercetin

This antioxidant and anti-inflammatory flavonoid found in apples, onions (especially red onions), red grapes, and other fruits and vegetables has been shown in lab studies to be a potent scavenger of free radicals, those particles in the body that damage cell membranes and induce aging. Quercetin helps the body to increase IGFBP-3 levels. It also interacts with phytochemicals to create health-beneficial synergies.

Quercetin supplements may also have some benefit for physical endurance. A study published in a June 2009 issue of *International Journal of Sports Nutrition and Exercise Metabolism* found a 13.2 percent increase in endurance among cyclists who took 500 mg of quercetin before exercising. The substance may also have benefits for the prevention of cancer, heart disease, prostatitis, cataracts, allergies, and respiratory diseases.

Astragalus

This herb root contains two molecules called cycloastragenois and astragalosides, which have been found to help your telomeres grow. Remember telomeres from the previous chapter? They exist on the ends of your DNA strands and are protective coverings that guard against degradation that comes with age.

Each time one of your cells divides, your telomeres shorten slightly, hastening the aging process toward eventual death. So astragalus, by reigniting the growth of some telomeres and preventing others from depleting, serve an anti-aging function if it's added to your diet as a supplement. Usually it's sold as a powder or in capsules. For thousands of years, it's been a staple in Chinese medicine remedies.

In a 2010 study published in the journal *Nature*, Harvard Medical School researchers rejuvenated worn out organs in elderly mice, turning them back into healthy animals, by reactivating an enzyme called telomerase that stops telomeres at the end of each chromosome from getting shorter. The lab animals even grew new neurons in their brains. "What we saw in these animals was not a slowing down or stabilization of the aging process. We saw a dramatic reversal," commented study leader Professor Ronald DePinho. Though astragalus wasn't used in this particular experiment, the results did provide more evidence that telomeres are one of the keys to anti-aging.

Omega-3 Fatty Acids

These are found in flax, flaxseed, and salmon. Evidence has emerged that omega-3s may protect you at the cellular level against the effects of aging. In the *Journal of the American Medical Association* (Jan. 20, 2010, issue) scientists reported on the results of a five-year study that found people with the highest levels of omega-3 fatty acids in their bodies had the slowest rate of telomere shortening. That meant the omega-3s may be protecting the body against cellular aging.

Andean Maca
Root

Long considered a powerful libido enhancer among native peoples of Peru, it contains a potpourri of chemicals that may offer anti-aging benefits. In particular, this root has many essential amino acids such as aspartic acid, glycine, arginine, and glutamic acid. Its components also include alkaloids, sterols, and other chemicals important to health, vitality, and longevity. Research indicates that the root helps to regulate those hormone-secreting organs: the adrenal and pituitary glands.

Cordyceps Mushroom

The latest anti-aging evidence for a super food has emerged for a traditional Chinese mushroom called *Cordyceps sinensis* (Cs-4). This mushroom had been promoted for centuries in China as having anti-aging properties and now Western medical studies have uncovered impressive evidence to underscore the truth of these claims.

Two University of Wisconsin professors and their LifeGen Technologies lab did a series of experiments in 2010 and found the mushroom may not only be a treatment for cancer, as other studies determined, but its consumption also encourages human genes to express themselves in ways that promote longevity.

Around the age of thirty, certain gene clusters in the human body slow down producing cellular mitochondria, an energy factory for cells and muscles. This decrease in energy metabolism results in fatigue and loss of endurance as we age. Chemicals in the mushroom apparently stimulate these genes back into productivity, reactivating energy metabolism, as well as increasing antioxidant activity to reduce free radical oxidative damage to cells.

Proper Nutrition Helps to Keep You Youthful

Remember that as we mature, our ability to appear and feel young involves more than human growth hormone replacement therapy, though that can certainly be an essential key. Exercise, proper sleep, food selections, minerals, and vitamins all combine in a synergy to play integral roles as biostimulants in this process. People who employ a balance of these factors position themselves for healthy, quality-filled aging—while lessening the possibility of chronic degenerative diseases like cancer.

Whether you are young or advanced in age, a nutritious diet is indispensable to maintaining exceptional health and a longer life. That's why I put so much emphasis on your absorption of healthy nutrients. Nutrition literally defines what you are made of because it is the foundation for every living cell and organ in your body. Nutrition in the blood supplies the body with the very fuel for existence. It supplies strength, energy, and vitality, while empowering the body to fight disease and illness.

Hunger is more than just a reason to consume food. This vital craving serves as your body's essential communication, conveying a basic need for important nutrients. When you consume natural, nutrient-dense foods, you satisfy your body's need for high quality fuel and that empowers your immune system to combat illness and disease.

Want to know more about the most nutrient rich foods on earth? Here is a list of nature's super foods:

NINE GROUPS OF ORGANIC SUPER FOODS
YOU NEED IN YOUR DIET

(Caution: Avoid genetically modified foods, whose long-term safety is unproven; GMOs are becoming especially common in soybeans and corn.)

- greens such as kale, spinach, broccoli, beet tops, and all dark green leafy vegetables in both whole and juice form; also nopal cactus, nettle leaf, and cabbages
- maca root from the Andes and maca root juice
- mushrooms, in particular these: reishi, cordyceps, maitake, chaga, mesima, lion's mane, turkey tail, shitake
- spirulina and chlorella: these include Klamath Lake Blue-Green Algae
- herbs and spices such as garlic, dandelion leaf, nettle, and parsley: the most potent spice is curcumin from the turmeric plant, a staple in Indian cuisine
- bee pollen and royal jelly

- dark red and purple fruits and berries: these include blueberries and raspberries. Also, goji berry juice and Hawthorne berry
- kelp and sea plants
- taro root, orange tomatoes, carrots, and orange vegetables

Other additions to the super foods list include cacao (raw chocolate), sweet mesquite pod, beetroot juice, and sprouted flax.

I also urge our patients to consume healthy smoothies that they prepare at home on a regular basis. Most of these recipes include soy milk, nonfat yogurt, berries such as blueberries, blackberries, or strawberries, bananas, and a raw egg, plus a couple of tablespoons of flaxseed oil and whey protein. Many patients consider such smoothies delicious, and they're also good for digestion.

TWO REASONS TO ALWAYS EAT
ORGANIC SUPER FOODS

1. Wise consumers will want to avoid the residues of pesticides, herbicides, and other synthetic chemicals applied to plants and fruits. Washing the produce with water will not remove all of the residues. These chemicals can cause health problems in humans, including neurodegenerative disorders like Parkinson's disease.
2. Organically (nonchemically) grown super foods contain higher levels of phytochemicals. These nutrients have been documented in thousands of medical science studies as being important to good health and a long life. Phytochemicals are produced by plants in response to stress and to protect against insects and disease. When pesticides and other chemicals are applied during the growing process, plants produce lower levels of these important phytochemical nutrients.

MAKE YOUR FOOD SELECTIONS
A FIRST LEVEL OF DEFENSE

Adopting a proper food selection or diet program should be your primary biostimulatory step in any serious anti-aging program.

While maintaining a trim, ideal weight might sound merely vain or narcissistic, various medical studies through the years strongly indicate that excessive or unnecessary weight contributes to cancer, cardiovascular disease, and diabetes mellitus. Maintaining an ideal body weight can go a long way toward preventing or at least lowering the probability of such negative health factors.

The South Beach Diet, Zone Diet, and Modified Atkin's Diet strive to reduce simple sugars, while increasing proteins and healthy fats. Another food-selection program, the Mediterranean Diet, also has been deemed effective. These diets often prove useful as low-glycemic or in supplying the healthiest form of carbohydrates. Medical professionals can measure the impact that carbohydrates have on blood glucose levels, using a system called the "glycemic index."

WHY I STRESS THE IMPORTANCE
OF CERTAIN FOODS

Whenever possible I recommend vegan or near-vegan diets, eliminating or significantly lowering the amount of animal flesh and animal products that you consume. However, occasional broiled or baked lean meats, fowl, or fish become acceptable when eaten in lower quantities.

In anti-cancer diets and for weight management, vegetables have proven especially beneficial and healthy, especially cabbage, cauliflower, carrots, beans, broccoli, and brussels sprouts. Foods containing natural digestive enzymes, including bromelain from pineapples and papain from papaya are also highly desirable.

You should always avoid fried foods, simple sugars, salt, flour, and any cured meats such as salami, sausage, bologna, pepperoni, canned meats, Spam, hot dogs, and similar foods.

Among other primary foods that we highly recommend to treat or prevent certain aging-related conditions:

Citrus foods: While also helping to prevent cancer, citrus foods containing bioflavonoids, terpenes, limonene, and citrus pectin aid the cardiovascular system while serving as antioxidants.

Red grapes: These fruits contain plant flavonoids called "pycnogenol," also present in pine bark extract. Red grapes serve as one of the strongest antioxidants, also helpful in strengthening bone and cartilage tissue while enhancing immune function.

Red wine: This beverage contains nutrients, which preserves telomere integrity—vital in enabling the body's cells to divide or reproduce with efficiency, thereby promoting longevity.

Hawthorne berries: This food and extracts from such fruits help strengthen bones, tendons, cartilage, and cardiac muscle, while serving as a natural treatment for hypertension.

Green tea: Three or four cups per day have long been known to Asians as helpful in preventing cancers—even common killers like lung cancer.

Flaxseed lignan fibers: An excellent hormone regulator, this food source helps protect against breast and prostate cancers.

Healthy oils: Selections such as corn, olive, canola, and soy are monosaturated, which is important in the production of good cholesterol.

Oat bran and wheat germ: These natural foods help lower "bad cholesterol," while increasing "good cholesterol."

Green "super foods": These selections include wheat grass, rye grass, barley grass, and blue green algae, nutrient and trace elements, and are an excellent source of making the body more alkaline than acidic. These foods also combat acidosis, a hallmark of inflammatory conditions and cancer. Remember that active cancers lower the body's PH and promote acidity, a condition that favors cancer growth

Soybeans: We know that this excellent anti-aging food, which is high in protein, remains a delight to people who prefer to avoid eating meat. The chemicals in soy contain strong antioxidants, hormone regulators, and cancer-prevention qualities, especially in battling breast and prostate cancers. Many people eat soy products, thanks to the cancer-therapeutic properties of these foods. (Be sure to avoid genetically modified soybeans by purchasing only certified organic products!)

Healthy dark chocolates: Derived from natural cocoa, chocolate without sugar or milk products serves as an essential antioxidant.

Foods You Should Eat

While all these various health food opportunities might seem limitless, in summary your food selection list should include:

raw or lightly cooked whole grain cereals
raw or lightly steamed vegetables and sprouts
raw or fresh fruits, including the skin
lightly cooked beans, lentils, and peas
preferably unsalted raw nuts and seeds
low-fat dairy products, especially low-fat cultured yogurt
occasional lean meat, fish, or poultry, usually limited to one or two
    times weekly
an occasional glass of red wine

Foods You Should Avoid

The list of foods and drinks to avoid remains extensive:

more than two ounces of alcohol daily, especially whiskey, scotch,
    vodka, and gin
bacon and cured meats
canned or frozen fruits
canned soups
fried foods in any form
all types of gravies
whole milk ice cream
salted peanuts
processed cheese products
processed luncheon meats
saturated fats
soft cheeses
soft drinks and sodas
tuna that is canned in oil

canned or frozen vegetables with salt additives

white or brown sugar

white flour products

white rice products

white vinegar

fruit syrups

Aspartame and other synthetic sweeteners

high fructose corn syrup, which appears not only in many soft
   drinks but also in thousands of other processed food products.

Avoid foods high in fat content, including cake, cookies, doughnuts,
   ricotta cheese, cream cheese, crescents, regular crackers, breaded
   or fried fish, whole milk ice cream, butter, mayonnaise, sour
   cream, de-boned or chuck steaks, dark meat from turkey or
   chicken, bologna, salami, hot dogs, and sausage.

A Sweet Tooth Prematurely Ages You

Medical evidence is overwhelming that sugar is addictive, and the more you eat of it, the faster you prematurely age. That includes not just an effect from white sugar, but from the high fructose corn syrup found in most carbonated beverages and processed foods.

Want some evidence? Consider these studies:

- The journal *Clinical Dermatology* reported in July 2010 that sugar ages skin by the simple act of cross-linking the skin's collagen fibers, making them incapable of easy repair.
- When lab animals were fed sugar-sweetened beverages, according to a May 2008 report in the journal *Bone,* severe effects on bone mass and strength were measured.

- In the *Annals of the New York Academy of Sciences* a 2007 study found that premature aging occurred in skin cells called keratinocytes when they were exposed over three days to sugar treatments of glucose.
- Consumption of fructose severely affected a range of factors involved in the aging process among lab animals exposed to it over the course of a year in this 1998 study published in the *Journal of Nutrition.*

Your Food Choices Can Determine Skin Wrinkling

Consider this additional evidence for the good anti-aging and bad faster-aging food groupings that I listed for you earlier in this chapter.

When it comes to skin wrinkling, a February 2001 study published in the *American College of Nutrition* found a direct connection to the quality of the nutrients that you absorb. Groups of people living in Greece, Australia, and Sweden had their skin condition and nutrient intakes assessed by a team of researchers.

Here is what they found: Less skin damage and wrinkling occurred with age for persons who had a higher consumption of vegetables, olive oil, fish, and legumes. Those who ate more butter, margarine, milk, and sugar products exhibited much more skin wrinkling and damage, which is to say, they looked older than their healthy-eating counterparts.

What Vitamins and Minerals Should You Take?

Most people know that the government recommends a "required daily allowance" or RDA of specific vitamins and minerals. By law, through a required packaging and labeling process, distributors of foods, vitamins, and minerals must specify the percentage of these substances that a particular product contains.

However, in all these instances—everything from cereal boxes to milk cartons—the term "100 percent" refers to the least amount of a vitamin or mineral that the government deems necessary to sustain good health. Medical professionals consider these minimum levels as the lowest amounts essential to prevent a wide variety of diseases including scurvy, rickets, pellagra, beriberi, pernicious anemia, and many other afflictions.

When developing these FDA requirements, medical professionals used nutritional studies that were conducted as far back as the 1940s. However, at the time scientists and physicians lacked precise methods of testing or determining the levels of vitamins and minerals in tissue and blood. Modern equipment gives much more accurate results.

The minimum RDA levels specified by the government fail to meet the human body's requirements, especially amid the increased onslaught of serious cancer, severe cardiovascular disease, environmental toxins, and virulent viruses or bacterial illnesses. Severe stress that afflicts people in today's society compounds these problems.

RDA and optimal daily allowances can vary significantly for specific vitamins or minerals. For instance, the RDA for Vitamin C is 60 mg per day, compared to an optimal daily allowance of about 1,000 mg daily for the same substance. Vitamins A and E also are among many individual vitamins and minerals with optimal daily doses significantly higher than the RDA listed for each of them. Vitamin D_3, considered essential for preventing most cancers, now requires up to 5,000 IUs per day.

TAKE THESE NINE IMPORTANT
MINERALS

When following all the various recommendations already mentioned for an anti-aging diet, your body still may need vitamins and minerals from other sources. As a result, you should take the following minerals, listed alphabetically:

Boron: This trace mineral activates Vitamin D while aiding the body's ability to absorb and use calcium essential for bone strength and estrogen for metabolism. Take at lease 3 mg daily.

Calcium: As the body's most abundant mineral, this essential substance gets absorbed best in its ionized form such as: citrate; lactate primarily from milk products; gluconate from fruits, honeys, teas and wines;

aspartate from sprouting seeds, oat flakes, and avocadoes; and orotate. Dietary supplements are often excellent, or single sources of calcium. Women, especially shortly before, during, and after menopause, should take 1,500 mg of calcium daily, usually in three doses of 500 mg each every eight hours.

Chromium: Prevalent in mushrooms, yeast, prunes, nuts, and asparagus, this mineral helps sugar metabolism by generating insulin. Without any known toxicity, chromium helps the body lower triglycerides or bad cholesterol. Take at least 400 mcg daily.

Copper: The body needs this essential trace element for enzyme function or vital biochemical reactions. The body stores or uses most of its copper in the brain or liver. Important in anti-aging therapy, copper's best food sources include fish, dark meat, and colored vegetables. Take at least 3 mg daily.

Magnesium: This plays an essential role for several hundred enzyme reactions throughout the body. Bones contain 60 percent of the total of this mineral within the body, while muscles have 25 percent. Medical experts find other high concentrations of magnesium in vital organs including the brain, heart, liver, and kidneys. Like potassium, most magnesium is intracellular or within the cells. The best magnesium supplements are glycinate, aspartate, or taurinate. Common foods that contain magnesium include wheat bran, wheat germ, almonds, cashews, Brazil nuts, peanuts, walnuts, tofu, soybeans, and brown rice. Take 400 to 600 mg daily. Excessive quantities may cause diarrhea.

Manganese: Multiple enzyme systems throughout the body use this mineral, necessary for the metabolism's glucose, for energy production, and for thyroid function. Common food sources include nuts, whole grains, split peas, green leafy vegetables and dried fruits. Take 1,500 to 2,000 mg daily.

Potassium: This essential mineral serves vital roles throughout the body, including the performance and functions of the heart and muscles—plus multiple enzyme systems and the balance of electrolyte or free ions within cell structures. Common food sources include bananas, figs, leafy green vegetables, and citrus fruits. Take 1,500 to 2,000 mg daily.

Selenium: This essential anti-aging trace mineral serves as a strong antioxidant, acting in concert with Vitamin E to prevent free radicals from damaging cell membranes. Useful in cancer therapy and anti-aging therapy, selenium—proven for its antiviral action—often is recommended for preventing prostate cancer. Physicians also recommend selenium for enhancing immune function and for relieving anxiety. Common food sources include Brazil nuts, sunflower seeds, whole grains, meat products, garlic, and seafood. Rare side effects include dizziness, nausea, brittle nails, and hair loss. Take 100 to 200 mcg daily.

Zinc: Often found in shellfish and red meats, this mineral plays an important role in the functions of vital hormones including insulin, sex hormones, thymus gland hormones, and human growth hormone. Essential for vision, taste, and smell, zinc becomes essential for prostate function and male fertility. Especially after surgery, zinc aids protein synthesis and cell growth while also fighting viruses. Citrate, glycerate, and picolinate are good zinc supplements. Take 25 to 50 mg daily.

WANT TO KNOW A DIRTY LITTLE SECRET?

Most of the health industry keeps a dirty little secret from you—the vast majority of vitamins and supplement products sold in the world today fail to work effectively.

Our bodies simply can't break down and assimilate many supplement products because they are synthetics created in pharmaceutical industry laboratories. More than 90 percent of all the supplements sold in the United States are synthetics, as opposed to natural, plant-based, according to nutrition expert Dr. Brian Clement, director of the Hippocrates Health Institute and author of the book *Supplements Exposed.*

As a result of this synthetic overload, our digestive system ends up passing most vitamin supplements through our system virtually unabsorbed!

Food provides the best, most direct way to get healthy nutrition that the body can readily absorb. That means plants, fruits, vegetables, and herbs. But most of us fail to get enough of these in our daily food intake.

Worsening matters, many industrial food farms add harmful chemicals to our fruits and vegetables in an effort to preserve crops through the long transportation process, from farms to the supermarket, and eventually to your table. Those pesticides, preservatives, and other synthetic chemical residues pose health risks.

When you purchase supplements, always try to find natural, organic products that come directly from plant-based sources. Look for labels that say "Naturally Occurring Standard" to indicate the ingredients come straight from plants rather than chemical laboratories. This helps to ensure that you absorb only the highest quality and densest nutrient supplements.

THE ANTIOXIDANT LINEUP
YOU NEED

Antioxidants reign as the most important anti-aging vitamin supplements, especially vitamins A, C, E, and coenzyme-Q_{10}. Medical professionals consider these vitamins as antioxidants thanks to their unique ability to inactivate free radicals that can accumulate in the body—especially in mature people. When left unchecked, free radicals can damage multiple tissues throughout the body, promoting the growth of abnormal cells that can cause cancer or accelerate the signs of aging.

Recall that free radicals become reactive substances formed when energy gets produced. Amid a search for its missing electron, a free radical becomes unstable while randomly attacking healthy molecules in the body. Free radicals cause extensive damage unless stopped by antioxidants.

Worsening matters, free radicals can attack the energy factory or mitochondria, interrupting important enzyme and hormonal systems. This interferes with the body's ability to grow and repair, and to cope with stress.

As a result, antioxidants become necessary to neutralize all free radicals within the body. Among antioxidants that I strongly recommend:

Vitamin A and beta-carotene: Take these together; since beta-carotene causes less toxicity to the liver, you should consider beta-carotene the preferred supplement for Vitamin A. Excellent food sources for beta-carotene include dark leafy vegetables such as spinach, broccoli, and peppers—plus dark yellow or orange fruits and vegetables like sweet potatoes, pumpkins, papayas, oranges, and apricots. Heavy smokers should avoid large doses of beta-carotene; numerous studies show a propensity for lung cancers among smokers who ingest large doses of beta-carotene and Vitamin A. However, this remains controversial.

Vitamin C: While serving as an excellent antioxidant and anti-aging weapon, Vitamin C strengthens blood vessel walls and promotes wound healing, and it also stimulates hormonal regulation and brain chemicals. Adding to these many benefits, Vitamin C also increases immune function and protects against toxic chemicals such as potentially cancer-causing nitrosamine chemical compounds. Excellent food sources for Vitamin C include citrus fruits, green or red peppers, broccoli, brussels sprouts, potatoes, spinach, strawberries, tomatoes, and papayas. Rare side effects from Vitamin C include kidney stones. But negative impacts of Vitamin C are rarely seen, even in large doses of 10 to 15 grams per day. I recommend 1,000 to 1,500 mg daily.

Vitamin E: Along with Vitamin C, this becomes part of a strong anti-aging and antioxidant team. Vitamin E attacks free radicals, blocks the oxygenation of bad cholesterol and other fats, and prevents heart attacks and strokes. Adding to its firepower, Vitamin E keeps arteries free from potentially harmful plaque, increases immunity, and blocks the growth of cancer cells. In addition, homeopaths strongly recommend Vitamin E for preventing the progression of degenerative brain diseases, improving the systems related to arthritis, counteracting cataracts and preventing certain impairments in our ability to walk. Good natural food sources for Vitamin E include seed oils, leafy green vegetables, liver, whole grains, wheat germ, egg yolks, butter, and nuts. Vitamin E has a mild ability to prevent blood from clotting. So, you should avoid taking Vitamin E with blood-thinner medications like warfarin and Plavix. For anti-aging purposes, I recommend 400 to 800 IU of Vitamin E per day.

Coenzyme-Q_{10}: Also known as Vitamin Q or ubiquinone, this plays an integral role in heart function—particularly congestive heart failure or cardiomyopathy. While lowering blood pressure, Coenzyme-Q_{10} also enhances the immune system, reduces gum disease, and increases energy levels. Common food sources include eggs, rice, bran, wheat germ, fatty fish, organ meats, soy oil, and peanuts. Coenzyme-Q_{10} lacks toxicity side effects. I recommend 300 mg daily.

MORE SUPPLEMENTS FOR YOUR
ANTI-AGING COCKTAIL

Anti-aging medicine becomes fun when we add or mix some or all of these important vitamins with a wide variety of substances that scientists know will slow the signs of aging. Thanks to modern science and cutting-edge production techniques, you can ingest these various substances in supplement form or from certain foods. Listed in alphabetical order, some of the most prevalent include:

Acetyl L-Carnitine: Serves as a powerful antioxidant for the central nervous system and peripheral nerves, in doses of 500 mg daily.

Alpha lipoic acid: An important amino acid essential in transferring energy among cells, this unique antioxidant synergizes, enhances or magnifies B vitamins. Useful in treating various disorders of the central nervous system—called "neuropathies" by physicians—this acid improves the body's regulation of insulin. This, in turn, improves the metabolism and enhances the functions of essential systems like the liver and muscles, recommended at 500 mg daily.

L-carnitine: This vitamin-like substance serves a necessary role in helping the body metabolize or process fatty acids, some essential in producing various hormone-like substances. Fatty acids regulate everything from immune responses to blood clotting and even blood pressure. In addition, L-carnitine helps produce energy in the mitochondria, vital in generating the body's essential chemical energy. You should take 4 to 6 grams daily.

Folic acid: Necessary in the production of neurotransmitters, chemicals that regulate signals between cells and neurons, this substance also enables the body to transfer essential methyl gasses within the body. Working in synergy with Vitamins B_6 and B_{12}, folic acid reduces levels of homocysteine—which, in elevated amounts could lead to thrombosis or cardiovascular disease. You should take 400 to 600 mcg daily.

Ginkgo biloba: The many positive anti-aging benefits of this extract include improved memory, blood flow to the brain, and vascular function. You should use care when using ginkgo biloba, derived from a unique Chinese tree species, and avoid using the extract with blood-thinning agents like warfarin. You should take 60 mg daily.

L-arginine: This amino acid stimulates growth hormone production and improves erectile function. You should take 3 grams daily.

L-glutamine: An abundant amino acid, this can work as a "brain fuel" during stressful periods and also serves a vital role in producing muscles and repairing the lining of the intestine. You should take 3 grams daily.

L-glutathione: Hailed by some medical professionals as a "life-extending master antioxidant," this serves a useful role in cancer prevention and in detoxifying the immune system. Also a powerful scavenger of free radicals, L-glutathione serves beneficial roles in treating the conditions of many ailments or physical problems. These include autism, cardiovascular disease, autoimmune diseases, asthma, diabetes, lung disease, colitis, hepatitis, chronic fatigue syndrome, multiple sclerosis, Parkinson's and Alzheimer's disease. Abundant in the cytoplasm within the plasma membranes of cells and in mitochondria that generate chemical energy, L-glutathione also helps patients with degenerative eye diseases like cataracts and macular degeneration. You should take 100 mg daily.

Lutein: Allied with Vitamin A, this substance comes from carotenoids or organic pigments found in various plants. Physicians consider lutein important in preventing and treating prostate cancer and degenerative eye disease. Medical professionals recommend eating natural sources of lutein, including green leafy vegetables, tomatoes, potatoes, spinach, carrots, fruits, and algae.

Lycopene: You can find abundant amounts of this powerful antioxidant, anti-cancer substance—also good in treating prostate cancer and degenerative eye diseases—in tomatoes, carrots, green peppers, pink grapefruits, and apricots.

N-acetylcysteine: A powerful antioxidant that becomes active when ingested with Vitamin C, medical professionals consider this helpful in brain and cardiac function. You can take 500 mg daily.

Quercetin: An antioxidant or bioflavonoid found primarily in plants, this strong anti-viral performs an anti-tumor activity while also helpful to people with severe allergies, asthma, and allergic rashes. You can find quercetin in abundance in yellow and red onions and broccoli. You can take 500 to 1,500 mg daily.

Turmeric: Also known as curcumin, abundant in curry powder and mustard, this antioxidant with anti-cancer and anti-inflammatory qualities has a positive impact on the intestinal tract plus the immune and cardiovascular systems. You should take 500 mg per day.

Vitamin B_1: Also called thiamine, working in conjunction with magnesium and found in abundance in coffee and alcohol, this serves a necessary role in optimal brain function. You should take 100 mg daily.

Vitamin B_2: Commonly called riboflavin, this serves as a natural "glutathione," a term used by physicians to describe something that protects cells from free radicals or toxins. Also vital in the body's energy production, this vitamin is found in abundance in brewers' yeast, almonds, wheat germ, mushrooms, whole grains, and soy. You should take 30 mg daily.

Vitamin B_3: Also called niacin, this performs an essential role in fifty enzyme reactions within the body. Besides performing an important role in producing sex hormones and adrenal hormones and energy, niacin performs essential work in metabolizing sugar, fat, and cholesterol. You should take 500 to 1,000 mg daily.

Vitamin B_5: Also called pantothenic acid, necessary to metabolize sugar and energy, this vitamin plays a necessary role in the production of adrenal hormones and red blood cells. This metabolism process emerges as essential, a process enabling cells to maintain life, grow, and reproduce. Working with coenzyme-Q_{10} and L-carnitine, Vitamin B_5

also helps metabolize fat. Excellent food sources include brewers' yeast, calf liver, peanuts, mushrooms, soybeans, peas, pecans, oatmeal, sunflower seeds, lentils, oranges, and strawberries. You should take 1 gram daily.

Vitamin B$_6$: Commonly called pyridoxine, this plays an important role in treating neuropathies and regulating neurotransmitters, the chemical process that regulates signals between cells and neurons. Medical professionals also use Vitamin B$_6$ to treat elevated levels of homocysteine, a condition that could—if left unchecked—lead to thrombosis and cardiovascular disease. The body also needs Vitamin B$_6$ for making proteins and for immune system function. Food sources include sunflower seeds, wheat germ, soybeans, walnuts, lentils, beans, whole grains, bananas, spinach, potatoes, and cauliflower. You should take 50 to 100 mg daily.

Vitamin B$_{12}$: Sometimes called cobalamin, this methyl donor responsible in the vital transfer of certain gasses helps the body maintain cell membranes and neurotransmitters—while also serving a necessary function in the production of normal red blood cells. Vitamin B$_{12}$ works in synergy with Vitamin B$_6$ and folic acid. You can find Vitamin B$_{12}$ in abundance in animal foods, liver, lamb meat, shellfish, salmon, and cheese. You should take 200 mcg daily.

Vitamin D$_3$: The hydroxyl form of Vitamin D and optimal for cancer prevention, this vitamin displays such power that even allopathic physicians administer doses to breast, prostate, and colon cancer patients. You should take 80 to 100 mg daily, or 4,000 to 6,000 IUs per day.

Vitamin K$_1$: Also called phytonadione and commonly found in green leafy vegetables, this has special anti-aging qualities and aids in treating osteoporosis, and is important in coagulating blood.

Use Natural Treatments
for Good Colon Health

Poor dietary habits emerge as the primary cause of poor colon health, which contributes to poor overall health.

It's important to eliminate or greatly reduce unhealthy foods from your diet. Foods to avoid or curtail include unsaturated fats, dairy products, excess starches, sugars, and red meat.

Among keys to getting the colon into good shape:

- **Enemas and colonics:** Colons serve as massive honeycombs that can harbor year's-old waste. As gross as this might sound, several pounds of bacteria-laden fecal matter can become attached to the colon walls. This can cause chronic fatigue, flatulence, bloating, skin disorders, breathing disorders, arthritis, and even constipation. Colonic cleanses help remove these wastes and intestinal parasites, restoring youthful qualities to the intestines and bowels. Meantime, hydro colon therapy and good diets can cure flatulence.
- **Probiotics:** While antibiotics fight against unwanted bacteria, probiotics serve an opposite chore—promoting the restoration of healthy bacteria within the body, including intestinal flora. Acidophilus and bifidophilus serve as the most common probiotic flora. In fact, these rank as so important to the colon that it's essential to take probiotics when using antibiotics, doing a colon cleanse, or undergoing chemotherapy. Probiotics enable fauna and flora to regenerate in the colon and intestines, thereby helping you ingest and absorb food. Keep in mind that antibiotics kill everything within the bacterial realm including good bacteria in your body. The lack of a healthy body flora promotes Candida yeast infections.
- **Fiber and raw foods:** Nutritionists know that fiber from raw foods can clean the intestines. Raw or lightly cooked broccoli, brussels sprouts, and cabbage often work best, while grains and seeds also prove beneficial.
- **Cholesterol connection:** Excessive cholesterol can cause gallstones in the liver and gallbladder, resulting in poor digestion and deterioration of the essential need to process fats and proteins. Unless efficiently processed into or out of the body, fats and proteins can get stuck in the colon, mucking up the works.

Coffee serves as one of the most widely used agents for enemas and colonics. In fact, coffee stimulates the lining of the colon, causing it to excrete more proficiently—while also cleaning bile ducts between the colon, liver, and gallbladder. Just as important, coffee also rejuvenates the deep peristalsis, the natural movement through your entire digestive tract.

Remember that the colon works as one of our main detoxification routes. As you've learned by now, a sluggish bowel breeds toxicity that seriously and adversely affects the entire body's health. Regular bowel movements and a clean colon signal that your organs are functioning at superior levels, the way nature intended.

The second step in this cleansing process involves pulling toxins from the digestive and intestinal tract with zeolite clay, activated charcoal, slippery elm, and other herbs. A cleansing product can add fibrous bulk while nourishing, soothing, and lubricating the intestines as it moves through. You also can benefit by using the cleanse for indigestion after meals; the activated charcoal and other ingredients help control acid indigestion and bloating.

After finishing your enema or colonic cleansing, you can introduce liquid chlorophyll—very healing, energizing, and soothing—back into your colon. You can also use wheatgrass juice, which is almost pure chlorophyll. Molecularly the closest to the substance to hemoglobin in your blood cells, chlorophyll possesses superior regenerative and healing benefits. Among colon cleanse supplement programs that also are available, most are multiday processes that use herbs to help remove waste from the intestines. Some key ingredients used in these programs include ground black walnut shell husk, garlic extracts, psyllium husk, bentonite clay or liquid, pau d'arco, wormwood, yellow dock, citric acid from lemon or grapefruit, cayenne pepper, and slippery elm.

Although colon work might seem embarrassing or something only done in secret, many people who first administer enemas on themselves subsequently find no problem when such applications are administered by a professional practitioner. From my experience, hydro colon therapists perform this task in a very gentle and professional manner.

While colon therapy is great for most people, those with intestinal tumors, Crohn's disease, ulcerative colitis, diverticulitis, or severe hemorrhoids should avoid enemas.

Keep Yourself Informed About Natural Health

Accurate information is a potent weapon if you desire to make positive changes in your health and in your life. To remain an informed consumer, I recommend the Natural News Network (www.naturalnews.com), which operates as a nonprofit company composed of public education websites.

Founded and edited by Mike Adams, who is known as "The Health Ranger" for his crusades on behalf of natural health and consumer choice, you will find on the website more than twenty-five thousand free articles and special reports, and daily news stories on every aspect of the natural health movement and the threats to its existence.

Among the special report topics you will find to be useful: super foods, food toxins, nutrition choices, bioidentical vitamins, herb use, and dozens more. This website also provides frequent coverage of FDA abuses and gives advice on how to protect yourself if you are an alternative health user and provider.

Note to Readers: You can also find the most up-to-date information on the latest anti-aging discoveries and products with my monthly Anti-Aging Cures newsletter. This entertaining and highly informative newsletter is packed with practical advice on cutting-edge medical science research and the health problems associated with aging. It's the closest thing to a personal visit with me each month. Go to www.anti-agingcures.com and subscribe now!

CHAPTER 5

More Natural
Cures for Aging

You've probably heard the old expression "I've got to get my beauty sleep," though I bet you never imagined how literally true that saying can be. Medical research is showing us that having healthy sleep habits is directly related to your ability to maintain a youthful appearance of beauty. Sleep, along with exercise, a positive state of mind, and the quality of your relationships, all act as biostimulators to support the work of anti-aging substances.

Here is how the journal *Sports Medicine* characterized the medical evidence for the benefits of sleep in a 2003 issue: "A number of physiological stimuli can initiate human growth hormone secretion, the most powerful, non-pharmacological of which are sleep and exercise."

A good night's rest rejuvenates the body—we all know and feel that. But there is much more to it. During your rapid eye movement dream states each night, your pituitary gland reaches its peak production of human growth hormone, the key to youthfulness. The less restful your sleep, the less dreaming that you will do, which means your hormone production process will be affected and so will how you look and feel.

It's clear that along with eating and breathing, sleeping is essential to human existence. As I point out in my book, *Sleep and Grow Young*, sleep quality affects every aspect of life—our personal relationships, our

75

job performance, our mental health, and our outlook on life. Our overall physical health is directly affected because the neuroendocrine system heals our bodies during sleep, producing the therapeutic hormones HGH, DHEA, and melatonin during the deepest levels of the sleep cycle. Sleep deprivation depresses the immune system and renders us more susceptible to diseases and other health challenges, hence the physician's traditional prescription of "get some rest and sleep."

Getting quality sleep is an antidote to stress, which is important to any anti-aging program because prolonged stress ages us. As the legendary comedian George Burns, who died at the age of one hundred, once put it, "If you ask what is the single most important key to longevity, I would have to say it is avoiding worry, stress, and tension. And if you didn't ask me, I'd still have to say it."

A deficit in the amount of deep sleep, known as stage four or delta brain wave sleeping, can leave anyone in a state of emotional stress the next day. A build-up of this stress over time can turn into a vicious cycle of insomnia—an estimated one-quarter of all adults experience some form of it—and this chronic condition can further accelerate aging. For women, this problem with insomnia and sleep deprivation often comes in the perimenopausal years, ages forty-five to fifty-five, when there is a sharp decline in the sleep-promoting hormone called progesterone.

It's probably no coincidence that in the nations where afternoon napping, or siestas, has been the cultural norm, we find the longest life expectancies. While the United States ranks thirtieth from the top among countries in life expectancy, according to the *CIA World Factbook*, cultures with much longer lifespans, such as Greece and Okinawa, value afternoon napping.

Since on average we spend one-third of our lives either sleeping or in bed trying to do so, we can't overlook the essential role that sleep plays in life's aging process. So let's do a brief examination of what's involved in this ritual.

Sleep researchers have determined that we undergo four levels of sleep during each sleep cycle. The first is light sleep, from which most sounds will easily awaken us. Then we undergo a slightly deeper level for a few minutes. That is followed by a third level in which a deeper state of relaxation sets in to quiet all of your thoughts. Finally, a fourth level of deepest relaxation occurs when the brain creates a delta wave pattern. We repeat this whole cycle an average of five times over the typical eight hours of sleep.

You may have heard stories about famous people who need much less sleep than the average person. The inventor Thomas Edison, for example, needed only two or three hours of sleep a day. That was apparently because he slipped immediately into the delta stage of deepest sleep. It's this deep level and your time spent in it, not just your total number of hours spent sleeping, that determine how rested and rejuvenated you will feel when you wake up.

As we grow older our sleep cycles change until, by about age sixty, our time spent in delta stage sleep may be reduced to just a few minutes each night. Because we sleep lighter, we wake up more often during the night, and that makes it difficult to fall easily back to sleep. This can make us grumpy and tired the next day. Added to this condition over time is a domino effect in which sleep deprivation accelerates the aging process characterized by bone deterioration, skin wrinkling, and decreased heart and lung efficiency.

Therapist and sleep researcher John Selby, in his 1999 book *Secrets of a Good Night's Sleep,* provides a wealth of practical and effective relaxation techniques and exercises to induce deeper and higher quality sleep. He recommends that we focus on the first three hours of sleep, which is when we get all of the delta stage rest we will get for the night, and not worry about staying in bed for a full seven or eight hours. Don't be rigid about your sleeping habits, says Selby. Why not get up and do something productive or fun after those three hours of delta time rather than tossing and turning restlessly?

"Many people simply cannot have a deep dream experience when they are sleeping with someone in the same bed," notes Selby. "The very presence of another being so close beside them disturbs the peace they need in order to relax into a deep dream state, not to mention into delta sleep." This is a common problem for long-married couples. Selby advises that they consider sleeping apart for some or most of the time, just to get the anti-aging deep sleep and dream time that their bodies need.

Also keep in mind that insomnia is not just a condition; it's a symptom of something. That "something" is often a generalized and free-floating form of anxiety. People experiencing chronic insomnia should seek professional help to discover the source of this anxiety, which can be a big step toward resolving it and returning to a healthier sleep pattern.

Seniors who take supplemental growth hormone often report they resume the ability to sleep more soundly each night. Many also report that they start enjoying and recalling multicolor dreams just as they did as children and as young adults. This is the sort of positive feedback loop we should all be striving to achieve. With our access to biostimulators and injectable growth hormone, combined with quality sleep, we can stimulate our body's own natural production of human growth hormone, to whatever extent possible, to help delay or reverse the aging process.

A Natural Sleep Aid

Sleeping pills that you get by prescription may knock you out, but they don't provide you with restful stage-four delta sleep. These pills have the additional disadvantage of being habit-forming or even physically addictive. You also wake up in a drugged state of mind.

Melatonin supplements are a natural alternative sleep aid available for you to try along with John Selby's relaxation techniques. They are most often publicized in relation to airline personnel and frequent travelers who have made melatonin a favorite recommended treatment for jet lag.

But it's not just important for getting restful sleep. It has numerous other well-documented advantages. Russian studies, for instance, have shown that melatonin replacement therapy expands the lifespans of mice by up to 25 percent, a finding that may have human applications.

Melatonin regulates the body's circadian rhythm, the daily twenty-four-hour cycle that mandates vital functions. Within humans, the pineal gland, about the size of a date pit and shaped like a tiny pinecone at the center of the brain, produces melatonin. The famed seventeenth-century philosopher Descartes called this gland "the seed of the soul." Surrounded by a rich blood supply, the pineal gland contains one hundred times more serotonin than any part of the human body.

Serotonin acts as a kind of thermostat system in the body. An essential neurotransmitter, relaying and amplifying signals between neurons and other cells, serotonin serves as an important precursor or direct parent of melatonin.

Melatonin also regulates the secretion of the stress-regulator cortisol and the sex hormone testosterone, which manages energy, libido, and red blood cell production—while also protecting the body against osteoporosis. The daily circadian rhythms regulated and controlled by melatonin include the secretion of growth hormone. Most important for anti-aging, melatonin stimulates the pituitary gland's production of it, which peaks during rapid eye movement sleep.

Just as with growth hormone, the body's production of melatonin decreases as people age. Melatonin levels peak from ages fifteen to twenty-five, before decreasing to 15 to 20 percent of those levels by age seventy. The problem becomes more complex because serotonin levels remain high in mature people. As a result, the balance between melatonin and serotonin weighs in favor of serotonin the older we get. Among mature people, a variety of negative symptoms can emerge from this imbalance, most notably interrupted sleep patterns, central sleep apnea, sexual dysfunction, depression, and a tendency to develop type 2 diabetes mellitus.

The eventual dominance of serotonin in mature people emerges as a harmful development, largely because melatonin plays a vital role in enhancing the essential sleep process, important to the body's healing. Remember that physicians know a good night's sleep serves as nature's best healing medicine. It's no coincidence that most heart attacks occur in the early morning hours, or that women are most likely to go into labor early in the morning.

Though researchers began studying melatonin in the 1950s, they didn't really realize this hormone's many benefits until the late 1980s.

Clinical results consistently show how this hormone battles free radicals hidden in toxic substances absorbed from food, water, and the environment, toxins that can contribute to the aging process.

Melatonin also defends brain function by warding off free radicals. It may also decrease heart disease and immune deficiency diseases. In a study at the University of Texas Health Center in San Antonio, rats given carcinogens before melatonin treatments had 50 percent less genetic damage than those without such therapy. Melatonin boosts the immune system while helping AIDS patients and people suffering from chronic depression.

MELATONIN SUPPLEMENTATION
MAY WORK FOR YOU

Physicians have found that mature people who have never taken melatonin have decreased quality and duration of sleep, while their immune system functions, their vitality and longevity diminish as well.

Thanks to the pineal gland's strategic location within the brain, the body secretes melatonin directly into the cerebrospinal fluid and the general circulatory system. However, our bodies markedly reduce the production of melatonin during daylight hours, following its usual peak at about 3 o'clock in the morning. Medical professionals say that melatonin acts as the body's biological clock due to the hormone's relationship to light and dark cycles. Seasonal changes impact this process, when daylight hours expand during summers and shorten during winters.

These biological changes cause fluctuations in the secretions of HGH, the stress-regulator cortisol and major sex hormones. Like a nighttime burglar, melatonin seemingly comes alive during the dark when performing its work, before fading at the light of day.

People older than fifty who use melatonin supplements should start such regimens by taking lower doses, such as 1 to 3 mg at bedtime. This process usually entails taking melatonin every other day or a maximum five to six days per week. Be sure to avoid taking melatonin at least one day per week in order to allow the pineal gland to continue making this hormone uninhibited.

After initial regimens have progressed for a while, some individuals can easily tolerate nightly bedtime melatonin doses of 10 to 30 mg. But it's important for pregnant or nursing mothers or women trying to conceive to avoid taking over-the-counter melatonin.

Sleep apnea is a disorder marked by potentially dangerous pauses in breathing while asleep and it affects up to 20 percent of people older than fifty. Physicians have been unable to find or develop an effective prescription drug to treat this condition. But melatonin in higher doses, as much as 10 or 20 mg taken before bedtime, may lessen the negative effects of sleep apnea.

A few other natural nonaddictive sleep remedies to consider include Valerium, Chamomiles, passion flower, 5HTP, and Kava-kava. Some homeopathic sleep remedies you might investigate include Arsenicum album, Cocculus, Ignatia amara, Lycopodium, Nux vomica, Silicea, and Sulphur taken from St. John's Wort, and certain teas.

Your Thoughts and Beliefs Influence Aging

What you think about age and aging, along with how the people in your life treat the aging process when around you, may have a surprising impact on the effectiveness of the anti-aging substances that you choose to take. Your state of mind can be a powerful biostimulator in your anti-aging arsenal of weapons.

It's no secret that our mind's thoughts—intensified by the beliefs we hold—affect us physically, helping to determine how often we get sick, or how quickly we get well. Sometimes this "mind over matter" ability gets labeled as the "placebo response," which scientists have measured in medical experiments under a wide variety of circumstances.

A conventional definition of the placebo goes like this: It is any fake medical treatment without any known pharmacological action to treat a patient's disease or other medical condition. It can be a sugar pill, a saline solution injection, or an elaborate ritual and ruse designed to look like real surgery.

For instance, a study in a 1983 issue of the *World Journal of Surgery* described how one-third of all people in a placebo control group who thought they were getting a new chemotherapy drug, spontaneously lost all of their hair because they believed chemotherapy was supposed to result in hair loss.

Other studies appearing in peer-reviewed journals found that 60 percent of all gastric ulcer patients claimed cures after taking placebo tablets made of sugar, and large numbers of people with degenerative knee conditions, who were given fake arthroscopic surgeries, afterwards began to walk normally again without any pain.

Our thoughts and beliefs can exert a profound "mind-over-matter" transformative role based on nothing more than our imagination. A case in point involves a British woman who lost 56 pounds in 2009 after five sessions with a hypnotist who convinced her to believe that she had undergone gastric stomach band surgery. These hypnotic sessions invoking surgery were so vivid for thirty-five-year-old Marion Corns that she declared in an interview with the *Mirror* newspaper: "Bizarrely, I can remember the clink of the surgeon's knife and the smell of anaesthetic." Feeling certain that her stomach had tightened, she no longer had much of an appetite and as a result, she lost an average of three pounds a week while avoiding any of the side effects associated with real gastric bands.

Still more evidence for the mind's impact on the body comes from a study published in the *North American Journal of Psychology* in 2007 titled "Mind Over Matter: Mental Training Increases Physical Strength." Thirty male university athletes were randomly assigned to one of three groups: a control group that did no exercise, or a group that actually did the hip flexor exercise, or a third group that only did visualization exercises imagining themselves to have physically done the hip flexor exercise.

After two weeks, those who did daily physical training had increased their hip strength by 28 percent compared to no increase in strength for the control group. But what seems astounding is that the visualization group also increased their strength by an average of 24 percent, almost equal to the group that really exercised. Both the mental and physical training groups also produced similar decreases in systolic blood pressure and heart rate.

How far to fitness can our beliefs take us? The housekeeping staff of a major hotel was told by Harvard University researchers in 2007 that the exercise they got every day cleaning hotel rooms endowed them with superior fitness. A month later, as a group, these housekeepers had lost weight, lowered their blood pressure, their body mass index, and improved other fitness measurements, all without doing anything other than their normal routine. Their belief about being fit, based on indoctrination from "authority figures," had set in motion changes in their body chemistry.

Previous studies from 1977 to 1992 showed how hypnosis and visualization can be used to disintegrate warts and even enlarge a woman's breasts. From these experiments we know there are a very wide range of physical effects potentially triggered by thoughts and beliefs. So why can't it happen with the symptoms of aging, especially when anti-aging states of mind are combined with the anti-aging miracle substances— HGH and biostimulators—described in this book?

Here is some more evidence to consider in support of my contention.

You Can Reprogram Your Relationship to Time

Can elderly people isolated together convince themselves they are young again to such an extent that their bodies actually begin to reverse many of the symptoms of aging? You might be surprised to learn that the answer is yes!

Harvard University psychologist Ellen Langer decided to test whether the body clock of a group of men in their seventies and eighties could be reset to 1959 by their collective behaviors and state of mind. So she constructed a mind over body experiment some years ago.

A group of male senior citizens was placed in a sort of quarantine at a New England hotel. The interior of the hotel was decorated with only what the men would have seen there a half-century earlier, in their youth.

The participants in this experiment were instructed *not* to reminisce about that bygone period in their lives, but rather to actually talk to each other as if the Eisenhower era was really happening again in present time.

The men had access only to reading material and television programs from that period to reinforce the impression of that time period. They had no access to current events, cell phones, computers, or any other distractions from believing they had been transported back in time. They were encouraged to keep their thoughts focused on how they had acted and how they had felt when they were young men.

After just a week, those in this experimental group (compared with a control group of similar-aged men who weren't in isolation) measured significant mental and physical changes. As Langer reported, the men had the following:

fewer arthritis complaints
more joint flexibility
improved posture and gait
better hearing and eyesight
sharper minds and better performance on mental tasks
elevated spirits and optimism about life

Most remarkable of all, those in the experimental group even looked younger, as assessed in before and after photos judged by outside observers. This was after only seven days of pretending they were young again! It's fascinating to imagine how far they might have progressed if the experiment had lasted for months.

With Professor Langer's work, we have been shown how mental states in group situations have the potential for creating long-term health, more rapid self-healing, and the delay, perhaps even the reversal, of an aging process most people have taken for granted as irreversible and inevitable.

These findings may have tremendous implications for revolutionizing the nursing home and retirement home industries. Instead of seniors wasting away in front of televisions and playing nothing but cards and bingo, Langer's findings show us opportunities for developing stimulating activities that challenge seniors to think and act in more creative and youthful ways, which in turn might give life more joy and meaning.

You can try some of these techniques on your own. Keep your mind sharp by exercising your memory. Don't dwell on events from your past that are traumatic or troubling, but periodically put yourself into a period from your past and try to recollect everything you can—the people you knew, their faces and voices, the interiors of homes or offices, the smells you experienced, the tastes from restaurants you used to enjoy. It's a mind and memory exercise that draws upon your imagination.

You can try the same technique in reverse. Project your imagination forward in time to visualize a goal. Give yourself permission to feel the exhilaration of its completion. See the new circumstances of your life in as much vivid detail as you can summon.

There are also group activities to reinvigorate you with youthful enthusiasm. Maybe you've had the experience of attending high school or college reunions where you come away feeling energized from the sharing of memories of good times with classmates. Create something similar in your current life. Whether it is playing cards or taking group walks, use these opportunities to share what you have experienced together in a way that affirms a positive outlook on life. Youthfulness can truly be developed as a state of mind.

Positive Social Relationships
Extend Lifespans

Another key to biostimulation and living longer comes from the quality and satisfaction level of our relationships with other people. Both psychological research findings and just plain common sense inform us that positive attitudes, such as happiness, tend to spread virally in social networks. Being around happy people makes us happier, just as constant exposure to sad or unhappy people can be a downer for us.

People with good social relationships have a 50 percent greater likelihood of living longer than people with poor relationships, according to a July 2010 study in the journal, *PLoS Medicine*. What the researchers from Brigham Young University and the University of North Carolina did was analyze 148 different research studies going back several decades that examined the connection between relationship quality and a longer life. These studies involved a total of 308,849 people, almost equally divided between male and female, with an average age of sixty-four years, who were followed for an average of seven and a half years to assess their social interactions, disease incidence, and mortality.

The consistent finding across the board was that having good relationships was comparable to quitting smoking in its effect on extending lifespan. One reason may be because healthy social relationships, which can come from group activities or close networks of friends, enable us to weather more easily the stresses of life produced by illnesses, loss of loved ones, and otherwise negative changes in our life circumstances. There is also the factor that more healthy behaviors are often promoted by social networks in which good habits and healthy thoughts are encouraged.

It should be pointed out that other social research has found that people with strong religious or spiritual beliefs also tend to live longer than those without such beliefs. That, too, may be a reflection of being involved in a group activity, whether in a church or other place of worship, where the mutual support system and common outlook on life reinforces faith and optimism so that the human spirit can be revitalized.

Researchers at University College in London tested this idea by interviewing 10,860 people over the age of fifty during the period 2008 and 2009, as part of the English Longitudinal Study of Ageing. They discovered that people in this age group who produce higher levels of DHEAS—dehydroepiandrosterone sulfate—in their brain, adrenal glands, and sexual organs, which slows down the aging process, also tend to be more affluent. These same successful people were also found to produce higher levels of growth factor I (IGF-1). One might jump to the conclusion that affluent people live longer because they can afford higher quality medical care, but you would be wrong!

This study provided evidence that people who produce higher levels of these two hormones have more and closer friends and family, lead a more active life with lots of hobbies or pastimes, and they do greater amounts of exercise. This is all part of a positive cycle of behaviors and attitudes that help to extend lifespans. Exercise combined with proper diet leads to feeling better and looking better, which boosts self-esteem. As a result, these sorts of people tend to be more successful in life.

Never Overlook the Vital Role Played by Exercise!

Some of you couch potatoes may not want to hear it, but here comes the admonition, anyway. You might be able to "think" and "imagine" your way to some level of greater fitness, as the studies mentioned earlier indicate you might, but that is no complete substitute for actually getting off your butt and doing real, physical exercise to keep yourself in better physical shape.

One of the best-kept secrets is that vigorous exercise helps to stimulate human growth hormone production. The scientific evidence is also overwhelming that exercise contributes to longevity with optimal health. Here are just a few among hundreds of study examples that I can cite for you:

- A September 2010 study in the journal *Geriatric Gerontology* examined physical exercise among 690 people up to eighty-five years of age and showed that the intensity of aerobic exercise not only increased physical fitness, which improved health, but the exertion improved scores on cognitive performance. Your mind and memory work much better when you increase blood flow in the brain.
- Older frail women who combined ninety-minute twice-weekly exercise with DHEA supplementation substantially improved their body strength along with significant improvements in all hormone

production levels. That was another September 2010 finding, this time published in the *Journal of the American Geriatric Society.*

- A year earlier, researchers in the Netherlands, writing in the *Journal of Applied Physiology,* described how the progressive loss of skeletal muscle mass and strength with age, a condition that increases the risk of chronic disease, can be thwarted by intense exercise and physical activity. As the scientists wrote, "Prolonged resistance type exercise training represents an effective, therapeutic strategy to augment skeletal muscle mass and improve functional performance in the elderly."

When you increase growth hormone production in your body, either through biostimulator action or injections, you experience a huge motivation to exercise your body to channel some of that boundless energy you will feel. If you exert yourself by walking, running, or doing cardio and weight programs, then you can't wait to exercise again. The more you exercise, the more you want to exercise, and the healthier you feel, and the more you naturally produce growth hormone.

Your body will love the physical exertion! The more intensely you exercise, especially with weight training, the more your body will be primed to produce more growth hormone naturally. Exercise supports the biostimulators you take, and the growth hormone you subsequently produce supports your exercise regimen. So it's an upward spiral.

Additional benefits to weight training, especially for women, involve a reduction in the risk for osteoporosis. Stressing your muscles and bones acts to strengthen them. Don't limit the muscle groups you exercise. Work all of your major muscle groups—back, chest, arms and shoulders, and legs and abdominals.

As a general rule, I refrain from recommending extremely stressful or overly vigorous activities, such as fast-paced marathons that can cause severe wear and tear on muscles and joints. Seniors on treadmills never need quick-paced rates of between 2.5 and 3.5 miles per hour for extensive periods. Instead, limit the pace to 3 to 3.5 miles per hour in thirty- to forty-five-minute daily workouts up to five days a week. This enables seniors to maintain movement of muscles and joints. Also, lifting light weights, stretching, and enjoying Pilates can become extremely important, but don't overdo it. Also try a variety of physical activities such as yoga combined with meditation and stretching.

FOR WOMEN—WHICH EXERCISES RAISE GROWTH HORMONE LEVELS THE MOST?

Middle-aged women fifty to sixty-five years of age were divided into three groups: one did aerobics training and walking only; the second group did combined exercise that included resistance training and walking; and the control group did nothing. Exercise sessions occurred three times a week for twelve weeks. Each group of women was periodically tested to measure their growth hormone production, body fat percentage, fasting glucose, and blood pressure. The combined exercise of walking and re-sistance training "significantly improved" growth hormone production and the other health measures, compared to the aerobics and walking group. ("Twelve weeks of combined exercise is better than aerobic exercise for increasing growth hormone in middle aged women." (D. I. Seo, et al., *International Journal Sport Nutrition Exercise Metabolism 1* [Feb. 2010]: 21–26.)

Another 2010 study evaluated the effects of bicycle exercise on growth hormone secretion in both younger women (twenty-six to thirty years) and older women (forty-two to forty-six years.) It included sedentary lifestyle subjects as well as athletic persons. The researchers concluded that "exercise induced similar growth hormone responses in younger sedentary and exercise-trained subjects and in older exercise-trained subjects, with mean peak levels 7.5 times higher than baseline (baseline being when they started the exercise experiment). In contrast, in older, sedentary women peak growth hormone level was only 4.4 times higher than baseline." The overall effect of cycling was clear whether the women were young or older, sedentary or athletic. Intense prolonged cycling "ex-erted protective effects against age-dependent decline in growth hormone secretion." (V. Coiro et al., "Effect of physical training on age-related reduction of GH secretion during exercise in normally cycling women," *Maturitas* 65, no. 4 [Apr 2010]: 392–395.)

FOR HEALTHY MEN AND WOMEN—HOW IMPORTANT IS RESISTANCE TRAINING AND AEROBIC EXERCISE TO GROWTH HORMONE SECRETION?

In the journal *Sports Medicine* a study was published that concluded, "Exercise is a potent physiological stimulus for growth hormone secretion, and both aerobic and resistance exercise result in significant acute increases in growth hormone secretion . . . regardless of age or gender, there is a linear relationship between the magnitude of the acute increase in growth hormone release and exercise intensity." The study went on to assess results showing that "the combination of exercise and administration of oral GH secretagogues may result in greater GH secretion than exercise alone in individuals who are older or have obesity." ("Growth hormone release during acute and chronic aerobic and resistance exercise: recent findings." L. Wideman et al., *Sports Medicine* 32, no. 15 [2002]: 987–1004.)

FOR OVERWEIGHT MEN AND WOMEN— HOW VITAL IS EXERCISE TO GROWTH HORMONE PRODUCTION?

People with excessive abdominal visceral fat suffer from reduced spontaneous growth hormone secretion, while simultaneously raising their risk for type 2 diabetes, cardiovascular disease, and metabolic syndrome (risk factors which include obesity, increased levels of triglycerides, high blood pressure and raised fasting plasma glucose.) A 2009 study of thirty-four adults, median age of forty-nine years, all with metabolic syndrome symptoms, had them undergo sixteen weeks of endurance training while measuring their spontaneous, twelve-hour overnight growth hormone production. Regardless of whether they engaged in low-intensity or high-intensity exercise training, they significantly increased their spontaneous nocturnal secretion of growth hormone as they reduced their abdominal fat. ("Effects of exercise training intensity on nocturnal growth hormone secretion in obese adults with the metabolic syndrome." B. A. Irving et

al., *Journal Clinical Endocrinology Metabolism* 94, no. 6 [Jun 2009]: 1979–
1986.)

Tip For Success: To exercise longer and develop more stamina, drink
beetroot juice, which is high in nitrate, and eat more nitrate-rich foods
such as spinach and lettuce. Two medical studies conducted at Britain's
Exeter University in 2010 found that cyclists who drank a half-quart of
beetroot juice several hours before racing increased their endurance by
20 percent because nitrate in the juice reduced the energy requirements
on muscles. Other studies revealed that beetroot improves heart performance by lowering blood pressure. (Be sure to drink organic juice!)

One final thought. Try exercising after a light meal of nutrient-dense
food. An organic super food smoothie is a great choice before working
out. In some cases, it may actually help to stimulate your growth hormone
production.

Summary of Anti-Aging Lifestyle Ingredients

1. Use biostimulators and use them until they no longer work for you.
   When that happens, consult Part Two of this book and investigate
   taking the injectable form.
2. Adopt a nutritious diet with anti-aging super foods being consumed
   throughout your life, irrespective of your age. Make this part of your
   biostimulating dietary lifestyle.
3. Train yourself to have healthy sleep patterns. Stress ages us. Good
   sleep and rest are the antidotes to stress and help to produce growth
   hormone. Use melatonin to help induce sleep if you're having sleepless
   nights. It's a supplement that deserves to be in your life.
4. Be a joiner! Get yourself involved in both physical and spiritual pursuits that involve group activities that keep you inspired about yourself and life. Do youthful activities and have youthful thoughts. Don't
   allow yourself to "think" old.
5. Stay active with an exercise routine. No matter how limited you might
   be in your physical capabilities, there is always some level of exercise

you can perform each day to keep growth hormone stimulated and your life-force energy circulating.

Note to Readers: You can have the most up-to-date information on the latest anti-aging discoveries and products thanks to my monthly newsletter, *Fountain of Youth,* which provides practical advice on how to apply cutting-edge medical science research on aging and the health problems usually associated with aging. Go to www.getfountainofyouth .com and subscribe now!

PART II

≈

USE AN
ANTI-AGING
SILVER
BULLET

CHAPTER 6

Clinical Results Provide Irrefutable Evidence

REST ASSURED THAT THE SAME FORCES THAT TRIED TO JAIL ME WOULD rather you didn't know about the evidence supporting the benefits of injectable human growth hormone that I am about to share with you. They would prefer that you continue taking all of those expensive pharmaceuticals to treat mature-age-related symptoms. They want you to continue spending money on all of those drugs for hypertension, high cholesterol, age spots, and osteoporosis—all of whose symptoms that legally prescribed growth hormone can reverse, curtail, or eliminate at much lower cost. They also don't want you to know that its safety and use is backed by clinically proven results.

Because our bodies naturally produce growth hormone, the substance is tolerated and effective in mature people when administered in appropriate doses. The same cannot be said for most of the pharmaceutical drugs foisted on us by Big Pharma, which kill thousands of people every year.

(**Important Note to Readers:** Anyone considering the use of injectable growth hormone should first be tested by a qualified physician to determine your body's actual production level of the hormone. Although the FDA-approved Forsythe protocol for growth hormone deficiency syndrome provides for minimal basic testing, which includes IGF-1 levels over two separate days, plus a twenty-four-hour urine growth hormone level test, it's useful to perform the more extensive pituitary stimulation tests that are detailed in the protocol. Each physician can independently and in concert with their individual patients make these decisions for further testing.)

Before I go deeper into detail about the injectable form, it might be worthwhile for you to know why Earlene and I got involved with it in the first place. This background information may give you some insights into why we stuck with this anti-aging treatment in the face of a concerted federal government effort to drive us out of the health care business and put me in prison.

Both of us had served our country in times of war and peace. I graduated from the U.S. Army's medical school program at the University of California at San Francisco and did a tour of duty in Vietnam at the height of the war, where I rose in the ranks to become a major and the chief of pathology at a jungle hospital. Earlene joined the U.S. Army Nursing Corps in 1969 as a private first class. She later served in the U.S. Army Reserves as a Second Lieutenant and the Nevada National Guard as a major while pursuing a master's degree in nursing.

Following my honorable discharge from the military in 1970, I remained in the Army Reserves while receiving training in hematology and oncology at the UCSF. Then I practiced as a cancer specialist in Reno, Nevada, developed cancer wards at the city's two major medical facilities, served as medical officer in charge of the local U.S. Army Reserve Hospital, taught as an associate professor at a University of Nevada medical school, and spent a decade as Nevada State Surgeon for the National Guard. I retired from the Active Army Reserve as a full colonel. Earlene resigned about the same time as a major, having spent a decade as State Nurse.

Starting in the late 1980s, I became disenchanted with the "slash and burn" tactics that mainstream medicine relied upon in treating cancer. The situation I confronted in the field of oncology was depressing. Among patients suffering advanced stages of cancer, only a few emerged as long-term survivors of more than three to five years after treatment. Those lucky enough to survive often experienced symptoms of toxic chemotherapy, suffering from conditions that ranged from chemo brain syndrome to peripheral neuropathies.

Chemotherapy also caused cardiac, liver, or kidney damage among many survivors. They sometimes suffered chronically low blood counts, requiring periodic transfusions. Others had their health endangered by persistent low white blood counts that caused frequent infections. Chronic bleeding episodes occurred when platelet counts dipped to seriously low levels.

The quality of their lives, even though they had survived cancer, was often very low, and so I wondered if it was worth the price to pay for survival. There is an old saying in oncology, "We cured the cancer, but the patient died."

Despite the odds against them due to limited treatment options, cancer patients usually retained a fighting spirit, and that gave me cause for hope. Since entering the field of oncology, it had often surprised me that there were very few patients of mine—and I can think of only two—who actually committed suicide because of their advanced disease. A cancer patient in general is a real fighter who will go to extremes to do everything he or she can to beat the disease.

So I set about trying to find more treatment options for our patients. I decided to "push the envelope" by training as a homeopath so I could use both conventional and complementary therapies to broaden the care afforded cancer patients. Though I continued my standard oncology practice, giving patients chemotherapy when I felt they needed it, I treated other patients with complementary therapies when they seemed well suited for it. For each cancer patient, I offered three standard options of treatment:

1. Conventional chemotherapy alone.
2. Conventional chemotherapy with complementary therapy.
3. Complementary therapy alone.

After more than two hundred thousand patient visits in three decades of practice, my treatment criteria amassed a record of achievement. My most recent treatment regimen resulted in a 63 percent survival rate among breast cancer patients and up to an 80 percent survival rate among patients with extremely serious stage four cancers after five years. This track record for cures and concerned care turned our clinic into a nationally recognized destination for patients who had reached a dead end with the rigid conventions of allopathic medicine.

The next field of health care that Earlene and I tackled was the one that has fascinated and perplexed humankind throughout recorded history—how to stop, or at least slow down, the aging process.

What the "Powers That Be" Want Silenced

Since you were a child, your body has naturally produced a hormone that kept you youthful and strong. But as your natural production of growth hormone declines decade by decade, your sex drive decreases, skin wrinkles, brain function deteriorates, body fat increases, and your body becomes susceptible to fatigue and disease. You get old and you feel old!

Medical science is capable of discovering and creating miracles, and that's what happened in the mid-1980s when improved technology finally enabled physicians to mass-produce injectable HGH in laboratories. This innovation eliminated or severely curtailed the necessity of using the previous process of laboriously extracting this substance from cadavers.

Once Earlene and I got involved in this field, we became advocates for the idea that every one of us should have unfettered access to this extraordinary substance, under proper medical supervision, to turn off the aging clock. Gradually, I began prescribing Master Hormone supplementation to patients, but only after medical tests confirmed that their bodies no longer produced an adequate amount of the hormone.

The results we began to see in our patients were nothing short of remarkable. Almost unanimously, patients who used it reported phenomenal or at least greatly improved increases in energy and vitality, enabling them to do things they had never done once past mid-life.

Skin wrinkles were reduced along with unsightly age spots. Their libidos were re-energized. They reduced body fat, increased their muscle mass, and improved cardiac efficiency. Medical tests consistently showed decreases in bad cholesterol and a corresponding increase in good cholesterol. Bone density increased, which sharply diminished the probability or risk of severe fractures that a high percentage of mature people suffer.

A Range of Documented Benefits

There is no more convincing evidence than seeing someone up close and in person who has defied conventional "wisdom" and radically transformed their health and their life. I've seen it with friends of mine who are in their seventies and eighties. They run marathons. They take human growth hormone.

Some years ago I encountered a wealthy patient with a heart problem, a dilated heart, who couldn't spend five minutes on a treadmill walking at less than two miles an hour before wearing himself out. The gentleman started taking HGH and was able to normalize his heart rate so that he could exercise longer and more vigorously. He did these things so well and his health improved so much, that he no longer had to take heart medications.

Seeing this transformation firsthand tweaked my curiosity to examine the benefits of this natural substance. The more I asked questions and studied the substance, the more cases I found where it had become the silver bullet for a wide range of health problems.

A doctor patient of mine had rheumatoid arthritis so bad that he developed a hand deformity, which prevented him from taking film out of X-ray jackets and placing them on a screen, which is a task that's a professional necessity for radiologists. Six months after being on the Master Hormone, he no longer needed to take any of his rheumatoid medications.

These are not isolated or unusual cases. In fact, these sorts of health miracles are an everyday occurrence among people who have embraced the use of human growth hormone to combat the challenges posed by the aging process.

At least five hundred medical study articles have been published in reputable medical journals verifying the many benefits of HGH. You will find many of these studies referenced in my protocol document in Appendix A of this book.

At our Century Wellness Clinic in Reno, we have seen hundreds of positive results, treating everything from arthritis and liver disease, to bone density and body fat. We have carefully and scientifically listed the benefits of human growth hormone for people of all ages. The clinic has also charted what happens to our bodies at each stage during the aging process.

Keep in mind that the beauty of a growth hormone prescription is that it's nontoxic as well as effective. How many pharmaceutical drugs can make that claim? If you use the proper dosing and do so after a physical exam and blood testing, you can expect no long-term adverse side effects, just long-term benefits.

As a benchmark using what happens naturally with the Master Hormone during the growth and aging process, we're able to provide here a list of specific benefits that growth hormone can provide you. Here are the Century Wellness Clinic's findings showing what happens to you during the "normal" aging process and how this miracle hormone can positively influence these changes.

YOUR SKIN

Youth through young adult. Often called the body's largest organ, your skin protects you from outside invaders while performing many vital functions that include sweat glands for heating and cooling, plus the vital senses of touch. Healthy skin keeps essential fluids within the body while shielding or protecting other organs. Except for acne during the teens and young adult period, the skin of most young people is relatively blemish-free and wrinkle-free.

Mid-twenties through maturity. Your skin gradually begins to wrinkle—a process that becomes more progressive as time passes from your forties and beyond. The incidence of cancerous or unsightly moles or lesions increases markedly. Age spots, commonly referred to as liver spots, begin appearing on the back of the hands, neck, face, and other regions.

Upon getting HGH during maturity. Many wrinkles diminish somewhat or disappear altogether. Most or all liver spots disappear. Clinical results remain inconclusive on how much—if at all—the advent of HGH reduces the incidence of skin cancers. In my experience, the injectable form lessens the likelihood of such diseases, but more studies are needed to prove that.

YOUR LIBIDO

Youth through young adult. In healthy individuals, the libido increases in intensity as the years progress, particularly past puberty. People's desire for physical intimacy peaks during the late teens through the mid-twenties.

Mid-twenties through maturity. You gradually have less desire for physical contact. The libido's intensity steadily wanes to the point where many women during menopause never think of sex. Many men begin feeling less passionate. Despite the advent of erectile dysfunction drugs such as Viagra, a large percentage of men become unwilling or physically unable to pursue sexual intercourse.

Upon getting HGH during maturity. Both genders, particularly men, report increases in sexual desire. Although, overall, women report less of an increase in libido, many experience an increase in desire.

YOUR ENERGY LEVELS

Youth through young adult. Healthy people possess increasingly boundless energy, in some instances even when eating little or no food for limited periods. Some children play so much they lose any sense of time. College students and young adults are legendary for going days at a time with just a few hours of nightly sleep.

Mid-twenties through maturity. Energy levels decrease slowly through the early thirties, before dropping off at a steadily increasing rate from the early forties and beyond. For some seniors, exercise and restricting foods to low-calorie, high-protein meals can boost energy somewhat. But most people experience a sharp decrease in vitality, especially during their sixties and seventies. Many have difficulty exercising due to physical challenges caused by aging.

Upon getting HGH during maturity. Many—but not all—patients report a significant increase in vigor. Some resume games or sports they had once dropped such as golf. Others begin low-intensity exercise like walking. Overall, men report a greater increase in energy than women. Most females become more vibrant as well.

YOUR BONES

Youth through young adult. Beginning from childbirth, the bones grow until emerging as our mature primary adult lifetime physical frames in the early twenties. Thanks to natural HGH, during this twenty-five-year period most bone fractures heal fast, sometimes amazingly so. The bone marrow also plays the essential role of creating blood-forming precursors for red blood cells, white blood cells, and platelets.

Mid-twenties through maturity. Due to the aging process coupled with decreasing HGH, bone density steadily decreases, greatly increasing the probability of fractures among people sixty and older. Particularly in women, severe cases of osteoporosis make the bones look like hole-ridden Swiss cheese. Hip fractures are a leading cause of death among mature females; most women who suffer hip fractures die of other related complications within a few years.

Upon getting HGH in maturity. On a consistent basis, for both men and women bone density increases, sometimes up to 1 percent per year. This decreases the likelihood of severe fractures, a significant development, especially among women.

YOUR HEART'S EFFICIENCY

Youth through young adult. In healthy individuals, with each beat, the heart's left ventricle pumps out most blood into the aorta, thereby increasing the likelihood of good overall cardiovascular health. Physicians use the term "ejection fraction" when measuring this degree of efficiency. Most healthy people from their teens through early twenties have an ejection fraction level greater than 55 percent of blood that had been in the heart.

Mid-twenties through maturity. Partly due to a decrease in the body's production of HGH, ejection fraction levels begin to decrease as the heart muscle's efficiency decreases. In some individuals, this change emerges as a primary or secondary factor leading to heart disease, which is fatal in some instances. For the most part, people with ejection fractions of less than 50 percent are considered to have heart disease and may have congestive heart failure.

Upon getting HGH in maturity. Among healthy individuals whose hearts have not yet been irreversibly damaged, patients experience a marked improvement in their ejection fraction. This, in turn, can result in overall improvements in health throughout the body. However, at this point, medical professionals have yet to complete comprehensive research, partly due to restrictions the federal government imposes on the use of HGH in the general population—other than in cases where physicians issue "off-label" prescriptions.

YOUR MEMORY

Youth through young adult. Healthy, young children have remarkable memories, particularly as they learn languages and other vital skills. Teens and young adults sometimes hone their memories, often capable of answering basic queries almost from the millisecond that they hear a question. These cognitive abilities also help them respond fast to sudden dangerous situations, such as while driving a car that goes out of control—using their brains to make vital instant decisions.

Mid-twenties through maturity. Your brain responds to emergency situations much slower than during youth. Mature people react slower to life-threatening situations, such as slamming the brakes when it's too late—while young people lack such problems in some similar situations. Also, the memory fades, and people gradually lose cognitive skills they once took for granted. Beginning in their forties, many people start forgetting phone numbers they once knew in a flash, or they lose car keys or other possessions with greater frequency. Even people who lack early signs of Alzheimer's disease sometimes walk into rooms only to suddenly forget why they went there.

Upon getting HGH during maturity. Century Wellness clinical results show that these people enjoy an increase in mental acuity and sharpness, while experiencing a greater overall interest in life. These changes make them feel better about themselves, and many even feel like learning again. More studies are needed, but for now, I believe that the injectable form may delay or eliminate the onset of dementia.

YOUR EYESIGHT AND HEARING

Youth through young adult. For most children and young adults, eyesight is keen at around 20/20 vision, while many can hear well from long distances. Of course, plenty of children need corrective eyewear or hearing aids, but a vast majority of them lack such problems.

Mid-twenties through maturity. Your overall quality of eyesight and hearing decreases with age. In the late twenties through forties, many people get their first eyeglasses or contact lenses. A small percentage of people at that age discover that they need hearing aids.

Upon getting HGH during maturity. Again, partly as a result of the history of restrictions imposed by the federal government on the ability of physicians to issue "off-label" prescriptions for HGH, there are few conclusions or opinions on whether this hormone decreases the incidence of cataracts, glaucoma, or retinal detachments or if it improves hearing. Even so, I think that injectable HGH strengthens eye muscles, reducing certain vision problems while also decreasing the need for reading glasses.

YOUR CHOLESTEROL

Youth through young adult. For the most part, in healthy individuals, the body regulates the levels of HDL, commonly known as good cholesterol, and LDL, the bad cholesterol that can lead to heart problems or coronary artery disease. By contrast, HDL works to diminish harmful triglycerides, thereby making arteries healthier.

Mid-twenties through maturity. As the aging process progresses, the vascular systems of most people begin to deteriorate. The body's control of HDL and LDL levels gets off kilter, increasing the incidence of coronary disease. Life-debilitating or fatal afflictions emerge, including the clogging of arteries.

Upon getting HGH during maturity. On a consistent basis, the lipid profiles that I take on these patients show improvement in their levels of HDL and LDL. I have never prescribed HGH as a treatment for cholesterol problems. Yet these improvements have been discovered to be a positive, consistent side effect when issuing "off-label" prescriptions of HGH for anti-aging treatments.

YOUR MUSCLES

Youth through young adult. Your muscles enable you to move, while defining your body so that you can attract the opposite gender as young adults, and to perform vital activities such as physical labor. Sturdy muscles enable healthy people to keep their balance, often providing flexibility and strength. The muscles serve as significant tools for young people as they suffer falls or attacks, in some cases enabling them to avoid or ward off potential injury.

Mid-twenties through maturity. Your muscles lose their previous size and strength as natural levels of HGH decrease. Mature people in their sixties and seventies sometimes lack enough strength to keep their balance, increasing the incidence of accidental falls. Since the muscles and tendons also play a key role in maintaining healthy joints, some people begin suffering problems in these areas.

Upon getting HGH during maturity. On a consistent basis, muscles throughout the body increase in size and strength. In the vast majority of individuals, Century Wellness tracks the growth in biceps, triceps, calf muscles, quadriceps, and the neck muscles. Many joint problems decrease or disappear. And people find they're able to resume strenuous activities. Men, particularly, consider this benefit as significant as they resume favorite sporting activities ranging from golf, tennis, bicycling, and walking. Some women report similar results.

YOUR BODY FAT

Youth through young adult. Even during infancy, childhood, puberty, and the young adult stage, we all need healthy amounts of body fat—primarily to store energy. Young people who eat too much food often gain excessive weight, sometimes becoming obese. For the most part, a majority of healthy, young people find it relatively easy to lose weight fast, and some never gain excess pounds at all, thanks largely to their naturally high energy levels.

Mid-twenties through maturity. As the years pass, the body has less energy, burning off increasingly smaller percentages of fat. Calorie-restriction and exercise become less efficient during the thirties and forties. Losing weight becomes increasingly difficult for people older than fifty. Occasional weight loss becomes short-term as low energy levels persist.

Upon getting HGH during maturity. An increase in energy levels, coupled with larger muscle mass, burns off calories and decreases the body's overall percentage of fat. This makes the person look more attractive, while increasing the ability to move about and expend energy. At Century Wellness, our clinical results regularly and consistently show decreases in body fat.

YOUR HIP-TO-WAIST RATIO

Youth through young adult. Especially during the late teens and young adult period, an excellent hip-to-waist ratio is often considered a sign of attractiveness. Even more important, many physicians view a good ratio as a sign of superior overall health—less prone to diseases such as diabetes or prostate cancer. Waists usually are smaller than hips or posterior areas. Young women have a greater hip-to-waist ratio than men in order to endure the birthing process.

Mid-twenties through maturity. The sizes of bellies and posteriors often increase outside the range of ideal ratios. The advent of disease rises, while people become less physically attractive.

Upon getting HGH during maturity. Hip-to-waist ratios improve thanks to the increase in muscle mass and the overall decrease in body fat. This makes mature people who take HGH appear more attractive. Yet for now, studies are lacking on whether this improved hip-to-waist ratio correlates to any decrease in disease.

YOUR HEALING ABILITY

Youth through young adult. Healthy individuals heal amazingly fast, largely because HGH levels are surging through their bodies. The growth factor often enables them to recover within days or mere weeks. Young people injured in car accidents or wounded in combat often fully recover from trauma that could have easily killed a much older person.

Mid-twenties through maturity. People from their mid-thirties and beyond heal much slower from severe wounds, thereby increasing the probability of extreme or fatal infections. Also, older people recovering from surgeries tend to heal much slower than young people who receive the same operations.

Upon getting HGH during maturity. I am unaware of any formal studies on what impact this hormone has on the abilities of mature people to heal. However, some patients tell me they recover much faster from sports injuries such as muscle strains. Comprehensive studies are necessary before a definitive conclusion can be reached.

YOUR IMMUNITY

Youth through young adult. In healthy individuals, the body creates white blood cells to ward off infections. Various white cell types each employ "T" cell receptors that fight invaders and help eliminate infections. At times, invading viruses such as the flu, measles, or the common cold cause adverse symptoms ranging from fever to sore throats and runny noses. Most of the time the immunity system prevents or destroys the worst symptoms, with recovery coming relatively fast, usually within a matter of days.

Mid-20s through maturity. Due to the natural decrease in growth hormone, the immune system becomes less efficient. Abnormalities appear in the blood's anti-infection "B" cells and "T" cells, resulting in increased infections. During outbreaks of severe flu, authorities warn that the worst symptoms often target mature people. Infections including pneumonia are among leading causes of death among seniors.

Upon getting HGH during maturity. On a consistent basis, we at Century Wellness have seen a decrease in abnormalities in the vital anti-infection B cells and T cells. Although there have been no studies on whether these improvements decrease the probability of infections, I certainly believe that's the case. Comprehensive research is still needed.

YOUR OVERALL ORGAN
FUNCTION

Youth through young adult. An extremely small percentage of children suffer from problems with vital organs such as the heart, kidneys, and pancreas. Thanks largely to this hormone naturally produced within the body, organs grow to their mature size during this stage.

Mid-twenties through maturity. Decreased growth hormone output can contribute to the advent of heart disease. Yet, barring this, as an overall group, in most people the internal organs continue to function well enough to keep a person alive—until inevitable and eventual death. Even in people as old as ninety, unless they already suffer from such maladies as heart or kidney problems, for the most part the organs function fine up to the end of life.

Upon getting HGH during maturity. Other than chronicled improvements in cardiac function, no evidence has been found that the Master Hormone improves the organs individually and as an overall group—although it's likely the hormone contributes to healthy organ function.

YOUR LIFE EXPECTANCY

Youth through young adult. A person born in the United States today can expect to live about seventy-seven to eighty-one years.

Mid-twenties through maturity. Barring cataclysmic events such as war, famine, or the onset of new horrific diseases, the average person born in the United States in 2009 should expect to live to about 2086 to 2090.

Upon getting HGH during maturity. There isn't yet any hard clinical evidence to indicate that mature people who use the injectable form live longer than should otherwise be expected. HGH researchers do think they will live at least somewhat longer, and my studies clearly show that the overall quality of their lives improves while taking it. Even so, the jury is still out on this, and far more research is necessary.

CHAPTER 7

Users Voice Support

DO YOU STILL HAVE DOUBTS THAT HUMAN GROWTH HORMONE, STIMulated either by biostimulators or injection, can work wonders for your health, your libido, and your vitality?

Studies and clinical research findings tell only part of the story about the Master Hormone and its many benefits. Some of the most compelling evidence comes from people with life challenges similar to your own who have experienced those benefits firsthand and who have been willing to speak about it.

At Century Wellness Clinic, we have collected a wealth of these accounts that demonstrate the wide range of positive changes in health and quality of life that ordinary people have seen and felt after using this amazing hormone. After just a few weeks of Master Hormone use, most of them felt like they were thirty-five years old again!

Let me share a few of those remarkable stories with you. In keeping with my Hippocratic oath to protect patients' privacies, only the initials of patient's last name will be used, but you can rest assured that these are real patients whose case studies are on file.

———

"HGH has changed my life for the better, in a relatively short period of time," said Jonathan M., a seventy-three-year-old retired casino executive.

"For me, the most important benefits were a good increase in energy and what I think is a pretty significant improvement in my ability to recover from strained or sprained muscles. People notice my weight loss, most of all, and the change has given them a more positive impression of me."

After conducting the necessary tests to determine if his HGH levels were substandard, I issued him a legal prescription for the hormone shortly after the man's seventy-second birthday. At five feet ten, he weighed 233 pounds during his first visit to the clinic, significantly overweight for a man of his age and height.

For the previous eight years, Jonathan had been unable to participate in long, quick-paced walks, which was by far his favorite exercise. Nagging leg cramps and a sharp decrease in energy made him gradually lose interest in walking, until he stopped his daily strolls all together. His weight problems only worsened, gaining an average of five pounds each year. But today, with use of the Master Hormone, Jonathan describes himself as happy and vibrant following a fifty-one-pound weight loss. When visiting the clinic for regular yearly checkups, he always remarks, "I'm never going to stop taking HGH for as long as I live."

Our patients universally give positive statements about their experience. Some achieve the results they had hoped for, while others say things like, "With all the hype I've heard, I had expected more." No more than 10 to 20 percent of patients voluntarily choose to discontinue their prescriptions.

———

"Everyone keeps telling me how much more attractive I look than before," said Marilyn Z., a sixty-one-year-old receptionist for a major law firm. "I just smile, and never tell them my secret, that this all happened for me thanks to HGH."

For privacy reasons, Marilyn asked us not to reveal her before and after weights. With Marilyn's permission, we can report that she had a healthy 35 percent decrease in overall body fat and an 18 percent increase in muscle mass. The wrinkling on her neck, chin, and chest has also noticeably subsided.

———

"I want to thank you for this miracle," Veronica B., a seventy-eight-year-old housewife told us during her most recent patient visit. When Veronica first arrived a few weeks before her most recent birthday, unsightly age spots riddled her arms, the back of her hands, her face, and scattered sections of her neck. Nine months later, following her steady injectable treatments, 95 percent of the markings disappeared.

Veronica's blood tests showed a definite, measurable 35 percent improvement in her hormone levels. In results typical for mature people who use appropriate doses, our clinic also noted an increase in Veronica's good cholesterol, and a decrease in her bad cholesterol—plus a 15 percent improvement in her heart's ejection fraction, the ability of the heart's left ventricle to pump out blood.

It's important to emphasize that there has been no indication whatsoever that injectable HGH can cure, stall, or reverse heart disease. As a result, we will never issue an off-label prescription of HGH as a specific treatment for cardiac problems until more thorough and convincing studies are done.

———

"I never get colds any more," said Dorothy S., an eighty-two-year-old woman who lives in the home of her daughter and son-in-law. "Before getting HGH, during the past seven years or so, it seemed I was always getting colds or the flu." Dorothy's blood tests concluded that after starting her HGH regimen, the abnormalities in her natural T cells improved. With no conclusive evidence to say otherwise, I believe this change improved her body's ability to fight infections.

———

Lillian S., Dorothy's seventy-eight-year-old next-door neighbor who has osteoporosis, visited the clinic after suffering a severe leg break from a fall. Still in a cast during her initial visit, Lillian asked if she could receive an HGH prescription to strengthen her bones. She was told, "No, we never issue off-label prescriptions for such uses." She was informed that a prescription would be possible to improve the HGH levels in her body.

Following the appropriate blood test, Lillian was given an HGH prescription. Just one month later, she was able to declare that her fracture had healed twice as fast as her family doctor had told her to expect. Tests showed that her bone density had increased within twelve months. "There has been another change that I hadn't anticipated," Lillian related. "Everyone in my family is amazed because my mind definitely is much sharper than before."

Three months after beginning her HGH treatments, for the first time in years, Lillian started playing board games like checkers and began watching the TV game show *Jeopardy* with her grandchildren—occasionally belting out correct answers before some of the brightest contestants. Before taking HGH, Lillian never came close to displaying such sharpness.

Until more conclusive studies are complete, I would never consider injectable HGH as a treatment to prevent or delay the onset of dementia. Yet, the sort of regular and consistent results on mental acuity such as those enjoyed by Lillian have been reported by numerous HGH users as an unexpected fringe benefit.

———

Byron B. is a sixty-seven-year-old patient who always refers to his growth hormone prescription as "The Fountain of Youth that no one else knows about." His reaction is a common one. While more intensive studies are needed to confirm such claims, the evidence is accumulating that the Master Hormone is about the closest thing to a fountain of youth that medical science has ever uncovered.

More Stories Demonstrate Wide-Ranging Benefits

For more clues to what the Master Hormone might do for you, let's examine the case history of a typical seventy-year-old woman who started taking the injectable form on a regular basis, as prescribed by a certified physician.

By this stage in life, the woman—whom we'll call Alice—has slowed down considerably in all of her physical activities. Like clockwork, she retires to bed at 9 o'clock sharp each night, a few hours earlier than her pattern from a few decades earlier. Heavyset with large bags under her eyes, Alice usually awakens by 6 o'clock in the morning, but still feels tired through much of the day.

Retired like her husband, Fred, she handles their grocery shopping but always feels fatigued by the time she gets home. Alice's decreasing strength, endurance, and agility forced her to function within a boringly predictable routine.

Proclaiming Alice as "typical" may be stereotyping and unfair, since many seventy-year-old women feel far more vibrant than she does— while others show even less energy. Yet, from my clinical experience, her physical decline is far more ordinary than not.

Alice doesn't like to believe it or accept it, but she has gotten "old," at least when compared to many women her age, and especially when compared to young adults. While many people scoff at the mere mention of the word "old," as if it's nothing but a state of mind, that's how she was perceived by much of society and even by herself.

Then Alice made a decision to transform her attitudes and her life. At age seventy-one, one year after beginning an injectable regimen, Alice glowed with confidence. People who had not seen her for several years instantly proclaimed how much better she looked and acted. She openly admitted that she felt they were right. She did feel that way.

You see, her routine and her life had changed. By this point after using the Master Hormone, she was not only slimmer than before, but she stayed up late watching TV, or went out to the theater with her husband. Once they got home, she enjoyed intimate time with Fred.

Unlike just a year ago, Alice often extends her grocery shopping trips by taking leisurely strolls through their community's largest shopping mall—sometimes to buy lingerie or luxurious evening gowns. For the first time in a decade, she arranged a two-week ocean cruise for two, surprising her husband.

Before taking the injectable form, Alice occasionally became frustrated at her frequent inability to open something as simple as a pickle jar. Back then, she had no choice other than to ask Fred to help with such chores. Today marks a far different atmosphere in their relationship. Alice's improved muscle mass enables her to open these containers by herself with little effort.

About six months after Alice started taking the injection, Fred began noticing that she smiled much more frequently than before. This devoted husband realized that his wife had found a new sense of happiness. Should the credit go to HGH? All Fred knew for certain was that Alice looked better than ever, and their relationship had improved.

One Spouse's Example
Can Inspire the Other

During Alice's first six months of taking the Master Hormone, Fred balked at her continual suggestions that he try the hormone. Initially, pride prevented him from showing much curiosity, at least openly. Finally, Fred sneaked out one morning to the same physician's office that Alice had been visiting.

Fred did the necessary blood test to determine whether his natural growth hormone levels had decreased below those of average young adults. As soon as the physician told him that "your levels are low," Fred asked for and got a prescription for a one-month supply.

At first, Fred gave these injections little thought, administering the hormones when alone in the bathroom late at night so that Alice wouldn't know. During those first few weeks, Fred went about his typical daily routine, which pretty much meant staying home glued to their TV set. At age seventy-five, he had little energy or motivation for much of anything else.

Then, a few weeks after beginning his regimen, everything changed. Fred began bounding into the kitchen for snacks. Re-energized, he finally confessed to Alice that he had been taking the hormone.

"I've noticed this positive change in you the past several days," she conceded. She insisted that Fred take up golf again, and he made his first trip to the golf course in a decade. When in his mid-sixties, this retired civil engineer had stopped participating in his favorite sport due to nagging aches and pains. His aging body usually took weeks or months—if at all—to recover from these bothersome discomforts.

This time, just a few months after his seventy-fifth birthday, Fred enjoyed a full round of golf while suffering only minor discomfort in his left shoulder. A single aspirin made the pain go away, and since then he has had a blast in weekly excursions to his favorite links. As an added benefit, during the months that followed, Fred developed solid friendships with newfound golfing buddies. This is how the unexpected benefits of the Master Hormone show up—first physically, then mentally, and then in social relationships.

Alice and Fred are an ideal couple with whom we can show the contrasting reactions to growth hormone that sometimes occur. At age seventy, Alice began her regimen, but it took a full year until her muscles had improved enough to open pickle jars by herself. Meantime, her libido took a while to click into higher gear. Fred, however, experienced almost immediate and much more diverse reactions. Despite their different results, Alice and Fred each became dedicated to using the Master Hormone because it deepened their satisfaction with all aspects of life.

(**Important Note to Readers:** Anyone considering the use of injectable growth hormone should first be tested by a qualified physician to determine his or her body's actual production level of the hormone. Although the FDA-approved Forsythe protocol for growth hormone deficiency syndrome provides for minimal basic testing, which includes IGF-1 levels over two separate days, plus a twenty-four-hour urine growth hormone level test, it's useful to perform the more extensive pituitary stimulation tests that are detailed in the protocol. These decisions for further testing can be made by each physician independently and in concert with their individual patients.)

CHAPTER 8

How to Acquire
and Use It

REMEMBER THAT THE NATURAL CURE FOR AGING IS HUMAN GROWTH
hormone, and there are two ways to increase the levels in your body—
use one or more of the natural biostimulators that I described in Part
One, or use the injectable form.

Here is what you need to know if you've been persuaded that this
miracle hormone will help counteract the effects of aging so you can
enjoy a higher quality of physical and mental health. But before I tell you
how to obtain it, how to use it, and what you can expect by way of costs
and other issues, let's take a quick look at where it actually comes from.

Physicians began injecting growth hormone that had been extracted
from cadavers into children who were dwarfs during the mid-1970s. The
youngsters' bodies had produced insufficient amounts of the hormone
for them to grow to average heights. Many of these children initially
benefitted from the injections.

However, by the early 1980s, some of these children began suffering
from viral dementia, a complication caused by contaminated HGH. Partly
in order to reverse the problem, scientists developed or expanded technology enabling them to safely produce the hormone in sterile laboratories on a massive scale rather than extracting the substance from cadavers.
Recombinant DNA technology kicked into gear in the mid-1980s.

During production, scientists isolate and amplify DNA or genes before injecting them with precision into another cell, creating a transgenic—or genetically engineered—bacterium. This hormone creates seemingly perfect replications of this vital substance; the exact replica, 191-chain polypeptide, is produced.

Why Are Injections Necessary?

Many of our senior patients receiving growth hormone prescriptions for the first time naturally wonder why they must administer the hormone via injection, rather than orally with pills or even by drinking liquids. I tell all of our patients that—other than when using certain oral sprays—the digestive process breaks down the vital, working characteristics of growth hormone that would have made it effective in the body.

Bear in mind that when produced naturally, the Master Hormone is a 191-amino acid, single-chain polypeptide or protein hormone. Hydrogen, oxygen, nitrogen, and carbon create a chain of amino acids, longer than the majority of molecular characteristics displayed by other hormones.

Your digestive system—except when using certain oral sprays—cannot absorb these long chains from the growth hormone in their original forms because of acid and enzyme degradation. Hydrochloric acid within the stomach would cleave or break up the essential amino acids. The digestive process would prevent any viable HGH from getting to the liver, a vital step in the body's process of creating IGF-1, the working component of human growth hormone.

Perhaps someday medical experts will be able to develop HGH-laden slow-release capsules or pellets that physicians can insert or implant into your body. Then your metabolism would slowly absorb the capsules in a time-release system, similar in many ways to a process that physicians now use to treat prostate cancer, or as long-acting birth control hormones.

For patients receiving it, this would eliminate the need to administer injections from three to six times weekly, while also ending the hassle of transporting injectable forms of the substance in cool or refrigerated containers when traveling.

LEARN VITAL BASICS

Upon getting your first, legal prescription for injectable human growth hormone, you'll need to know some basics on everything from costs to acquisition methods, plus mixing necessary substances, administering injections, and storing HGH while traveling.

Average costs. For now, most patients with prescriptions for injectable HGH spend $400 to $600 per month for this natural substance. That comes out to $4,800 to $7,200 per year. Each person's exact cost depends on how much the physician prescribes or recommends, or on the amounts the patient can afford or wants to use within parameters of what is prescribed.

A majority of adult patients must pay for the Master Hormone supplementation themselves. Medicare, Medicaid, and insurance companies authorize these payments for adults needing treatment for any one of only three specific types of FDA-approved uses: AIDS wasting, adult short bowel syndrome, and the continuation of childhood growth hormone deficiency syndrome.

The cost usually averages out to about $25 per injection; most patients receive from three to six injections per week. Some patients write off these expenses on their U.S. income taxes at amounts the government allows for each income bracket for health care—related costs.

Special Note About Insurance—If you experienced head trauma as a child, you might qualify for insurance coverage for growth hormone supplementation, since such trauma could result in dramatically lower growth hormone levels during adulthood. The experience of Bruce Somers provides a case in point.

Bruce is the son of actress Suzanne Somers, who wrote the foreword to this book. At the age of five, he was struck by a car in Sausalito, California, and suffered a severe concussion that also required 108 stitches. Blood work done when he was thirty years old showed a level of HGH that was below normal. Some years later an endocrinologist gave Bruce a battery of tests, and the correlation between his childhood head trauma and an HGH deficiency was found to be quite high. Consequently, Bruce's insurance company approved his use of the injectable form of HGH, and his only out-of-pocket expense has been a $20 a month co-pay.

Delivery methods. After receiving a prescription for injectable human growth hormone, the substance usually is dispensed by a compounding pharmacy—rather than from a standard pharmacy such as at Wal-Mart. Pharmacists or physicians at compounding pharmacies use long-standing processes to mix drugs or substances to fit a patient's unique needs.

Most patients have their injectable delivered at home via FedEx or UPS, usually in amounts just enough to last for one month. The potency of unused HGH decreases after thirty days.

Mix ingredients. When you receive growth hormone, it's usually sent in an unreconstituted form—one vial containing powder and a separate vial of liquid. After receiving proper training or instructions from a physician or from a compounding pharmacy, you must mix contents from the vials. The resulting mixture usually is placed into other vials, each holding up to 10 milliliters.

INJECT YOURSELF

Anyone initially concerned about the process of injecting themselves has little to worry about. There is minimal pain. Among those in our family using it, none has felt any discomfort. Here are basics you need to know about self-injection:

Quick process. While careful to conduct each step the right way, the entire task usually takes less than a few minutes. Most physicians give their first-time clients fast and easy lessons on this process at the time these patients receive initial prescriptions.

Injection time. Always administer injections late at night, or shortly before bedtime. The body absorbs HGH best during your deepest sleep, commonly called the rapid eye movement or REM period. An alternate but equally effective protocol is to inject one-half the dose in the morning and the other half at bedtime.

Environment. Choose a private, well-lighted place so that you can see clearly. Administer injections when alone, out of sight from children in order to avoid sparking their curiosity.

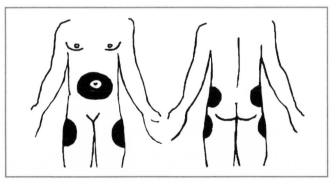

Handle syringe. First, push out any air that might be in the 1 milliliter syringe. Then, pull back the syringe pump, sucking air into the device. Stop at the indicator showing the dosage you need, such as one-half (0.5) milliliter or 2 milliliters.

Displace air. Push the needle through the small "bull's-eye" in the center of a rubber diaphragm on the vial, and then inject the air into the vial containing HGH.

Fill syringe. Invert the positions of the syringe and the vial, so that the container is now on top. Then, pull back the syringe pump to the amount of your prescribed dosage. Pull out without pressing the plunger.

Administer injection. Poke the needle at a ninety-degree angle fully into your belly fat or love handle at or around the sides of your waistline. There is rarely any pain when this is done right. People with little or no belly fat can inject at their rumps or fatty areas of their thighs.

Restore material. Right after completing the injection, replace any remaining HGH in the vial back into the refrigerator while still in the vial.

RECOMMENDED STORAGE METHODS

Because the effectiveness of injectable human growth hormone decreases at room temperature, you should store your HGH and syringes in a refrigerator. If possible, use a compartment that children have difficulty finding or reaching.

When traveling, take your HGH in a refrigerated or cool container, packed inside check-in luggage. Avoid taking your prescriptions inside carry-on luggage or purses in order to avoid unnecessary questioning from authorities unless you are carrying a letter or prescription from your doctor.

CARRY YOUR PRESCRIPTION NOTE

To prevent any unwarranted accusations, keep your prescription papers or a physician's permission slip on hand, in case you're stopped by airport security personnel or even by a traffic cop. If you're stopped and searched, be sure to tell authorities that HGH and syringes are legal when prescribed by a physician and obtained from the state where that medical professional practices medicine. *Remember, injectable HGH is illegal when obtained via the Internet or when sent direct to you from other countries.*

NUMBER OF WEEKLY DOSES

Injections are usually given once a day, and the usual dose a physician prescribes is six injections per week. This gives the pituitary gland the opportunity during a full day each week to continue its own natural production of HGH without benefit of injections—and enabling the gland to remain active on its own.

Many patients start their treatment regimens at five or six injections per week, before tapering off to three or four weekly. This course of action often is used for either or both of two reasons:

1. **Conditioning:** At the start, get your body used to these injections, before cutting back to lower levels.
2. **Economy:** Some patients request the lower frequencies for financial reasons.

Although these basics are easy to learn and implement, be sure to do them all the right way. From the start, make a habit of using these suggested procedures. This way you can position yourself to get the greatest benefit from your prescription.

PRODUCTION WILL ACCELERATE

More than a dozen manufacturing facilities worldwide produce enough injectable HGH for an estimated 160,000 Americans, with each patient spending an average $6,000 yearly for the hormone. That brings the current annual industry to around $1 billion, a total that we foresee booming to $100 billion, or perhaps even $1 trillion, within a decade.

By some estimates, at least 7,900 baby boomers in the United States reach age sixty every day—or a whopping 2.8 million people per year. If just 5 percent—approximately 140,000 individuals per year—start receiving injectable HGH, the total expenditures could easily grow by a minimum $1 billion yearly.

Of course, these totals pale by comparison to the overall world population, estimated in mid-2008 at 6.68 billion. At the current average prices of about $25 per injection, a vast majority of people from other nations would lack resources to obtain injectable HGH.

As with other pharmaceutical products, we anticipate that the overall worldwide price per dose will decrease significantly from current levels as burgeoning overall demand generates increased production. Meantime, we expect demand within the United States to double, triple, or even surge to far greater levels.

A Major Issue:
Off-Label Prescriptions

Many consumers would benefit by knowing the definition and importance of "off-label" prescriptions. This seems especially vital, since most HGH prescriptions are for off-label treatment of anti-aging characteristics. When a physician or medical professional gives a prescription "off-label," the substance, device, or drug gets issued as a treatment different from those authorized by the federal government.

Medical professionals insist the practice of giving "off-label" prescriptions is widespread. By some estimates, about 60 percent of U.S. domestic legal drug distribution in any given year is issued off-label. This especially holds true with HGH, since the only authorized direct use of the hormone is for dwarfism, AIDS wasting syndrome, and short bowel syndrome. When prescribing HGH as treatment for anti-aging, physicians or medical professionals are issuing "off-label" orders to pharmacies.

The Physicians Desk Reference, a book considered the Bible on pharmaceuticals for medical professionals, clearly indicates that physicians can issue off-label prescriptions for virtually any of the many thousands of drugs it describes. There is no ethical problem issuing "off-label" prescriptions, and merely issuing drugs "off-label" does not constitute malpractice. In an oncology practice such as mine, between 70 percent and 80 percent of prescriptions are written "off-label."

From my perspective, the issuance of HGH as an "off-label" treatment to a mature patient with low natural levels of the hormone is proper, ethical, and highly advised.

An Illegal or Underground Market

According to some official estimates, at least thirty thousand licensed medical professionals nationwide prescribe injectable HGH. We believe the actual number of distributors is nearly fifty thousand, or perhaps more. Many doctors distribute the hormone covertly or surreptitiously in order to stay out of range from the public radar. Since my trial, case law has established that it is a legal precedence.

In the past, a growing number of Internet sites have offered HGH in a wide variety of forms and distribution methods. Keep in mind that federal or state laws make obtaining HGH illegal unless prescribed by an appropriate, licensed medical professional and obtained within the state where the prescription was issued.

Some medical professionals who legally issue such prescriptions are homeopaths that practice forms of alternative medicine, licensed in only a limited number of states including Nevada, Arizona and Connecticut. Professionals licensed to practice naturopathy—which emphasizes the ability of the body to heal and maintain itself—can prescribe HGH in states including Washington, Oregon, and California.

As you might imagine, the laws on human growth hormone are murky from state to state. For instance, by some accounts, a doctor of Oriental medicine would be breaking the law if he prescribed HGH in one state, but the same professional could issue a perfectly legal prescription for the same substance in another state if he holds a license there for that profession.

How to Obtain Legal Prescriptions of Injectable HGH

I strongly encourage you to obey the law when seeking and subsequently obtaining injectable HGH. To begin this search, you can contact the American Board of Anti-Aging Medicine or the American Anti-Aging Association; each organization maintains a lengthy list of licensed practitioners. You can also check the yellow pages section of your phone books under the listings of anti-aging physicians.

After selecting one or several licensed professionals to contact, ask them basic background questions. Can the practitioner legally issue prescriptions for injectable HGH within the state where he or she practices medicine? Also inquire about experience, the types of testing this professional requires before issuing a prescription, and whether the professional has ever given prescriptions to people of your gender within your age group.

Once you get an appointment for an initial visit, the cost for that first exam usually ranges from about $150 to $300. Unless seeking a prescription for dwarfism, AIDS wasting, or specific lower intestinal problems, most standard insurance companies plus Medicare and Medicaid will refuse to pay for the actual prescription of HGH. A vast majority of people must pay out-of-pocket for this phase of the ongoing process. Add to these costs an additional $200 to $450 that you'll need to pay out-of-pocket for medical tests that are necessary for the medical professional to determine if your body's HGH levels have decreased enough to justify issuing such a prescription.

For the standard blood tests, licensed professionals look for IGF-1 levels below 300 to 350 in males and 250 to 300 in females, the maximum amounts that their bodies produced as young adults. In addition to blood tests, some practitioners also require twenty-four-hour urine tests, measuring the amount of HGH that passes through the body in a full day. A wide variety of other intricate tests for measuring HGH levels also are possible but not necessarily required.

(**Important note to readers:** Anyone considering the use of injectable HGH should first be tested by a qualified physician to determine your body's actual production level of the hormone. Although the FDA-approved Forsythe protocol for HGH deficiency syndrome provides for minimal basic testing, which includes IGF-1 levels over two separate days, plus a twenty-four-hour urine growth hormone level test, it's useful to perform the more extensive pituitary stimulation tests that are detailed in the protocol. These decisions for further testing can be made by each physician independently and in concert with their individual patients.)

Is the Price Worth the Results?

Sad but true, many seniors on low incomes never will have financial resources to obtain injectable HGH on a regular basis. With average costs ranging about $6,000 per year, the expenses remain far too high for many mature people to even consider. At least that is the current situation for injectable HGH.

But let's put the cost factor into some perspective. Economists say that average monthly car payments have ballooned above $500 since 2007. So, in monetary terms, for many seniors the decision on obtaining HGH mirrors the choice of whether to buy a new car.

Some mature people might ask themselves questions like: "Do I already have too many vehicles, or would I be willing and able to forego having a car in order to feel more vibrant and healthy for the rest of my life?"

Other seniors might consider trying HGH for a limited period, just to see if it'll give them the boost in vitality and various hoped-for physical improvements. Then, after checking results, they could decide whether to continue treatments.

Still other seniors might choose to sell off limited assets such as an older, seldom-used vehicle in order to amass the $6,000 average yearly expense. This way they could wait until after taking the hormone for a full year before making a final decision about its long-term use. Your choice must hinge on your personal desire and financial situation.

Ask yourself this question: How much do I already spend each month for pharmaceutical drugs, and how many could I discontinue once I start experiencing the benefits of HGH? You may surprise yourself at the answer.

Many economists agree that Americans pay more for pharmaceuticals than people in any other country. For instance, in mid-2008 a single ninety-pill supply of the cholesterol drug Lipitor cost $335 to $361, according to various surveys. Coupled with the steep prices of other drugs, the average annual prescription drug costs paid by mature people or their insurance companies sometimes exceeds $10,000 or much more.

According to the *Washington Post*, the U.S. Customs Bureau estimates that 10 million Americans receive their drugs from other countries in order to lower costs. Meanwhile, large pharmaceutical companies argue that they must impose high prices in order to pay for vital but expensive research.

Imagine the wrath of Big Pharma once legal and natural HGH gets thrown into the mix. In instances where the hormone would decrease, reverse, or remove any adverse characteristics of aging, how much potential revenue would these conglomerate companies lose? Their loss would be your financial and health gain!

So when considering whether to spend your money on HGH, also factor in the extent to which such expenditures would help offset or decrease your long-term medical costs. Depending on how much money you already spend on pharmaceutical drugs, their replacement with HGH might prove to be a dramatic cost-saving step toward better and more youthful health.

CHAPTER 9

~~

Dispelling Growth Hormone Myths

YOU MAY HAVE HEARD OR READ SOME OF THE BAD RAP AGAINST THE use of human growth hormone. Usually the rumor mongering goes like this: Injectable HGH will make your jaws protrude, give you huge eyebrows, trigger heart problems, or even give you cancer.

Sounds outlandish, doesn't it? That's because it is. The scary myths being spread about HGH are designed to do one thing—discourage you from spending money on HGH rather than on Big Pharma's drug offerings, such as all of those widely advertised erectile dysfunction, cholesterol, and osteoporosis drugs.

Endocrinologists are allopathic medical practitioners who specialize in the body's excretions of hormones. Along with Big Pharma, endocrinologists are the ones leading the charge when it comes to spreading fear about the use of HGH. They either openly or unwittingly create many negative perceptions about the use of this hormone in an attempt to protect their professional turf. Mostly it's an opposition based on unfounded fear "of the unknown" stemming from their lack of education or personal research into the Master Hormone's potential benefits. Many of them just simply "want" to believe that everything negative they've heard about HGH is true.

Endocrinologists absorbed much of their anti-HGH paranoia and propaganda while still in medical school. Then, following three years of intense training in internal medicine in order to become certified endocrinologists, they undergo an additional two or three years in fellowship training, all of which further reinforces their conditioning to resist HGH as playing a role in anti-aging medicine. By the time they finish their formal studies, many endocrinologists feel protective of what they've learned and jealous of any other medical professionals who would "intrude" upon their hormonal turf.

It's true that an increasing number of practitioners of other medical specialties—from internists to gynecologists and sports medicine doctors—have been seeking to prescribe HGH for their patients as word has been spreading about its proven benefits. Feeling threatened by these "encroachments," endocrinologists as a specialized group of professionals began forming an alliance with Big Pharma and exercising influence with medical associations, government regulatory officials, and politicians to spread the fabrication that anyone who prescribes HGH as a treatment for hormone deficiencies is practicing bad medicine.

Compare this situation with that of another hormone—estrogen. Under federal guidelines, physicians have the option of prescribing estrogen as a replacement therapy for menopausal women. Endocrinologists prescribe it with regularity, as do other types of physicians. In fact, if a menopausal woman suffers hypothyroid disease—symptoms experienced by 20 to 30 percent of women during menopause—a physician could face legal action for *not* prescribing replacement thyroid hormones as therapy.

Somatopause is a term that refers to the body's lowering of growth hormone production, a condition that comes with age. To treat it, HGH should automatically be considered. But HGH remains illegal to prescribe specifically and directly as a replacement hormone—the way estrogen is distributed in pharmacies. This makes absolutely no scientific sense whatsoever!

Behind the resistance to HGH (besides Big Pharma's obvious profit motive) is this ugly little secret—a lot of uninformed people simply don't believe that aging should be regarded as if it were a treatable disease. They think we should just roll over and die when our time comes. That point of view reared its head in my trial when the prosecutor told the jury: "Doctor Forsythe treats aging, and we all grow old and die. Why treat aging?"

Like many opponents or skeptics of HGH, this prosecutor was far behind the curve in his knowledge of medical science's advancements. The use of HGH for anti-aging is not some form of quackery, as endocrinologists and Big Pharma would have you believe. It's a legitimate response to the realization that medical science *can* slow down the aging process by treating the core reason for the symptoms of aging, which is a bodily deficiency of this natural hormone.

In prosecuting me, the federal government took a very narrow view about what modern medicine is all about. Prosecutors tried to make it sound like I was merely and only a physician who prescribes it. In reality, I prescribe a wide range of bioidentical hormones, and I also strongly emphasize the need to complement HGH use with the other biostimulation keys to life extension and good health—proper nutrition, sleep, healthy thoughts and relationships, and exercise.

The following are the most common myths about human growth hormone and how I dispel them based on the medical evidence.

Ten Most Common Myths About HGH

IT CAUSES CANCER

Fear mongers. People who use the injectable form of HGH suffer a higher incidence of cancers. The resulting disease riddles the body, sharply decreasing life expectancy.

The facts. When taken in proper doses no greater than the maximum allowed, injectable HGH in mature people causes no increase in cancer incidence. As an oncologist, I would never consider giving HGH if the hormone had even a slight chance of inducing cancer. Though studies still need to be done, there's a real possibility that HGH may actually lower the rate of cancer in mature adults because it improves immune system functioning. Some studies indicate that the incidence of prostate cancer might be lower among men taking injectable HGH. In general, there seems to be an inverse relationship between higher rates of cancer and the levels of HGH in the body. Children, also, have not shown any higher levels of cancer by taking HGH.

IT CAUSES ACROMEGALY

Fear mongers. HGH causes acromegaly (a disfigurement disease), particularly the enlargement of the brow, jaw, hands, and feet. This growth could make the person appear grotesque. HGH could cause excessive growth resulting in severe health problems, including heart disease and early death from an enlarged heart.

The facts. Gigantism only occurs in children who have not experienced full bone growth. Symptoms of acromegaly would emerge only in extremely excessive doses. When taking HGH at proper levels, mature people experience no such changes. Also, bear in mind that the adult dose is only 14 percent of a child's dose.

IT CAUSES GIGANTISM

Fear mongers. Mature people who use injectable HGH could grow excessively tall, perhaps up to 8 feet, resulting in severe health problems such as heart disease and early death.

The facts. Users of HGH never grow excessively tall. Actually, a positive benefit of HGH is that it may curtail the body's natural shrinking process that affects most seniors in the form of osteoporosis. HGH increases bone density. That helps to offset the effect of aging, which compresses the spine like an accordion, causing people advanced in age to lose three to seven inches of their former height.

Healthy people have seven vertebrae in their necks, twelve in the thoracic spine, and five in the lumbar spine. When and if each of the twenty-four vertebrae compress by just a quarter-inch as part of the natural aging process, a person can lose six inches in height. Studies show that HGH increases bone density in mature people by 0.5 percent to 1.5 percent per year, thereby preventing or decreasing the likelihood of osteoporosis-related fractures. One doctor-patient with severe rheumatoid arthritis experienced a complete remission after six months of HGH therapy.

Children of short stature or with dwarfism who receive injectable HGH as a treatment often grow in height, but never to the point of becoming extremely tall. Once again, it should be pointed out that the doses mature people receive are only 14 percent of those administered to children suffering from short stature.

IT CAUSES DIABETES

Fear mongers. The use of HGH promotes or causes diabetes and all of its attendant medical complications.

The facts. When given in proper doses, HGH never results in diabetes. Insulin problems could occur only in instances where the hormone gets administered in excessive amounts beyond the recommended dosage. Though studies still need to be done, I believe that injectable HGH actually lowers the risk of diabetes because—as shown by clinical results on a consistent basis—the hormone reduces body fat, a major contributing factor in generating the disease.

IT CAUSES HYPOGLYCEMIA

Fear mongers. Unlike people with diabetes, whose bodies fail to produce enough insulin, people with hypoglycemia produce too much of the substances resulting in glucose levels that are too low. The claim is that HGH forces the body to produce more insulin than necessary.

The facts. These problems rarely happen in healthy children, and the same is true for mature HGH patients. At Century Wellness Clinic, we monitor the blood of patients during regularly scheduled follow-up visits and any increase in insulin levels would be noticed. Such increases never happen.

IT CAUSES CARPAL TUNNEL SYNDROME

Fear mongers. Primary symptoms of carpal tunnel syndrome supposedly caused by HGH include over-growth of the wrist tendons, pinching the median nerve in the wrist, and numbness in the middle fingers.

The facts. I know of only one case where such symptoms occurred, and that happened when a physician administered the hormone to himself in excessive amounts. The symptoms subsided when he decreased the dosage to acceptable levels. If HGH causes carpal tunnel syndrome, all children who take HGH would suffer from the condition. None of Century Wellness Clinic's patients have experienced the symptoms.

IT CAUSES MUSCLE OVERGROWTH

Fear mongers. HGH makes people too big or muscular to the point of being candidates for a circus sideshow.

The facts. While HGH consistently increases muscle density in mature users, muscle mass never becomes excessive if doses are in proper amounts. Retired baseball star Jose Conseco, an admitted HGH user, never complained about looking "too ripped."

IT CAUSES JOINT PAIN

Fear mongers. People suffer severe joint pain as a result of injectable HGH, causing excessive growth throughout the body.

The facts. None of my patients—who did not previously suffer from arthritis or other joint disease—have ever experienced new problems in these areas of the body. Anyone complaining of joint pain may have exceeded the intake of appropriate doses.

IT CAUSES EXTENDED BELLIES

Fear mongers. Bodybuilders who use HGH experience extended bellies, an unsightly physical condition.

The facts. Some bodybuilders have administered HGH in excessive amounts. Patients at Century Wellness never experience this phenomenon.

IT CAUSES PITUITARY TUMORS

Fear mongers. Tumors grow in or on the pituitary gland, cutting off or accelerating production of vital hormones, including HGH, and causing significant health problems.

The facts. Over many years of clinical research, I have seen no sign whatsoever that injectable HGH, administered in proper doses, causes anything resembling such tumors.

Some Commonly Asked Questions

Do I need to exercise and eat a healthier diet for HGH to be effective?

If you don't change any of your bad habits, if you continue doing what you're doing right now, not exercising, drinking alcohol and smoking, eating in fast food restaurants, et cetera, you will still experience some benefits from injectable HGH. Now, keep in mind that these behaviors and bad habits are not what we would recommend. Exercising and a healthy diet all enhance the effects of HGH on your body. But you should still feel better using HGH even despite your unhealthy lifestyle.

How soon can I expect to feel the effects?

Results vary from person to person, of course, but most people begin reporting positive results within a few weeks or months of taking injectable HGH. These results can be felt and seen. Usually it starts with an elevation of your energy level.

Can I purchase injectable HGH safely over the Internet?

We strongly discourage that! I don't treat patients over the Internet. It's important for you to see a physician and have your HGH levels measured as part of a physical exam. Only then can the proper amounts of HGH for your particular needs be determined and then prescribed safely so there will be no side effects. It's also important for a physician to periodically monitor your HGH use.

Will HGH help me to perform better in competitive sports?

I don't encourage the use of HGH for sports enhancement. I feel that it's a substance whose use should be directed toward health and wellness. I do, however, believe that HGH helps sports injuries to heal faster, so I advocate its use among both amateur and professional athletes to shorten recovery times before returning to competition.

Isn't HGH really a type of steroid?

No! That's a common myth. To be technical, HGH is a long chain polypeptide, a sequence of amino acids connected together. It's a protein. We produce it naturally in our bodies. We don't naturally produce the steroids in our bodies that are being sold today. Those are all synthetics.

At what age should I switch from biostimulators to injectable HGH?

I have picked the age of forty as the optimal year to switch from bio-stimulators to injectable HGH, but only HGH testing can determine for you individually, with any accuracy, the right age. I chose the age of forty as a general yardstick of when HGH production in the body declines because few pro athletes are able to compete effectively beyond that age in any sport.

How much will injectable HGH cost me?

For men, the cost will run up to $400 a month. Women usually require less HGH in their prescriptions, so their costs will be less. Biostimulators taken orally or as nasal sprays can cost as little as $10 a month.

What happens to me if I stop taking HGH after a few months or years?

No adverse effects should be expected from stopping its use. If you stop taking it, your energy level may change back to the level it was before you started the HGH injections.

PART III

∾

ENJOY YOUR
ANTI-AGING
BENEFITS

CHAPTER 10

You Can Take Pride
in Growing Old

GROWING OLDER ISN'T SOMETHING TO BE ASHAMED OF, NOR SHOULD IT be a reason any longer for you to be afraid of what will happen to your body and your mind.

We are at the frontier of a revolution in our attitudes and understanding of age and aging. Thanks to the wondrous anti-aging effects of biostimulators and HGH, we now know there can be far fewer limitations to our physical enjoyment of advancing years than our ancestors would have ever dreamed possible.

Many of you who are of the Boomer generation may recall a popular tune by Huey Lewis and the News, lyrics proclaiming "It's hip to be square." With the advent of HGH, many of these same people might now sing a new variation on these lyrics along the lines of "It's cool to be old."

The evidence for this colossal change in attitudes is everywhere around us. "Seeing Old Age as a Never-Ending Adventure" was the headline on a *New York Times* article (January 8, 2010) that described how people in their seventies and eighties are demonstrating pride in their age by embarking on adventure trips to the North Pole, hiking Mount Everest, camping in the Grand Canyon, riding biplanes across the English Channel. This new wave of active elderly, as they are called, have doubled the numbers of bike touring enthusiasts past the age of seventy over the last decade, and doubled the passenger volume of adventure tour companies over the same period. The global travel and leisure industry is racing to keep up with this demand from seniors.

Where some are fearless about adventuring forth, others share the vision and desire but struggle physically, and quickly give up hope of remaining vigorously active. As the old saying goes, where there's a will there's a way, and that's where a little help from our friend HGH and its allies comes in.

We feel confident that once people decide to seek a prescription for injectable HGH, they will quickly realize the significance of this life-changing decision. Part of this understanding is an education process. It's not just that you will see and feel the differences. It's also important to understand the forces within you that you have unleashed and then harnessed so you can educate others when they see those changes in you and begin to ask questions.

That is a primary role of this book—to provide you with the pertinent facts that you need to understand your own transformation and to explain those changes to others in your life, people who will naturally be curious, maybe even suspicious, about what is happening to you.

HGH Will Be a Hit Among Baby Boomers

As word spreads about the many amazing benefits of legal injectable HGH, we foresee a huge increase in the use of this substance by the baby boomer generation as it reaches what has traditionally been considered to be the retirement years.

Many of the whopping 78.2 million people born between 1946 and 1964 will seek any legal means possible to maintain their youthfulness and vitality. During their forties and fifties, many of the oldest boomers started hopping onto the get-youthful bandwagon. From the late 1980s to the present, swarms of these middle-aged people bought Jane Fonda's aerobic videos and Jack LaLanne's exercise equipment. Suddenly good-health enthusiasts, these consumers took up jogging while running through a maze of diets, including the Atkins Diet, the Zone Diet, South Beach, and more. Along the way, lots of baby boomers saw their parents wasting away in nursing homes.

Eager to avoid being sent to such demeaning human warehouses, huge numbers of boomers will flock to HGH. The effects of its use are hard to miss. Lots of people older than fifty who use HGH wake up early in the morning feeling rejuvenated, often after staying up late the previous night to dance, watch television, enjoy physical intimacy, or engage in a wide range of other pursuits. Many also enjoy taking up games that require mental sharpness, everything from chess to poker.

An added blessing comes to those unlucky enough to suffer minor or serious injuries. Injectable HGH enables mature people to recover much faster than they would have otherwise, while the chances of serious or debilitating injury actually decrease thanks to HGH. Our Century Wellness Clinic case studies show that bone density often increases by several percent after a few years of taking HGH, in some cases eliminating osteoporosis.

What About Regaining a Youthful Appearance?

Let's not fool ourselves. None of my HGH patients who are age fifty or older look like they are twenty-five years old. Nonetheless, a high percentage of these individuals look or feel ten or fifteen years younger than their actual age. Some significant changes occur in the look, feel, and texture of the skin, which becomes thicker—making these patients have a less weathered or wrinkled appearance.

Prior to taking injectable HGH, just about everyone over age fifty has what the general public commonly refers to as "age spots" or "liver spots," often on the back of their hands, together with ugly blemishes. These usually disappear after taking human growth hormone.

Many HGH patients regain a degree of elasticity in their skin. Much of the time, this makes the tone or constitution of the face, neck, and arms appear tighter and firmer. Because HGH improves liver function and the body's ability to ward off toxins, in some cases unsightly moles or warts also fade or disappear. These changes together project an unmistakable impression of youthfulness, since such blemishes have always been associated with the stigma of old age.

Enjoy a Glowing Aura

Have you ever bumped into someone after being away from them for a while, only to find they seemed more vibrant, youthful, and happier than before? Perhaps they've had a well-done facelift or recovered psychologically from a death in the family, or a divorce, or a job loss. Your instinctive reaction motivates you to tell them that they look fantastic.

Lots of patients who use injectable HGH report similar reactions. Surprised and smiling acquaintances might say, "Wow! You've changed for the better. Did you retire wealthy or something?" These patients enjoy greater vitality, a zestful energy they lacked before. This change, in turn, often enables and inspires older patients to get more exercise, engaging in activities as simple as strolls in parks or shopping malls.

Increases in your time spent exercising can improve your organ function, especially the heart. Think of this as a double bonus. Tests consistently show that HGH improves cardiac function, even among patients who get little or no additional exercise.

The improved heart function, in turn, re-energizes the flow of vital blood and oxygen to the brain. As a result, many HGH patients become joyful when their memories improve, they answer questions faster, and they start engaging in lively conversations again. Patients with positive mental attitudes and better brain function enjoy greater happiness and an improved overall quality of life.

Better brain function that results from the use of injectable HGH often leads to sharp improvements in the ability to make decisions. Boosted by higher energy levels, these patients often choose or engage in life-fulfilling activities.

Mature people who resume or start such interests often find a glow, energy, and pizzazz that had been missing from their lives. For many, these changes result in a new "meaning" or "purpose" for life—igniting the will to live.

Improved Exercise Tolerance

Most children heal extremely fast from minor cuts, scrapes, sprains, and even bone fractures, while mature people mostly lack such natural healing power. For the young, most of these seemingly miraculous recoveries result from large quantities of human growth hormones that their bodies generate.

To the delight of many seniors, our clinical results indicate that recovery rates from injuries increase markedly among mature people who use injectable HGH. A large percentage of them also insist that they suffer fewer aches after minor sports activities. Before taking HGH, many who tried to resume these activities made a sharp cutback in such exercise or quit altogether. Mysterious aches, strains, and sprains became too much to tolerate.

Mature women using human growth hormones are rarely mistaken for bathing beauties in Miss America contests. Nor can older men expect that by merely taking HGH they will soon end up looking like Charles Atlas strolling down Muscle Beach. But here is the good news. Studies regularly and consistently show that over a period of time mature people who use injectable HGH grow in overall muscle structure.

Just as in nature during their young adult years, an increase in muscle mass for seniors also generates a decrease in body fat. Love handles around the waist decrease in size or disappear. On occasion, posteriors shrink, while the thighs and neckline also tend to firm up. Such structural changes can make the person look far more attractive. Non-fatty increases in structural mass connote overall good health. Many patients proclaim, "I feel better than ever."

From several thousand years ago when the Greeks launched the first Olympic-style games, through the twentieth century to the present day, physical training experts have stressed the need for athletes to excel in three categories—strength, agility, and endurance.

When compared to those in the senior population, teenagers and young adults reign as far superior in these physical skills. As the decades pass, mature people lose much of their strength and their ability to move about at ease with little or no pain. Many seniors get tired often as their endurance fades.

Now, the good news is spreading that injectable HGH can stall or reverse these natural trends to varying degrees in each individual. The results that have been chronicled remain undeniably positive.

Everyone from middle-class families to movie stars contact our clinic for advice on how they can get this natural substance. People travel from around the country to visit us. Some of the world's most popular action movie stars come to receive the appropriate tests before possibly being issued prescriptions for injectable HGH. But remember, this isn't just a celebrity or rich man's pursuit. Average citizens just like you hold the same rights and opportunities for the use of prescribed human growth hormone.

What Should You Tell People?

Some patients find themselves so absorbed with getting their first HGH prescriptions that they initially put little thought into what to tell people about what they are doing and why.

One way of handling this dictates a keep-quiet strategy, since some people prone to envy or jealousy might pepper you with unwanted or bothersome questions. Pesky queries could spring forth, ranging from "Do you really think you look better?" to "Don't you think this apparent change is only psychological?"

These questions, in turn, might make you think more than necessary about the benefits. Could you end up asking yourself, "Am I really getting a lot friskier than just a few months ago, and do I really have a lot more energy—or is all this merely a placebo effect, something that's strictly in my head?"

Let results speak for themselves. You will know the difference between the old and new you. Concerning the question of what to tell people, consider these options:

- **Keep Quiet:** This often remains the best tactic. What people never know for sure lacks the potential to bother them.
- **Limited information:** Tell only a handful of people, heightening a sense of urgency by giving only sketchy details.
- **Openness:** Make this quest a tell-all journey, chronicling for your acquaintances as many details as you want, from changes in your blood results to the disappearance of age spots.

The Gender Trap

As a group using injectable HGH, men enjoy faster results than women in getting their desired changes. Within two to four weeks of starting their regimens, large numbers of men say their libidos are already re-energizing and they feel much more energy. Overall by this early stage, women often report that their results are far less pronounced.

No specific reason so far has been pinpointed as to why the changes seem more dramatic in men. My initial theory is that perhaps injectable HGH synergizes better or faster with male hormones than with female estrogen profiles.

Men often say they feel so much better shortly after starting these prescriptions that "I never want to get off of it." Conversely, in some cases, although women proclaim that they feel better, some of them do not seem as impressed with the changes. So a small percentage of women lack motivation to continue, forgetting the old adage that patience pays.

Perhaps an answer rests in the fact that, psychologically, many males seem more motivated to exercise than females. While there certainly are exceptions between the genders, as separate overall groups this might hold true.

Taking these concerns a step further, maybe the increase in energy levels afforded by injectable HGH motivates men to move their bodies more than the substance does to women, resulting in an overall sense of improvement among males. More studies should continue seeking answers.

While specific practices vary among people, countries, and cultures, overall the male is usually the aggressor when instigating physical relations with females. This is another area where men might sense a greater benefit from HGH than women, since men have more to gain—at least sexually—from the increased energy that this hormone provides.

Injectable HGH might naturally produce more muscle mass in mature males than the same hormone produces in older females. In addition, women's bodies generally have less of a need for the many benefits that human growth hormones generate. In nature, men have—and need—more musculature than women.

Many women like HGH because the hormone increases their strength. The substance gives females a measurable increase in bone density, a change that—as already noted—actually could prevent death. A large percentage of older females suffer falls, and women who break their hips often die within a few years of sustaining such fractures.

Women also like the fact that as an overall group, their cardiac function improves thanks to HGH. This helps improve the quality of their lives, while also possibly increasing their lifespans.

CHAPTER 11

Your Sex Life
Can Soar with Age

REMEMBER BACK WHEN YOU WERE A YOUNG ADULT AND YOU ENJOYED making love for hours on end? Those days shouldn't be considered over.

Engaging in emotionally satisfying sexual activity is one of the keys to good health and a long life. That's not me making this declaration. It's a conclusion reached by medical science after decades of studies showing how important our sexuality is to our well-being, irrespective of how advanced in age we've become.

The multifactor benefits of having sex later in life are really remarkable, and the impact—heightened or stimulated by human growth hormone— is the one natural high that keeps on giving. There are at least ten good health reasons why sexual expression should always be kept on your agenda.

Top Ten Reasons To Remain Sexually Active

1. **Heart Health:** Hormones produced by orgasms, along with the increased blood flow from sexual activity, help to keep your heart healthy. British researchers have found that people who engaged in

sex less than once a month recorded twice the rates of fatal coronary events than people their age who had intercourse twice a week or more.

2. **Blood Pressure:** Studies in journals such as *Biological Psychology* have established that, irrespective of age, people who engage in sexual relations more often experience lower diastolic blood pressure and less dramatic blood pressure spikes when under stress.

3. **Breast Cancer Risk:** European studies uncovered evidence that women who have infrequent vaginal intercourse experience three times the risk of breast cancer compared to women who are more sexually active. Additional studies need to establish exactly why.

4. **Prostate Cancer Risk:** Men who have more frequent intercourse and ejaculation tend to have better prostate function, along with a better ability to eliminate toxins from the prostate, later in life. There is study evidence that this, in turn, provides some protection against prostate cancer.

5. **Pain Relief:** Orgasms release hormones that help the body counteract pain from arthritic and other conditions. Sex researcher Dr. Beverly Whipple has done studies indicating that sex can help relieve migraines and lower back pain.

6. **Menopause Symptoms:** British sex researcher Stuart Brody points to studies showing that menopausal women experience fewer hot flashes when they engage in frequent sex, perhaps because sexual release contributes to the regulation of hormonal levels.

7. **Testosterone Levels:** "Use it or lose it" is especially true for men as erectile dysfunction often increases with age. Frequent sexual release enables men to increase their testosterone levels, which in turn helps to maintain firmer and longer-lasting erections.

8. **Weight Reduction:** We all know that burning calories can result in weight loss or weight maintenance. Dr. Whipple's research indicates that having sex three times a week for over a month can burn up to seven hundred calories per event, which is about what you would burn by fast-walking or jogging seven miles.

9. **Fertility:** For men who still intend to father children, several studies have found that frequent sexual activity results in not only a higher volume of semen, but a higher percentage of healthy sperm.
10. **A Longer Life:** A ground-breaking study in the *International Journal of Epidemiology,* published June 11, 2007, examined 2,453 elderly men and women and discovered that those who continued sexual relations had a much lower mortality rate than people of similar ages who stopped having sex.

Other studies have added additional compelling evidence that remaining sexually active extends your lifespan. A *British Medical Journal* survey on orgasm frequency in 1997 showed that men having sex less than once a month were twice as likely to pass away over a decade than men having sex at least once a week.

Similar results have been found for women. Duke University researchers surveying the sex lives of women in their mid-life and beyond discovered that those who continued to enjoy their sex life lived up to eight years longer than women who stopped having sex or who no longer had an interest in sexual relations.

These are significant findings that cannot be ignored if you really care about living longer!

Nor should you ignore other research demonstrating that when it comes to maintaining a youthful appearance, sex is much better than Botox!

Irrespective of your age, you will look younger to others the more regular your sex life remains. That was the finding from a long-term study of 3,500 people between 30 and 101 years old. Royal Edinburgh Hospital (Scotland) researchers devised a clever experiment. They presented photos of test subjects—half who regularly engaged in sex, half who didn't—to a panel of judges who were asked to guess their ages. Consistently the impartial judges guessed people who had regular sexual relations to be between four and seven years younger than their actual chronological age. It was clear that sexual release enhanced physical appearance and attractiveness. This was true even for the elderly volunteers in this experiment.

As you learned in a previous chapter from the glowing personal accounts of HGH users, this natural hormone stimulates the libido, giving you not only more sexual energy, but also more interest in sex. That's because orgasms increase your natural production of human growth hormone. It's a self-reinforcing cycle or feedback loop. The more HGH you use, the more sexual you become or remain, and the more sexual you become, the more HGH you produce naturally. One result is that you are better off physically, which translates into your good health encouraging more sexual activity.

See how it works? It's really quite a miracle of nature and human nature.

But don't forget all of the other benefits of sexuality.

Some of the world's most popular comedians joke that after sex, women often like to cuddle with their mates while many men find themselves dozing off. Endorphins that the body naturally creates due to physical stimulation can produce euphoric sensations that cause these behaviors.

These reactions, in turn, can also help contribute to overall good health among young adults and even seniors who enjoy consistent, good, and healthy sex. Orgasms aren't necessary each time, but they certainly go a long way toward generating euphoria and the hormones that bolster your immune system.

Our bodies were made to procreate, to repopulate the Earth and to ensure the survival of our species. In fact, much of the physical and psychological makeup of humans is centered on one thing: having healthy, physical intimacy and lots of it, too. That's where HGH can act like spark plugs for your sexual engine.

More on Why Older People Need Sex

Human beings are considered the only mammal that can engage in orgasmic sex long after mature females in the population lose the ability to reproduce. But why does nature afford us this wonderful opportunity long after sexual intercourse loses any practical use, other than for physical pleasure?

Some physicians and psychologists believe that nature wants us to bond with other humans as much as we want to throughout life. This, in turn, gives life itself some greater meaning for seniors—a motivation and purpose for sharing.

Yet, when the libido decreases, mature people find themselves unwilling or incapable of even trying sex, lacking the motivation. Nature, in a sense, is giving dual signals: "You've got the tools to get laid, but you don't want to have that fun."

Certainly, drugs such as Viagra, Levitra, and Cialis have begun to correct erectile dysfunction, making sex among seniors more possible than before. I predict that increasing numbers of elderly people will soon start getting amorous again due to the growing popularity of injectable HGH and bioidentical hormone replacement therapy.

CRAVING PHYSICAL CONTACT

Medical science presently lacks an aphrodisiac pill that could suddenly turn on mood intimacy for golden girls and senior men. However, our laboratory results and conversations with patients clearly indicate that injectable HGH consistently turns the proverbial "I-want-sex" switch back into the "on" or "green light" position.

A large percentage of senior patients, both male and female, tell us that they gradually begin to crave and even yearn for sex—in many instances for the first time in decades. Just as they did as young adults, some of these delighted patients awaken refreshed in the morning, thinking about sex and asking, "How am I going to get more of it?"

While masturbation emerges as an easy option or a quick fix for some, we all know that the greatest pleasures usually derive from physical contact with another person. This, in turn, inspires the motivation necessary to generate relationships, which make life seem fuller and more delightful.

Have you ever known a senior who became isolated or lonely? Perhaps you or your mature parents stay at home most of the time watching TV alone, or avoiding in-depth conversations with people you meet on an everyday basis. It's no stretch to say that injectable HGH will help to motivate a change in these self-limiting behaviors.

JUST HOW AMOROUS WILL
YOU GET?

While tests at the Century Wellness Clinic have not been comprehensive on HGH's impact on the libido, I have found that overall, patients report a higher sex drive. As many physicians or pharmaceutical companies like to say in such instances, "Individual results vary."

What's most important from the viewpoint of patients, though, is that their physical desire clicks back into full gear, or at least into a cruising mode. One patient might report a minimal or insignificant increase in libido, while another begins craving sex like a young adult.

Although we have not yet formally charted these results, I can say with a fairly high degree of certainty that men and women have similar results overall—at least when it comes to regaining physical desire.

For many people of all ages, there's a need to look good, or at least seem physically attractive in order to become amorous. Perhaps due to the high attention our media gives to the importance of a youthful appearance, many patients—especially women—hold a need to look beautiful or, at least, alluring in order to crave intimacy.

The higher energy that results from taking injectable HGH can play a significant role in increasing your self-esteem, enabling those vital mating juices to flow once again.

SENIORS BREAK STEREOTYPES

In findings that might make the grandchildren of many seniors blush, the August 2007 edition of the *New England Journal of Medicine* reported results of the first comprehensive survey on the sexual activities of people ages fifty-seven to eighty-five. The survey found that more than a fourth of those up to age eighty-five admitted to having sex at least once during the previous year.

These results show that many seniors can and want consensual sex, wiping out a long-held stereotype that sex is a fun activity reserved for the young.

As if these statistics weren't enough to stir the imagination, think of how these overall totals will increase once great numbers of seniors start using injectable HGH. Imagine the private screams of ecstasy that will reverberate within households of seniors across America.

The hit 1966 Broadway musical *Cabaret* made the phrase "money makes the world go round" popular worldwide. And in the same vernacular, even today you could argue that "love makes the world go round" as well. While equating sex with love might raise some eyebrows, there's little doubt that enjoying more sex can generate lasting relationships and good health, particularly when practicing safe-sex methods.

ADD MELATONIN TO YOUR LIFE

Without adequate sleep and rest, sexual desire and sexual performance can end up being shunted to the wayside of your life.

Here is a catch-22 situation to be aware of. After orgasm, both men and women experience a drop in blood pressure and this drop accompanies the release of endorphins, all of which combine to help induce sleep. With deeper quality and consistent sleep, you retain the capacity to produce more HGH naturally. So consider orgasms to be a sleep inducer to bolster your own natural growth hormone production.

A lack of sleep, which is a condition often accompanying unhealthy aging, can short circuit your sex drive. How to break the cycle? It starts with HGH, proper exercise, proper nutrition, and proper sleep. It should also include the use of melatonin, which is a multipurpose adjunct for your health, as I pointed out earlier in this book.

I strongly recommend that people who use injectable HGH also take melatonin, a natural, nonsteroidal hormone available over the counter. As indicated earlier, it's an admirable performer in the anti-aging process.

CHAPTER 12

Special Benefits for Women and Athletes

IT'S NO COINCIDENCE THAT THE ONE GROUP OF PEOPLE WHO ARE THE biggest users of HGH right now is physicians. They are smart enough to have investigated this hormone, and once they realized its benefits, they became part of the vanguard of users, though they don't usually reveal that to their patients.

If you're a woman, an athlete, or someone who aspires to become more physically active at any age, this chapter was created with you in mind because you should be in the vanguard of HGH users, too.

Life enhancement and health improvement can happen by using the power of HGH and its biostimulants alone, but the best results come when this anti-aging superstar has a good supporting cast of therapies and regimens. Let's look first at how the lives of women can be improved.

Women in their mid-fifties and beyond who use HGH can enjoy additional benefits by also adopting replacement therapies for other hormones. Women who employ these additional therapies often benefit from increases in muscle mass, decreases in body fat, and increased energy, plus better mental function, improved immune systems, and improvements in cholesterol levels and bone density.

Other than HGH, the most common bioidentical hormone replacement therapies for women involve:

- **Estrogen:** A naturally occurring steroid, estrogen serves as the main female sex hormone primarily produced within the ovaries—and by the breasts, liver, and adrenal glands. (Keep in mind that not all hormones, such as HGH, are steroids, but estrogen happens to be a beneficial and natural body-produced steroid.) Estrogen performs an essential role in regulating menstrual cycles and developing secondary female sex characteristics. Besides regulating height, estrogen plays an essential role in accelerating the metabolism to burn fat and increase bone density.
- **Progesterone:** This steroid hormone regulates the female menstrual cycle, pregnancy, and the formation of embryos. Progesterone is primarily produced by the ovaries, adrenal glands, the brain, and also the placenta during pregnancy. Also in nature, yams are the primary foods that generate progesterone.
- **Testosterone:** The well-being and health of a person hinges largely on this steroid hormone produced by the male testes, the adrenal glands, and female ovaries. While protecting against osteoporosis, testosterone increases red blood cell production and enhances the libido while increasing energy. Adult men produce forty to sixty times more testosterone than women, but females show greater sensitivity than males to this hormone on a behavioral level.

To varying degrees, the levels of estrogen, progesterone, and testosterone decrease in women as they age. In addition, individual women respond at different levels to bioidentical replacement therapy or BHRT. Every woman has a different level of absorption and varying degrees of metabolism.

Some controversies have arisen involving the use of bioidentical replacement therapy, particularly estrogen when it is applied as a cream. I say an emphatic "no" to people who ask if such therapy in the form of estrogen increases the rates of breast cancer and cardiovascular disease. I am pleased to tell patients that creams used in bioidentical hormone replacement therapy are effective in almost all women.

Understand the Impacts of the Female Life Cycle

Hormonal imbalances occur in women before, during, and after menopause, the period when a female's menstruation cycles ends. A bioidentical hormone replacement therapy regimen can address a variety of adverse physical symptoms that women sustain during each of these life phases.

Besides heart palpitations, racing hearts, moodiness, and depression, other symptoms can include erratic behavior or irritability, tender breasts, diminished sex drive, and pain during intercourse due to vaginal dryness.

Compounding these problems, during the perimenopausal period just before, during, and after menopause, some women also experience frequent urination, excessive weight gain, frequent vaginal yeast infections, and diminished bone density.

As if all these problems weren't already enough, many maturing women complain of decreased energy or vitality, memory loss, joint and muscle aches, lightheadedness, insomnia, hot flashes, and cold or clammy skin.

Bioidentical estrogen and progesterone hormones can be used to help battle these problems. They are created from plant products in a bio-engineering process.

Some medical professionals also recommend using synthetic hormones or the hormones from pregnant horses as supplements. However, synthetic hormones and hormones from mares, such as Premarin, fail to work as well as bioidentical products in the human female body.

BIG PHARMA AVOIDS DISTRIBUTING
THESE HORMONES

Similar to what happens with HGH and nutrients such as Vitamin C, large drug companies avoid distributing or actively marketing natural hormones through pharmacies—at least in large quantities. The reason is because these firms lack the ability to patent and profit substantially from naturally occurring substances like hormones.

In 2002, the Women's Health Initiative studied hormonal replacement therapy on women before, during, and after menopause. The study focused on Prempro, a combination of two synthetic female hormones—Premarin from mares' urine, and Provera, a synthetic progesterone.

There were stark differences. Premarin was 10 to 15 percent estriol, which naturally occurs in human females, serving as the main protective estrogen in women. By comparison, bioidentical estrogen produced in laboratories contains 60 to 80 percent of the level of estriol that naturally occurs in adult human females.

In addition, Prempro contains only 5 to 15 percent of estradiol sex hormone, compared to bioengineered products that contain 20 percent of the levels of this naturally occurring estrogen that women have. The synthetic drug Prempro, made from pregnant mare's urine and a synthetic progesterone hormone, contains only 10 percent of Estradiol, a safe estrogen, while bioidentical estrogen creams contain twice as much Estradiol, or 20 percent. On the other hand, Prempro contains up to 80 percent of the harmful estrogen, Estrone, which is considered carcinogenic. Based on these facts alone, biodentical estrogen creams are a safer and more natural product for women.

The Women's Health Initiative stopped its study of sixteen thousand women taking Prempro earlier than scheduled, citing results that showed severe risks of taking the product. Among the findings: a 20 percent increased risk of breast cancer among all women in the study; a 20 percent increased risk of coronary artery disease of women in the study compared to control groups; a 41 percent increase in strokes; and a 111 percent increase in the risk of blood clots in the lower body.

Although these products remain on the market, many physicians now avoid prescribing Premarin and Provera, given their known risks.

I am unaware of any studies revealing negative results involving bioidentical hormones intended to benefit mature women.

TOPICAL CREAMS ALSO BENEFIT WOMEN

Mature women also can benefit from a variety of topical creams developed as vital treatments within bioidentical hormone replacement therapy regimens. Compounding pharmacies create many of these creams by using natural foods or substances like soy or yam roots. Medical professionals prepare these substances, making exact replicas of female hormones that women's bodies naturally produce.

Using topical creams, estrogen replacement therapy can effectively diminish acne, facial hair, hot flashes, depression, and joint or muscle pain. Meantime, these same treatments often increase breast fullness, nipple sensitivity, bladder control, vaginal lubrication, the intensity of orgasms, and the clitoral size and sensitivity. Female patients additionally enjoy improved sleep, better mental function, and increases in bone mineral density.

Women also enjoy some of these benefits from low-dose bioidentical testosterone applied via bioidentical creams. Besides increases in energy, strength, bone density, and libido, these changes include decreases in moodiness, depression, and panic attacks.

Adding even more substantial benefits to these therapies, natural progesterone applied as bioidentical replacement therapy in the form of topical cream has many benefits as well. These include increases in appetite, fertility, and bone mineral density—plus decreases in premenstrual symptoms, mood swings, insomnia, anxiety, and depression.

To their credit, since the mid-1900s, gynecologists, homeopaths, and naturopaths have prescribed bioidentical hormone replacement therapies to mature women. But amazingly, despite the many benefits that maturing women receive from bioidentical replacement therapy, many allopathic medical physicians still refuse to issue such prescriptions.

Some medical professionals worry about the effects of too much or too little estrogen. Among potential negative outcomes in these situations are the following:

- **Too much estrogen:** Fluid retention, oily skin, overly tender breasts, bloating, overactive libido and sexual aggressiveness, increased sedation, and possible cancer promotion in breasts and uterus.
- **Too little estrogen:** Except for the libido, any or all the potential problems from having too much estrogen, plus increased moodiness and insomnia, and a decrease in sex drive.

UNDERSTAND THE VARIOUS
APPLICATION METHODS

Medical professionals use various methods and doses when applying estrogen, progesterone, and testosterone in bioidentical replacement therapy.

As a result, patients should understand the basics of applying each type of hormone. Among application methods for each:

- **Progesterone:** Partly because this medication will help you sleep, take it at bedtime as either a cream or capsule. Never apply creams to fatty areas of the skin. Rubbing thoroughly at least ten times, apply creams to clean, dry skin at the inner forearms, upper chest, and neck, where the body can easily absorb the hormone. The cream usually dries within five to ten minutes. Wait at least two hours to wash these areas, and avoid bathing, swimming, or exercising during this period. Unless directed otherwise by a medical staff, women still in the menstrual phase should take progesterone creams or capsules on days fourteen to twenty-eight of their cycles. Because homeopaths consider daily applications of progesterone as safe, they sometimes issue full one-month supplies at a time.
- **Estrogen:** The application of estrogen usually involves estriol, some-

times referred to as E-3, and the estradiol sex hormone, sometimes called E-2. Patients should apply estrogen-based creams the same way such ointments are administered for progesterone. Women still experiencing menstruation should take estrogen creams on days one through fifteen of their cycles. Some patients wonder why estrogen applications are applied via creams rather than capsules taken orally. The liver and digestive tract have difficulty absorbing the integral properties of estrogen when taken in capsule form.

• **Testosterone:** When applied as a cream, women should usually take this in the morning, preferably at the inner thighs, or behind the knees or lower legs. These creams can increase hair growth in areas where applied. So some women prefer to administer these treatments to areas where they normally shave. Just like with progesterone, avoid applying to fatty areas of the skin. Use all application and cleaning methods necessary with progesterone or estrogen creams. Unlike creams and progesterone and estrogen, those with testosterone can be used daily.

Diet and Exercise
Play Key Roles for Women

Professionals in anti-aging medicine emphasize how diet and exercise play key roles, enhancing the overall quality of life and health in maturing women. Homeopaths and allopathic physicians urge these individuals to engage in both aerobic and anaerobic exercise, Pilates, and yoga.

The general attributes of these types of activities are:

• **Aerobic exercise:** This involves a warm-up period, followed by a minimum twenty minutes of moderate or low-intensity exercise.
• **Anaerobic exercise:** These activities generally involve high-intensity activities such as cycling, running, swimming, and strength training for short periods.
• **Pilates:** Developed by Joseph Pilates of Germany, this physical fitness

regimen focuses on the body's postural muscles, including the spine as deep torso muscles strengthen.

- **Yoga:** Originating in India, offering various related mental and physical disciplines or philosophies, practitioners usually strive to control their bodies—while seeking to achieve a variety of goals from better health to losing a sense of self.

Before beginning any exercise program, you should first consult your allopathic physician or homeopath to determine if you're healthy enough for such activity.

Just as important as exercise, the diets of maturing women near, during, or after menopause should include organic fruits, healthy fats such as olive oil, and fish or poultry. Women also should strive to eat healthy carbohydrates in the form of vegetables and whole grains rather than from sugar, bread, or pasta. Also, the principles outlined in three primary food-selection programs are highly desirable:

- **Zone Diet:** Developed by biochemist Barry Sears, this food-selection program entails comprising your diet of 40 percent carbohydrates, 30 percent proteins, and 30 percent fats. Various studies indicate these ratios result in reasonable rates of weight loss.
- **South Beach Diet:** Dietician Marie Almon and cardiologist Arthur Agatston developed this diet or food-selection plan related to low-fat diets developed in the early 1980s that the American Heart Association advocates. This diet essentially involves replacing "bad" fats and carbohydrates with their good counterparts. Rather than grains and sugars that are heavily refined, this diet favors whole grains, beans, and vegetables that are relatively unprocessed. Meantime, unsaturated fats replace trans-fats.
- **Modified Atkin's Diet:** Developed by the late Dr. Robert Atkins, this low-carbohydrate food-selection system or diet—also low in saturated fat—attempts to make the body's metabolism burn stored body fat rather than burning glucose.

Government Tries to Smash Its Use Among Professional Athletes

Unless you've lived in a remote cave for the past decade insulated from the media, you've probably heard about the controversy and scandals in professional sports surrounding the use of performance-enhancing substances.

In his best-selling books, *Juiced* in 2005 and *Vindicated* in 2007, former professional baseball player Jose Conseco opened the lid on the clandestine use of HGH and steroids in that sport. Conseco estimated that during the previous twenty years, up to 80 percent of pro baseball players had used performance-enhancing drugs, including HGH.

Once heralded as professional baseball's golden boy, a former player of the year and an ex–most valuable player, Conseco earned two World Series rings. Coaches, players, teams, and the news media ostracized and blackballed Conseco following the release of his first book, labeling the athlete as a "has-been." Many people called him a jealous retiree with a chip on his shoulder, concocting lies about his former teammates.

The controversy intensified when the 2006 tell-all best-seller *Game of Shadows,* by Mark Fainaru-Wada and Lance Williams, alleged that former San Francisco Giants baseball star Barry Bonds used performance-enhancing drugs.

Game contends that former player Mark McGwire's record-setting seventy home runs in a single season in 1998—smashing the former records of Babe Ruth and Roger Maris—motivated Bonds to use such substances. Fainaru-Wada and Williams claimed that Bonds began using performance-enhancing drugs including HGH via his relationship with the Bay Area Laboratory Co-operative (BALCO).

In 2001, Bonds smashed seventy-three homers, a new single-season record. Yet the star power of this slugger who subsequently became a free agent diminished in the eyes of many when the *Game* book was released, perhaps inspiring authorities to step up a criminal investigation of his activities. In November 2007, a federal grand jury indicted Bonds on perjury and obstruction of justice charges, alleging that the athlete lied under oath about his use of steroids. This case remains unsettled.

Major League Baseball had launched a joint drug prevention and treatment program in 2002 to look into the players' use of performance-enhancing substances. Largely as a result of these findings, the sport added HGH and seventeen steroidal hormones to its list of prohibited substances.

McGwire refused to answer questions under oath in 2005 at a congressional hearing on steroids. In what some analysts attributed to McGwire's refusal to testify, despite his many various hitting records, he failed to get enough votes in 2007 and 2008 for induction into the Baseball Hall of Fame. Finally, in early 2010, McGuire confessed publicly that he had used steroids as well as HGH.

Earlier, as the controversy continued to swell, in March 2006 Major League Baseball Commissioner Allan "Bud" Selig asked retired former U.S. senator George J. Mitchell of Maine to investigate allegations that the sport's players illegally used steroids and other performance-enhancing substances.

During the next twenty months, investigators interviewed more than seven hundred people, including at least five hundred current or former team employees, team physicians, athletic trainers, and security agents. Officials attempted to contact five hundred former players, but only sixty-eight consented to interviews.

Issued in December 2007, the 409-page Mitchell Report, along with U.S. Senate hearings, resulted in several athletes falling from grace, while vindicating Conseco's earlier allegations.

WHAT IS OVERLOOKED ABOUT ITS USE IN SPORTS

The federal government and owners of major sports franchises should continue to develop and impose stringent bans of HGH among professional athletes. I strongly believe that competitors who abuse this natural substance to enhance their performance should face suspension or even expulsion.

However, we also argue that professional athletes should be allowed to use HGH to rapidly accelerate the time needed to heal from injuries. Team owners, the fans, and competitors deserve to have the most talented A-list athletes on the playing field or court rather than B-list or C-list team members that fewer people want to see.

Team owners make huge investments in their most popular players, sometimes tens of millions of dollars to attract and keep the best athletes. Fans that pay big bucks for season tickets in advance want and deserve the most talented competitors, and major advertisers want healthy athletes who are paid for endorsements.

The abuse of performance-enhancing drugs by Major League Baseball players as far back as the 1980s contributed to the costly delay in allowing HGH to be accepted by the federal government and by a majority of allopathic physicians as replacement therapy for age-related deficiency syndrome.

The controversial Mitchell Report did a horrible disservice to the public. Perhaps to scare teens and young adults from using HGH, the document exaggerated or flat-out gave wrong information about alleged health problems caused by the hormone.

Amazingly to me, when conducting research for the report, its panel interviewed hundreds of people, including baseball owners, athletic trainers, athletes, and clubhouse employees—but only a handful of medical professionals, none of them homeopaths from highly knowledgeable clinics such as our own, Century Wellness.

Adding to the public's misconception, the Mitchell Report incorrectly stated that HGH has never been approved for cosmetic purposes or for anti-aging medicine. Here we stress that the practice of anti-aging medicine involves far more than HGH, but also a variety of allopathic and integrative therapies.

In yet another grossly incorrect statement, the Mitchell Report says that "having a prescription for HGH for these unauthorized purposes (such as anti-aging) is a violation of federal law." The innocent verdict in the government's criminal prosecution of me clearly and emphatically indicates otherwise.

USE IT FOR RAPID HEALING

Remember, my own studies and various reports by other medical professionals consistently show that HGH rapidly accelerates the healing process, even in young adults. Under my proposal, sports teams could treat their injured players with this substance when conforming to the following conditions or criteria:

- **Doses:** Use only appropriate doses within recommended guidelines, in order to prevent adverse side effects.
- **Restriction:** Treat players while in the nonactive or injured reserve mode, away from competition.
- **End-time:** Stop giving HGH treatments immediately or shortly before a player resumes competition.
- **Supervision:** All treatment should be supervised or prescribed by a licensed medical professional.

By adhering to these basic criteria, professional sports can get its players back in action in a healthy condition much faster than would normally be expected, while avoiding any chance that HGH will significantly enhance their athletic performances.

When conducting interviews, investigators or lawmakers working on the Mitchell Report determined that players also used HGH to heal injuries. Prior to the newest restrictions and bans on performance-enhancing drugs in their sport, numerous Major League Baseball players explained that they chose HGH because physicians had difficulty detecting the hormone in blood, urine, or drug tests. Since then, enhancements in twenty-four-hour-long urine tests have improved the ability to detect the use of injectable forms of the hormone.

The Mitchell Report also cited additional health risks associated with obtaining steroids or HGH from potentially nefarious compounding pharmacies in Third World countries or China, providing drugs of "unknown or questionable strength, source, or contamination." Adding to concerns, officials noted that the sharing of needles in locker rooms could, in rare instances, result in infections, hepatitis-B, hepatitis-C, or even AIDS.

By implementing an approved manner of using HGH for healing injured athletes, while also imposing a strict ban on the substance in other circumstances within professional sports, officials would eliminate such health concerns—also efficiently monitoring players for any inappropriate use of the hormone.

ATHLETES FACE A DIFFICULT REALITY

Before and since the Mitchell Report, professional athletes have faced a quandary when considering whether to use HGH to enhance their performance.

Among the three primary questions many ask themselves:

1. **Dilemma:** Should I compete without performance-enhancing drugs, possibly losing my competitive edge against teammates or opposing athletes who have fewer scruples?

2. **Leave:** Should I abandon my sport altogether, unwilling to use performance-enhancing drugs that would put me on par with athletes who use them?

3. **Join:** Is it the best decision to start using these substances, largely in order to stay in my high-paid profession where people at this level have relatively short careers anyway?

As noted by the Mitchell Report, players who avoid steroids and HGH have "long complained that their teammates using steroids were taking their place on the starting roster." Taking this a step further, the report also noted that the illegal use of performance-enhancing drugs in Major League Baseball "victimizes the majority of players who do not use this substance."

Compounding the problem, again as noted in the Mitchell Report, extortionists or gamblers—many with inside knowledge of which athletes take performance-enhancing drugs—could seek to take advantage of the situation, sometimes via illegal bribery in hopes of rigging point spreads or game results.

Some lawmakers and investigators fear this could lead to poor performance and point shaving, plus an advantage in predicting game outcomes. Officials also worry that unscrupulous drug suppliers could dilute a drug or combine it with other substances, making a player dependent on the drug and its supply source.

By imposing the stringent ban on HGH and steroids, and implementing stringent testing, team owners sharply curtail these dilemmas and problems while keeping the playing field level for everyone. Just as important, the public should keep in mind that the legitimate and legal use of HGH for age-related human growth hormone deficiency syndrome has nothing to do with using this substance or steroids to enhance athletic performance.

OFFICIALS WRONGLY CRITICIZED IT

When blasting human growth hormone, the Mitchell Report largely cited complaints echoed by endocrinologists, whose fear-mongering assertions I've already addressed and repudiated in a previous chapter.

Bogus symptoms of HGH cited by the report, which never occur when given in proper doses, range from acromegaly to enlarged flabby hearts. Other supposed symptoms that I have never seen include osteoporosis, thyroid disorders, and menstrual disorders.

Because the report is loaded with misinformation on HGH, I urge Congress to create a special commission to investigate the erroneous and false conclusions about this vital and natural hormone.

By no means should the ban on HGH for the enhancement of athletic performance be construed as a strike against many clinically proven benefits, especially among mature people. Those who compiled the report are clearly off base when they claim that human growth hormone is a dangerous drug.

All along, we know that an athlete without an adequate medical background or lacking basic knowledge on administering HGH could double or triple the doses beyond the maximum-recommended limits. To their own detriment, some players might mistakenly believe that "if a little is good, then more is better."

However, while doubling or tripling doses in clinical medicine causes severe side effects, especially when using substances like cortisone or androgenic steroids, the same cannot be said about HGH. This difference holds true, even when users increase doses of the hormone two- or three-fold, usually without severe untoward symptoms.

Once again, allowing HGH for treatment of injuries while imposing stringent testing and restrictions among active players would sharply diminish such concerns.

KEEP THE BAN ON STEROIDS

Remember that HGH is not a steroid. In contrast to HGH, which never causes severe health problems when administered in proper doses, steroids create or promote debilitating or life-threatening maladies from heart disease to cancer.

As I have indicated previously, I've never heard of HGH causing life-threatening disease or death in any athlete. By contrast, many people have blamed anabolic steroids for causing the severe illnesses or premature deaths of athletes like former Oakland Raiders football player John Matuszak, who died in 1989 at age thirty-eight from apparent heart problems. Whether any alleged use of steroids caused Matuszak's death remains speculation. According to news reports, his sister also died young due to heart problems, pointing to a possible genetic disorder.

There is no doubt that steroids can cause severe health problems, especially when mismanaged or given in improper doses. These dangers hold true among androgenic steroids that control masculine characteristics, and among cortical steroids that impact everything from motor skills to vision.

Besides promoting cancer, steroids can create a susceptibility to viral or bacterial infections, diabetes, obesity in the middle section of the body, and thin or gangly arms and legs.

Worsening matters, people who take steroids develop or suffer from weakened capillaries, making them bruise easily, even when lightly bumping into something such as a chair. These people often suffer stretch marks, stomach ulcers, and yeast infections in the mouth or vagina.

Severe weakness in the upper or lower extremities may occur. For people taking massive doses of steroids, everyday tasks like getting out of chairs become difficult. A huge list of other potential maladies includes enlargement of the heart, congestive heart failure, glaucoma, thyroid disorders, hypertension, osteoporosis, menstrual irregularities, erectile dysfunction, and increases in bad cholesterol.

Adding to these woes, when given for performance enhancement, androgenic steroids or testosterone could cause increased aggressiveness or "roid rage," an unhealthy increase in red blood cell levels, testicular shrinkage, accelerated baldness, facial hair—a condition known as hirsutism—in females, facial or truncal acne, and a generalized increase in moodiness.

In my clinical opinion, all these various symptoms associated with steroids are never seen in patients receiving correct doses of HGH. Remember, the adult dose of HGH for age-related deficiency syndrome is an average of one-seventh or 14 percent of the childhood dose prescribed for childhood deficiencies. By extrapolation, HGH is seven times safer in an adult with a larger body than it is in children.

PART IV

PROTECT YOUR ANTI-AGING RIGHTS

CHAPTER 13

Why Our Government Tried to Imprison Me

IN SLOWING DOWN OR TURNING OFF THE AGING CLOCK, WHILE IMPROV-
ing overall health, this natural substance, HGH, reduces our dependence
on pharmaceutical drugs marketed to treat the ailments caused by aging.
You can imagine how Big Pharma feels about that!

The less we need pharmaceutical drugs, the more money that Big
Pharma loses. It's that simple! With huge profits at stake, these corporations will try to disparage and undermine anything and anyone threat-
ening their bottom lines, and the means at their disposal for doing this
are immense. If they can't stop the competition directly, they use their
influence with the U.S. Food and Drug Administration and other federal
agencies to thwart health care innovations they don't like. They do it
with scare tactics.

My bogus arrest and the trumped-up charges against me stemmed
from one overriding goal: to curtail or shut down altogether the legal
prescribing of HGH nationwide so that you won't have access to it. That
I went from being attacked by the U.S. Food and Drug Administration
over HGH to actually being asked to write the government's HGH protocol (standards for use) may be difficult for some of you to believe. But
it's all true and a matter of public record.

Here is what happened when our government sent its henchmen to arrest me for doing nothing more than making people look and feel decades younger.

The Story of My Arrest

My wife, Earlene, and I were in the kitchen of our home outside Reno, Nevada, cooking breakfast one morning in February 2005, when Earlene glanced out a window and noticed three dark SUVs roar up to the top of our driveway.

"Honey, what are those cars doing in the driveway?" Earlene asked. "Did you invite somebody for breakfast?"

"No, I'll go see," I replied, and hurried down a winding hallway to a back door leading to our garage.

I got to the door just as the intruders prepared to knock it down with a battering ram. They all wore black flak jackets, some with stocking caps over their heads, and carried a variety of weapons. They demanded to know if my wife or I kept any guns in the house.

Bewildered, but thinking maybe this was someone's idea of a prank, I blurted, "Is this a joke?" It obviously wasn't meant to be funny because a dozen federal agents then bolted into our home.

A U.S. Food and Drug Administration officer announced, "We have a search warrant for money laundering, smuggling, trafficking, and introduction of an unapproved drug into interstate commerce, and illegal distribution of an unapproved drug."

Treating me like a common criminal, an agent ordered me to kneel and then pushed a gun to my head.

"Is there anyone else in the house?" yelled another agent, part of a SWAT-like team that included authorities from the FBI, the FDA, and the U.S. Immigration, Customs, and Enforcement agency office.

"Just my wife," I answered.

The intruders intercepted Earlene as she came down the hallway to investigate the commotion. Horrified, I could only watch as one of the agents pointed a gun at my wife.

"What did my husband do?" she pleaded.

"He prescribed human growth hormone off label," an agent replied.

Earlene and I were stunned speechless by this revelation. We couldn't believe it. This just didn't make sense. Every single physician in the United States who writes prescriptions does so frequently off-label, which simply means that a drug listed in the *Physician's Desk Reference* can be used for more than one purpose other than what it was originally created for.

Now here was the U.S. government, without any sort of advance warning to us, without any notice of complaint, sending in agents who acted like storm troopers to single me out for arrest and prosecution, even though I had compiled a spotless medical record.

As they ransacked our home, even going so far as to measure the outside perimeter of the house looking for false walls where we might be "hiding" HGH, another federal agent team raided our medical clinic where they seized records and closed down our medical practice. For the so-called crime of prescribing HGH off-label, I faced up to five years in prison and a $250,000 fine.

I gazed out through a window of our home while I was being held at gunpoint and caught a glimpse of our family's six-foot by four-foot Old Glory, lightly flapping from a pole in the front yard.

"Is this really America?" I wondered. "What on earth is happening to our country?"

Government Treachery Emerges

Arrested at the age of sixty-eight for the first and only time in my life, I sat alone in a county jail cell, still mystified by the sequence of events that had turned our world upside down. I knew that I had done nothing illegal or wrong. The HGH that arresting agents found in our home refrigerator had been legally prescribed for me by another physician to treat a legitimate medical condition.

Even as I was in jail waiting to be released on my own recognizance, federal officials tried to portray me as a sleazy doctor who employed unethical and illegal techniques.

While occupying and searching our clinic, some federal government employees actually answered the clinic's phones and told callers that the clinic was under investigation for alleged criminal activity. Many of our worried and confused patients abandoned our practice as a result. Others took their business elsewhere after seeing the sensationalistic front-page newspaper articles about my arrest. But the most damaging effect resulting from my prosecution came in the loss of innocent lives. That's right! I am not exaggerating. Some of my patients were unable to find adequate or comparable care after my arrest. In other instances, cessation of treatment put patients off track from returning to good health. Though medical treatments for these cancer patients never involved injectable HGH, only integrative oncology protocols, the government attack on my HGH practice also severely impacted the treatment options for our cancer clientele. No one will ever know for sure whether these former patients would have lived. But I have reviewed the files on a dozen case histories, and I have little doubt that many or all of them would have survived if they had continued in our care.

Nor does this miscarriage of justice stop here. Neither before, during, or after my trial was I ever told the names of my accusers. When arresting me, agents failed to read me the required Miranda warning about my rights. All that the prosecutors would ever allege was that I had wrongly prescribed HGH to an undercover agent who never needed such treatments.

During the government's investigation, my clinic was ordered to duplicate the medical charts of more than two hundred of our patients and turn them over to prosecutors, an action that forced me to violate my Hippocratic oath that obliges every physician to protect the privacy of his patients. That tactic seemed partly designed to alienate our longtime patients.

When federal agents arrested me and raided our clinic, I had no more than twenty patients taking prescribed HGH at that time. By comparison, another Reno-area physician had an estimated one thousand HGH patients, and a local hospital had even opened an anti-aging facility serving just as many people.

The evidence indicates that I was singled out to provide the government with a test case, a show trial victim, because I had such a recognizable name in the medical field. Though many alternative medicine physicians prescribe injectable growth hormone, few are also credentialed allopathic physicians. So I am unique in this regard. I am a nationally recognized oncologist, as well as a proponent of alternative medicine techniques. I work at integrating these two traditions to benefit patients. A lot of conventional practitioners don't like that.

For the adherents of mainstream allopathic medicine, who view alternative treatments as nothing more than quackery, and for Big Pharma, which regards HGH and alternative treatments as a competitive threat, I needed to be publicly discredited and humiliated.

Most allopathic physicians are brainwashed to avoid issuing prescriptions of the Master Hormone as an anti-aging treatment. Instead, adhering to guidelines set by the American Medical Association and the FDA, these doctors issue millions of drug prescriptions just to treat the symptoms of aging—ailments ranging from brittle bones to high levels of unhealthy cholesterol. Though growth hormone costs much less than these pharmaceuticals, and even though it often provides better results for patients, mainstream physicians and medical institutions remain under the spell of Big Pharma and its prescription mill approach to consumer health.

Before I tell you how my wife and I eventually triumphed over this nasty attack on our character and our health care rights, it would be useful for you to have more information about how this conspiracy of economic self-interest works against the public interest.

CHAPTER 14

Four Fearmongers
Create An Unholy
Alliance

WOULD YOU LIKE TO KNOW WHO IS BEHIND THE ATTEMPT TO KEEP
growth hormone out of your hands? If you care about protecting your
health care rights, then you need to know what all of us are up against
and how this book can help.

Ask yourself this question. What economic and political interests
have the most to lose if you stop needing medical treatment, if diseases
go away, if you no longer use pharmaceutical drugs, or if you live longer
as a result? Some of the culprits are pretty obvious, but others may surprise you.

Our federal government doesn't want you to live a long life. Why?
Because if more of us live longer, it will put such a heavy budgetary strain
on the Social Security and Medicare systems that the bureaucrats fear
those institutions will go bankrupt. That's a sad commentary. Our government wants most of us to die on schedule so that the bureaucrats can
keep their jobs.

I am not here to give policymakers advice on how to keep Social Security and Medicare from going bankrupt. But I can tell you that if more
people live longer, and do so in much better health than they have today,
overall health care costs will go down and that is a big plus for both
government and private health insurance programs. Not only that, but

keeping a larger percentage of the population healthier means these citizens remain productive, and that helps to keep economic growth stimulated and as a result, creates tax revenues for all levels of the government.

Four institutions that have historically influenced if not dominated American health care policy-making—the media, politicians, physicians, Big Pharma—have been working together, usually with blatant scare tactics, to deny you the right to use growth hormone. Here is how the manipulative game they play works to your disadvantage.

Media. Huge conglomerates that control most of the media depend on advertising revenue from Big Pharma. Don't let media representatives try to tell you that advertising dollars never influence their news decisions. Money talks and big bucks from Big Pharma speak louder than other advertising dollars when decisions are made inside of corporate boardrooms. Were the mainstream media to report accurately the indisputable facts about the benefits of the Master Hormone, their major source of revenue from the pharmaceutical industry would be placed in jeopardy.

Politicians. Big Pharma provides more campaign contributions to federal and state officeholders of both political parties than just about any other industry. At the behest of Big Pharma's legions of lobbyists who operate at every level of government, laws and regulations are implemented that restrict health care rights in this country, including your right to unfettered access to growth hormone under a physician's guidance. Big Pharma also influences decisions made at the U.S. Food and Drug Administration where a "revolving door" has traditionally been in place that creates an incestuous conflict-of-interest relationship enabling pharmaceutical executives to take regulatory jobs in government, then after a few years, make a return to their old Pharma industry jobs.

Allopathic physicians. Standards and regulations imposed on allopathic doctors by Big Pharma and federal regulatory agencies discourage the use of natural substances such as growth hormone. Most Western-trained physicians are brainwashed into believing that their job is to promiscuously prescribe pharmaceutical drugs for every ailment; yet, according to even conservative estimates from the American Medical

Association, these same pharmaceutical drugs kill upwards of three hundred thousand patients every year. How many people have been killed by the Master Hormone? I challenge you to find any cases.

Big Pharma. You can imagine how much money the top executives make at pharmaceutical companies. Salaries and benefits in the tens of millions of dollars are commonplace. With so much money at stake, it's no wonder that greed runs rampant in this industry. For at least a decade, when surveys of the most profitable industries have been released, Big Pharma alternated with Big Oil at topping the list. Both physicians and politicians have been huge beneficiaries of Pharma's corporate wealth-spreading. Politicians get big bucks to be assured of re-election, while physicians receive gifts, junkets, and other perks as rewards for prescribing endless streams of drugs to their patients.

Ninety-nine percent of the employees of pharmaceutical companies are decent and well-meaning people. But they have a conflict of interest. They must work in a system where one objective is paramount—to increase shareholder profits. And healthy people don't buy drugs. If they use growth hormone, they aren't buying those heart and pain medications, those cholesterol and arthritis medications, or the Viagras and other virility drugs. If everyone were healthy, drug companies would be bankrupt. So that's the bottom line of why the pharmaceutical industry doesn't want you to know about or take advantage of the the Master Hormone anti-aging breakthrough.

We used to hear a lot about an Iron Triangle that operates in Washington, DC, composed of the Pentagon, defense contractors, and politicians, which soak taxpayers every year. Today, we also are up against something akin to an Iron Box that is composed of the media, politicians, big medicine, and Big Pharma. We health care consumers have been boxed in by these four institutions so that we are taken advantage of and soaked for hundreds of billions of dollars annually.

Working against the public interest and our collective health, this Iron Box of entangled vested interests poses a real and present danger to our future. The fear-mongers would tell you that we're exaggerating in making such statements. But check the public record for yourself. That's all you need to do to verify what I'm saying is true. The unsavory relationships between the institutions that comprise the sides of the Iron Box have been detailed everywhere from exposé books like my own, to drug company stockholder reports.

At the root of Big Pharma's resistance to natural substances, such as biostimulators, is the reality that natural substances can't be patented. Without patents so these substances can be owned and controlled, corporations can't protect their brand names and formulas. That means they can't ever make as much money from nature as they do from drugs created in their laboratories and then patented.

Federal regulations state that anything that prevents, cures, mitigates, or treats disease must, by definition, be a drug rather than a natural substance. Those of you who know something about natural cures understand the absurdity of this twisted notion and how arrogant it is for humans to believe that nature can't cure or treat any of our ailments, only medical science can.

Our bodies yearn to absorb natural substances, whether it's growth hormone or Vitamin C. No one has ever died from taking Vitamin C or growth hormone when it was prescribed and administered in proper doses, in contrast to the toxic and lethal effects of pharmaceutical drugs. Vitamin B_{12}, for instance, treats pernicious anemia, while Vitamin C treats scurvy. HGH creates muscle mass and decreases body fat, along with many other benefits. The list of natural cures goes on and on. Yet, the Iron Box of special interests would have us believe that HGH and other natural substances are unproven and unsafe.

Physicians like me, who encourage patients to use natural substances for treatment rather than relying solely on high-cost drugs, are viewed with suspicion, if not contempt, by Big Pharma and big medicine. Regulatory officials and state medical boards often label such medical professionals as "disruptive physicians" if they fail to diligently follow the narrow guidelines set in the *Physician's Desk Reference* for the use of prescription drugs. As punishment, "disruptive" physicians find themselves subjected to fines, censure, ostracism, and even expulsion from the profession.

To more clearly understand why the institutions that comprise the Iron Box went after our integrative medical practice and me, it's worth relating a short history of how and why HGH got regulated in the first place.

How the Law Governing HGH Got Complicated

U.S. amateur and professional athletes began obtaining manufactured HGH for their training regimens via illegal importation from Mexico, Canada, and overseas during the late 1980s. At this time, the U.S. Food and Drug Administration had not yet classified HGH as either a drug or natural substance, but the agency did empower physicians to administer the hormone as a prescription drug if the physician was handling the patient's immediate care.

At the FDA's request in 1990, the U.S. Congress revised the original law governing steroid use by adding a provision making the use of HGH as a general "anti-aging intervention" a criminal act punishable by up to five years in prison and fines up to $250,000. Ironically, at that time, there were no anti-aging physicians in the United States.

Just a few years later, the American Academy of Anti-Aging Medicine held its first meeting attended by a few dozen physicians, none of whom apparently knew that Congress had limited the use of growth hormone to very specific conditions. Meanwhile, a paradoxical situation developed. The *Physician's Desk Reference*, or PDR, the publication used by physicians to guide pharmaceutical use, decreed at the time that any drug approved by the FDA can be prescribed for off-label use. That meant a physician could prescribe a drug for a purpose other than a specific type of condition that the substance had been designated to treat.

So a catch-22 situation arose. Physicians were prohibited from pre-scribing the Master Hormone as a general anti-aging medication, but they could continue administering the hormone for specific conditions caused by aging. Making the standards for its use even murkier, the new law overlooked a proven medical fact—age-related growth deficiency syndrome is a bona fide medical condition that responds well to growth hormone treatment. A physician has an ethical duty to prescribe human growth hormone to each patient diagnosed with this condition.

Steven B. Harris, M.D., of the Life Extension Corporation, points out how the Master Hormone is the only substance defined as a pharmaceutical that is illegal to prescribe for off-label use. "Even FDA-controlled substances, including narcotics, are legal to prescribe for off-label uses."

This friction intensified a turf battle among many conventional board-certified endocrinologists and New Age "anti-aging" or "age management" physicians. The older, more rigid endocrinologists don't want family physicians, internal medicine physicians, or any other specialist encroaching on what has traditionally been their medical treatment territory.

With the emergence of the Internet in the late 1990s, people in the United States ordered growth hormone from international sources, which prompted the FDA to once again clamp down, this time with a requirement that only domestic-based doctors can issue the hormone on an individual basis to patients under their direct care. This regulation contradicts the FDA's own mission statement that clearly states that the agency "does not regulate the practice of medicine."

Numerous physicians interviewed for a *Forbes* magazine article in 2006 described how thousands of doctors had distributed the Master Hormone for anti-aging purposes, in part because the law banning the prescribing of the hormone for general anti-aging purposes was rarely if ever enforced. Primary care physicians and specialists in endocrinology, gynecology, and geriatrics have been prescribing hormone replacement therapy for thyroid deficiencies, sex hormone deficiencies, and for adrenal gland inefficiency. As a result, many physicians naturally began to ask, "Why is it illegal to prescribe—whether off-label or not—the use of human growth hormone for test-proven HGH deficiency syndrome?"

Clinical physicians directly involved in anti-aging medicine agree that the hormone, when used properly in deficient adults, provides numerous benefits to overall health, including body composition, and cardiac and cognitive functioning. Doesn't it make sense to use it not only for its curative powers, but also as a preventive therapy to ward off osteoporosis,

Alzheimer's, macular degenerations, and all of the other "symptoms" of age and aging before they develop into debilitating conditions? Of course it does!

Fair-minded, independent medical authorities concur that the hormone is a safe and effective therapy. "Given the state of scientific medical knowledge today, growth hormone is safe," observes Ronald Rothenberg, M.D., a clinical professor of family medicine at the University of California at San Diego School of Medicine, and author of a 2004 medical paper, "Anti-Aging Therapeutics." "There has been extensive documentation in the peer-reviewed medical literature on the benefits and low-risk profile of growth hormone replacement therapy for age-related human growth deficiency syndrome."

Dr. Steven Harris sums up the ongoing legal dilemma best when he says, "When your government determines for you, on penalty of long prison sentences, what is scientifically and medically correct—even on issues where reasonable, educated people disagree on the science—your society is in big trouble."

Despite extensive documentation in the peer-reviewed medical literature proving that the Master Hormone is associated with less cardiovascular disease, less inflammation, improved exercise capacity, and a better quality of life, the Iron Box of vested economic interests continue to resist and disparage its use. This is the conspiracy behind the attempt to drive our medical practice out of existence and put me behind bars.

CHAPTER 15

What My Legal Victory
Means for You

NOTHING MEANINGFUL IS EVER REALLY DONE TO PUNISH THE DRUG companies. Government regulatory agencies mostly treat Big Pharma with kid gloves. The FDA might send them a warning letter on rare occasions. That's about it.

But consumer advocates get the Gestapo treatment. They don't send us warning letters. The FDA and FTC send in SWAT teams with guns drawn to raid our homes and offices. Their intention is to scare and intimidate us and anyone else who might follow our lead.

Evidence for the weakness of the government's case against me came when the U.S. attorney's office made a settlement offer in August 2007, before the scheduled trial. In an amazing turnaround, the U.S. Food and Drug Administration had requested that I be enlisted by the U.S. attorney's office to write the agency's official protocol on the use of human growth hormone in age-related deficiency states. None existed, and I was the logical choice to write one since I was considered a leading authority in the world on growth hormone and its use. In return for authoring it, a settlement of the case would occur that wiped my record clean of any criminal indictment.

Taking this settlement offer seriously, Earlene, my attorney Kevin Mirch, and I, along with co-counsel Marie Mirch, went on a four-day fact-finding mission to Chicago for meetings with the executives of the twenty-thousand-member American Academy of Anti-Aging Medicine. These medical experts included some of the first physicians to prescribe the hormone to mature adults.

After a careful, methodical, step-by-step review of growth hormone criteria and data with these professionals, I returned to Nevada and wrote the official protocol for its use. My defense attorneys then submitted the document to federal attorneys, who confirmed that they passed it on to FDA officials in Washington, DC, for further review. The protocol was signed off by the federal judge and federal prosecutors' office. (You will find the complete protocol reproduced in Appendix One of this book.)

At this point something happened that shouldn't surprise any of us familiar with how agencies of government operate. Big Pharma apparently threw a monkey wrench into the whole deal. As the online *Health Freedom Alliance Newsletter* reported, henchmen for Big Pharma who had been following developments in my case were furious when they learned of the settlement agreement.

So the government buckled to pressure. At a pre-trial hearing in September 2007, the prosecuting attorney told the presiding judge that no settlement agreement had actually taken place. The judge then decided that the case must now proceed to a trial.

Big Pharma, its lobbyists, and the government employees who serve them still wanted me punished for something I hadn't done to make a public example. As the first and only physician in U.S. history to ever be charged with prescribing the Master Hormone to a patient for an off-label use as an anti-aging treatment, I was the sacrifice Big Pharma needed to scare physicians and keep the blossoming growth hormone industry under control.

Before a twelve-person jury in a federal courtroom, my attorneys dissected and dismantled the government's evidence, destroying its case. It turned out that a middle-aged undercover agent had been sent into our clinic as a "shill" by the government to seek a prescription. The man had been given a blood test, as required, that determined his body had an inadequate amount of the hormone. Only then was the man given a prescription. Nothing illegal had occurred.

The prosecution called a parade of traditional allopathic physicians to the witness stand that testified that injectable growth hormone wasn't a standard part of treatments they gave patients. But that tactical argument quickly fell apart when my attorney showed the jury a standard FDA medical book, the agency Bible of sorts, called the *Orange Book*, which listed it as legal and approved even for off-label prescriptions. That meant the physicians who testified could have written the same prescriptions if they chose to. There was nothing holding them back.

At another point in the trial the prosecution further damaged its own case by delivering to the court boxes filled with injectable HGH, displaying it as if this were somehow evidence against me. Each box was clearly labeled as having been shipped to the offices of other physicians, not to me. So the obvious question was raised in juror's minds: Why was Dr. James Forsythe being singled out for prosecution when other physicians continued to obtain and issue off-label prescriptions for a natural substance that had never been proven unsafe?

None of the government's case makes sense now, nor did it at the time to those twelve jurors. After a morning deliberation, they returned a verdict of not guilty on November 1, 2007, not only vindicating my medical practice and me, but also thereby clearing the way for medical professionals nationwide to issue legal prescriptions for HGH. The trial's outcome tore down a curtain of fear for thousands of physicians who were "under the radar" of regulatory scrutiny.

Mirch & Mirch, my husband-and-wife defense attorneys, issued a press release after the innocent verdict that pretty well sums up what happened: "This was the most obscene miscarriage of justice I have witnessed, and the jury agreed with us. The only reason the feds have been caught in this web of deceit is a brave and courageous doctor stood up and challenged their lies."

What the FDA Protocol Gives
Doctors and You

There is a silver lining to the dark cloud of what happened to me. The trial became an opportunity to educate physicians and health care consumers about how to improve their health and longevity using human growth hormone.

The jury's innocent verdict and the national protocol on HGH that I developed for the FDA established major, positive guidelines for the medical industry, expanding and solidifying instances where physicians can use this potent hormone for a range of treatments.

Due to minimal publicity about this significant protocol, many doctors and medical professionals are either unaware that the document exists, or else they are still afraid to utilize it for fear that federal regulators will launch unjustified reprisals. So here in these pages I am laying out for you and medical professionals the details of how the protocol expands on-label, medically necessary uses of growth hormone replacement therapy so that you can take advantage of this wondrous substance and the opportunities it offers for revitalized health.

As outlined by the protocol, the expanded uses are

- **Aging:** Therapy for adults older than forty with normally occurring declines in HGH levels.
- **Heart problems:** Treatment of congestive cardiomyopathies, or heart muscle diseases, and congestive heart failure.
- **Burns:** Treatment of severe burn patients.
- **Fatigue:** Treatment of chronic fatigue immune dysfunction syndrome, or fibromyalgia.
- **Weight gain:** Treatment of morbid obesity.
- **Brain:** Treatment of traumatic brain and spinal injuries.
- **Sports:** Treatment of professional sports injuries.
- **Sleep:** Treatment of obstructive sleep apnea (OSA).

Until I created and submitted this protocol to the FDA, the only established and approved therapies for HGH were for the treatment of AIDS wasting disease, short stature or dwarfism in children, and for short-bowel syndrome.

Under the protocol, when considering whether to implement growth hormone replacement therapy, physicians must continue to use standard and acceptable methods of discovering, reviewing, or charting the complete and comprehensive medical histories of patients to document hormonal deficiencies. This involves reviewing medical records to determine the prior use of hormone replacement therapies, and also checking the history of pituitary tumors, surgery, radiation therapy and trauma, or prior chemotherapy. Patients suffering from various pituitary deficiencies have an increased probability of having indications signaling a need for growth hormone replacement therapy.

Physicians need to check for signs and symptoms consistent with growth hormone deficiencies, such as easy fatigue, lack of energy, a decreased libido, poor exercise tolerance, and sleep disturbances. The protocol also instructs doctors to look for contraindications, factors, or conditions that increase the risk of use to patients. These include patients with active cancer, type 1 or type 2 diabetes mellitus, carpal tunnel syndrome, and a variety of factors known as metabolic syndrome.

As the protocol notes, there is no single perfect and reliable test that a physician can give a patient. Many methods for the testing of growth hormone are considered impractical, largely because the hormone is primarily produced during rapid eye movement (REM) sleep. Because it has a short life of less than twenty minutes in the blood stream, accurate hormone-detection methods become impractical.

The most reliable and practical test is the liver metabolite of HGH called IGF-1. There are a number of cumbersome, risky, or flawed tests that include the stimulation of growth hormone with arginine, clonidine, glucagon, L-dopa, insulin, and propanolol. Of these, the insulin tolerance test is thought to be the best predictor of growth hormone deficiency.

Patients who fail to respond to insulin-induced hypoglycemia are likely to have a deficiency in growth hormones. But this dangerous test carries all of the risks of hypoglycemia, including sweats, nausea, vomiting, mental aberrations, hypertension, and possibly seizures. Also, physicians should avoid considering patients with coronary artery disease as candidates for the insulin stimulation tests.

Clinicians should also remain aware that poor nutrition, hepatic disease, severe diabetes mellitus, and untreated hyperthyroidism can reduce IGF-1 levels. So far, attempts to measure IGF-binding proteins called IGFBP-3 have failed to achieve superior results when compared to conducting IGF-1 testing alone.

Though the FDA never officially responded to my protocol for HGH use and treatment, silence does give consent in this instance and legal experts believe this court victory establishes a clear legal precedent. Despite Big Pharma's opposition, my vindication and the HGH protocol cleared the way for landmark expansions in the legal, permissible, and ethical uses of HGH, nature's gift to human vitality.

This legal triumph opens up for you a new horizon of wellness options and youth-revitalizing opportunities that can transform your life for the better. No longer should you or your parents and loved ones be condemned to an old age that automatically results in poor health and institutional warehousing.

CHAPTER 16

More Actions to Safeguard Your Rights

UNTIL RECENTLY, IT WAS MONEY AND POWER THAT RESTRICTED YOUR access to human growth hormone. I would like to think that my court case helped to change all of that in support of your health care rights. But we all need to be constantly aware that freedom always comes with a price tag.

At some point in your life, you've probably heard the expression "eternal vigilance is the price of liberty." That certainly holds true when it comes to protecting our health care rights, no less than it does for the freedoms of speech, press, or assembly that we so often take for granted.

If your right to receive legally prescribed growth hormone is to be protected into the future, the vigilance we need to exercise must be accompanied by public policy reforms.

In that spirit, I encourage the president of the United States, the U.S. Congress, the FDA, administrators of various federal agencies, and the mainstream media to implement the following health care practice protections for the public:

Official Report. Congress should hold hearings on the growth hormone issue and on the unholy alliance between federal regulatory agencies and Big Pharma. Afterward, the panel should issue an in-depth report with full recommendations on how to cut back the influence of Big Pharma and to minimize its exorbitant drug prices. Officials should issue these findings with the same publicity that the widely reported Mitchell Report received.

The panel should interview Master Hormone experts, plus numerous doctors of homeopathy nationwide. These experts should get just as much attention and consideration as any given to allopathic physicians or representatives of Big Pharma. Homeopathic physicians should be given a method to dispute any inaccurate statements made by Big Pharma.

Professional Sports. The panel should correct various misstatements made about HGH in the Mitchell Report, while recommending ways that this natural substance could and should be used for the appropriate treatment of sports injuries.

Legalize HGH. Congress should strengthen laws legalizing supplementation with the Master Hormone, making it clear to the public that this substance is beneficial as an anti-aging treatment and never harmful when administered in proper doses. The FDA should fund and start a multiyear advertising campaign, applauding the use of natural substances, including legally prescribed growth hormone and vitamins.

In addition, the FDA should work with various state medical boards, ensuring that the laws on administering HGH are uniform from state to state—eliminating the confusion about certain professionals being able to issue the hormone's prescriptions in some jurisdictions but not in others.

The FDA. This federal agency should conduct, publish, and distribute various intensive studies and reports, stating the many benefits of individual natural substances including growth hormone and vitamins—while correcting its own previous statements that natural substances are harmful to people.

Allopathic Medicine and Homeopathy. Congress should force the FDA to allow standard-medicine physicians to work alongside homeopaths, or at least in the same office facilities. Such integrated treatment methods have been successful throughout Europe and China for centuries but never in the United States where such associations are prohibited or discouraged due to the unsavory influence of Big Pharma.

Pharmaceutical Lobbyists. As noted earlier in this book, many thousands of pharmaceutical industry lobbyists in Washington, DC, work full-time to convince lawmakers to shut out homeopathic medicine in favor of Big Pharma and allopathic physicians, and the high-priced drug prescriptions that they administer. Congress should work to curtail the influence of these lobbyists, while severely limiting or removing altogether the ability of such companies to contribute to political campaigns.

Accountability. Congress should impose stringent laws, making the executives of pharmaceutical companies accountable for the tens of thousands of deaths caused yearly by so-called legal prescription drugs. Remember, growth hormone and vitamins in appropriate amounts have never caused a single death. In our view, although it has never received adequate publicity, the damage Big Pharma has caused society rivals or far surpasses the Enron scandal, which resulted in the imprisonment of several executives of a former electricity, natural gas, communications, and pulp and paper company.

Advertising Restrictions. Big Pharma should be allowed to continue advertising in print, radio, TV, and on the Internet. However, in order to minimize the unfair influence these mega-corporations wield over the mainstream news media, the federal government should provide tax incentives to companies when they also advertise the benefits of natural substances.

Appendix A

The Forsythe Protocol

Prepared by James W. Forsythe, MD, HMD. Board Certified Internal Medicine; Board Certified Medical Oncology; Certified in Homeopathy.

This protocol was submitted to the U.S. Food and Drug Administration in 2007 by Dr. Forsythe, MD, HMD., as part of a pre-trial settlement agreement with the United States prosecuting attorney's office in Reno, Nevada.

Outline of National Protocol

1) Endorsing Organizations
2) Abbreviations
3) Mission statement
4) Introduction
     a) Approved products
     b) Proven benefits of GHRT
     c) Cardiovascular risks of GHD
     d) FDA approved uses of GHRT
     e) Proposed expanded uses of GHRT

5) Selection of Patients

    a) Appropriate face-to-face work-up

    b) Major consideration

6) Laboratory Testing

    a) General facts

    b) GH stimulation tests

    c) Multiple endocrine deficiencies

    d) IGF-1 and IGF-1-BP-3 testing

7) Therapy Considerations

    a) FDA approved conditions

    b) Usual dosages

    c) Injection instructions

8) Side Effects and Adverse Events Profile

    a) General facts

    b) Adult side effects

    c) Diabetes facts

9) Conclusions

    a) Obligations to observe federal and state laws

    b) Expanded guidelines

    c) "Off-label" prescription

    d) Overall benefits of age-related GHRT

Endorsing Organizations

Academy of Anti-Aging Medicine—China

Academy of Anti-Aging Medicine—Iberia

Academy of Healthy Aging

Academy of Optimal Aging

Academy of Successful Aging

American Academy of Age Management

American Academy of Anti-Aging Medicine (A4M)

American Academy of Longevity Medicine

American College of Longevity Medicine

American Society of Longevity Medicine

Anti-Aging Medicine Specialization

Asian-Oceania Federation of Anti-Aging

Austral Asian Academy of Anti-Aging Medicine (A5M)

Belgian Society of Anti-Aging Medicine (BELSAAM)

European Academy of Quality of Life and Longevity Medicine (EAQUALL)

European Organization of Scientific Anti-Aging Medicine Anti-Aging

European Society of Anti-Aging Medicine (ESAAM)

German Society of Anti-Aging Medicine (GSAAM)

German Society of Hemotoxicology

Hellenic Academy of Anti-Aging Medicine

Indonesian Society of Anti-Aging Medicine

International Academy of Anti-Aging Medicine

International Academy of Longevity Medicine

International Hormone Society (HIS)

Japan Anti-Aging Medicine Spa Association (JAMSA)

Japanese Society of Clinical Anti-Aging Medicine

Korea Anti-Aging Academy of Medicine (KA3M)

Latin-American Federation of Anti-Aging Societies

Romania Association of Anti-Aging Medicine

Society for Anti-Aging & Aesthetic Medicine Malaysia (SAAAMM)

South African Academy of Anti-Aging & Aesthetic Medicine (SA5M)

Spanish Society of Anti-Aging

Thai Academy of Anti-Aging Medicine

Thai Association of Anti-Aging Medicine

Anti-Aging Research and Education Society, Turkey

Center for Study of Anti-Aging Medicine—Udayana University, Indonesia

World Academy of Anti-Aging Medicine (WAAAM)

World Academy of Longevity Medicine

World Society of Anti-Aging Medicine (WOSAAM)

Abbreviations

AACE......American Association of Clinical Endocrinologists

A4M......American Academy of Anti-Aging Medicine

AIDS......Acquired Immunodeficiency syndrome

CEA......carcinoembryonic antigen

DHEA......dehydroepiandrosterone

CFIDS......Chronic Fatigue Immune Dysfunction Syndrome

FDA......Federal Food and Drug Administration

GH......growth hormone

GHDS......Growth Hormone Deficiency Syndrome

GHRH......growth hormone releasing hormone

GHRT......growth hormone replacement therapy

HGH......human growth hormone

HIV......Human Immunodeficiency Virus

HRT......hormone replacement therapy(ies)

IGFI......insulin-like growth factor 1

IGFBP-3......insulin-like growth factor binding protein-3

MPHD......multiple pituitary hormone deficiencies

PWS......Prader Willi Syndrome

SGA......small for gestational age

TS......Turner Syndrome

Mission Statement

The use of Growth Hormone (GH) in clinical practice is expanding in both clinical endocrinology and the new and expanding discipline of Anti-Aging medicine pioneered mainly by the American Academy of Anti-Aging Medicine (A4M) and the International Hormone Society. The purpose of this protocol is to establish a national and perhaps an international protocol through the worldwide scientific and medical societies that are dedicated to the appropriate use of GHRT in improving the quality and perhaps the duration of the human lifespan and the function of the individual's physiology and hormonal balance in order to achieve greater vitality, prevention of disease and overall greater health during the aging process.

Admittedly some areas of GHRT will remain controversial until more information and testing become available; however, it is the purpose of this protocol to provide the physician with a standard sanctioned by the FDA that allows him to act as an advocate for the patient's right for optimal health and freedom of choice in health care.

This protocol consists of recommendations for the clinical use of GHRT. These guidelines should be used by physicians in conjunction with standard history and physical examinations along with appropriate clinical testing in concert with their best clinical judgment.

It is the position of this protocol and its authors that use of GH solely for athletic enhancement constitutes a misuse of this hormone and thereby taints its appropriate usage.

Introduction

GH has been used to treat children with GHD for over forty years. The original source of HGH was from the pituitary glands of human cadavers. In 1985 it was discovered that this source was subject to contamination with the Creutzfeldt-Jakob virus causing a slowly developing fatal dementia. Fortuitously, about this same time Biosynthetic recombinant GH became available and consequently after 1985 production and distribution of cadaver derived pituitary GH was discontinued.

GH of recombinant DNA origin with an identical 191 amino acid chain sequence is now produced commercially by a number of pharmaceutical companies. At present only the following recombinant HGH products have been approved by the FDA:

The purpose of this protocol is to promote the appropriate application of advanced medical technologies in order to address the changes in hormonal, biochemical, physical and nutritional needs that occur with the aging process. Over 500 articles in the world's scientific literature support the benefits claimed by returning hormones to their optimal physiological state when determined by appropriate and reasonable testing to be deficient. It is also a well-established scientific premise that many critical hormones either decrease significantly with menopause and andropause but also like GH decline stepwise at a predictable 10 to 15 percent per decade after the second decade.

TABLE A.1 FDA-Approved Recombinant HGH Products

PRODUCT	CONDITIONS
Genotropin (Pharmacia)	Pediatric GHD PWS SGA Adult GHD
Humatrope (Lilly)	Pediatric GHD TS Idiopathic short status Adult GHD
Norditropin (Nova Nordisk)	Pediatric GHD Adult GHD
Nutropin (Genentech)	Pediatric GHD TS Adult GHD
Protropin Somatrin (Genentech)	Pediatric GHD
Saizen (Serono)	Pediatric GHD Adult GHD
Serostim (Serono)	AIDS wasting Cachexia
Zorbtive (Serono)	Short Bowel Syndrome
TEV-Tropin (Savient)	Pediatric GHD

The documented proven benefits of GHRT in adults over the past seventeen years, since Daniel Rudman's landmark article in the *New England Journal of Medicine* in July 1990, include the following:

1. Increase in lean body mass
2. Loss of body fat mass
3. Improved skin texture and tone
4. Improved lipid profiles (cholesterol, triglycerides, LDL ratio)
5. Improved cardiac ejection fraction
6. Improved bone density
7. Improved exercise tolerance
8. Improved libido
9. Improved sleep quality
10. Improved immune function in patients with HIV

Furthermore the deficiency of GH and IGF-1 leads to an increase in cardiovascular risk factors. These include:

1. Increase in visceral fat
2. Increase in carotid intima/media thickness
3. Increase clotting factors
4. Increase in serum CRP
5. Increase in insulin resistance
6. Increase in serum homocysteine

Adult GHD has been associated with an increased risk of fatal stroke and myocardial infarction.

At the present time the only FDA-approved "on label" or "medically necessary" uses of GHRT are for patients with the following conditions:

1. Follow-up treatment for documented GHD in childhood
2. Documented hypopituitarism as a result of pituitary or hypothalamic disease from tumors, surgery, radiation therapy or trauma

3. AIDS Wasting Syndrome
4. Short Bowel Syndrome

It is the objective of this protocol to expand the "on label" and "medically necessary" uses of GHRT to include:

1. Therapy in adults over the age of forty with normally occurring decreases in GH known as age-related GHD.
2. Treatment of congestive cardiomyopathies and congestive heart failure
3. Treatment of severe burn patients
4. Treatment of patients with severe Chronic Fatigue Immune Dysfunction
5. Syndrome (CFIDS) and / or fibromyalgia (FM)
6. Treatment of morbid obesity
7. Traumatic Brain Injury (TBI)

Selection of Patients

The same concerns that exist in any other area of medicine apply in the field of GHRT. These include

1. A history of documented hormonal deficiencies
2. Signs and symptoms consistent with a deficiency state: i.e. easy fatigue, lack of energy, decreased libido, poor exercise tolerance, sleep disturbances, etc.
3. Review of medical records to document prior hormonal replacement therapies
4. History of pituitary tumors, surgery, radiation therapy, trauma or prior chemotherapy

This protocol recommends a complete and comprehensive medical history, review of systems as well as a thorough physical examination. The major contraindications to GHRT are:

1. Active cancer patients
2. Patients with type I and II Diabetes Mellitus (relative contraindication)
3. Patients with metabolic syndrome (relative contraindication)
4. Patients with carpal tunnel syndrome

Laboratory Testing

In general it is the medical judgment of each physician based on a thorough comprehensive medical history, review of symptoms/systems, physical and laboratory testing to determine the medical necessity of prescribing GHRT. Unfortunately with GHD there is no single perfect and reliable test to measure GHD. HGH has a short half-life of less than twenty minutes in the blood and is produced mainly during deep REM sleep thus making it impracticable to directly test for GH itself. Short of this, the next most reliable and practical test is another hormone whose production is predominantly stimulated by growth hormones called IGF-1 (Insulin-like growth factor 1) and whose level is relatively stable in blood throughout the day. Even more reliable is the ratio between IGF-1 and its major binding protein IGF-BP-3 (IGF-1 binding protein 3). This ratio provides a better picture of the amount of bioavailable IGF-1 for the target cells. The higher the ratio IGF-1/IGF-BP-3, the more IGF-1 is available for the target cells. A twenty-four-hour HGH urine determination is also advised.

Stimulation Tests

1. Arginine
2. GHRH (Growth Hormone Releasing Hormone)
3. Clonidine
4. Glucagon
5. L-Dopa
6. Insulin
7. Propanolol

All of these are cumbersome and puts some patients at unnecessary and unacceptable risks for little diagnostic return. The Insulin Tolerance Test is felt to be the best predictor of GHD. Failure to respond to insulin-induced hypoglycemia is indicative of GHD but carries all the risks of hypoglycemia—i.e. sweats, nausea, vomiting, mental aberrations, hypotension and possible seizures. Of note, if the patient has coronary artery disease the insulin stimulation test is contraindicated.

Along with a low serum IGF-1 level the documented presence of at least three other pituitary deficiencies (i.e. ACTH, TSH, LH) is, in itself, an indication for GHRT.

In summary the IGF-1 level, especially if documented to be below 200 on two separate testing days, is the most practical, cost effective, and safest test. The International Hormone Society, the world's third largest physician endocrine society, (www.intlhormonesociety.org) and the A4M (www.worldhealth.net) recommend levels in the 300 to 350 microgram/ liter range for serum IGF-1 as optimal for average sized men, while a slightly lower level of 250 to 300 is recommended for a medium sized woman. Taller or bigger persons may need a higher level, while smaller and thinner persons, a lower serum IGF-1 level. The best IGF-1–BP-3 is an average level, around the 3,000 microgram per liter mark.

Regardless of which stimulation test is used, the cutoff point of 5 micrograms/liter is used for all provocative stimulation tests.

The clinician should be aware that IGF-1 levels may be reduced by poor nutrition, hepatic disease, severe diabetes mellitus, sex hormone deficiencies and untreated hypothyroidism.

Measurements of IGF binding protein (IGFBP-3) alone have thus far not been proven to offer superior results than IGF-1 testing alone.

Therapy Considerations

In 1996 the FDA approved GH for use in adult patients with GHD. In addition to the aforementioned indications there is a small group of patients with other kinds of pituitary-hypothalamic diseases including Sheehan's Syndrome, auto-immune hypophysitis and sarcoidosis.

Initiation and titration of GHRT is left to the skill and care of the individual doctor trained in GHRT. Recombinant HGH is dispensed in mgm doses where 1.0mg equals 3 units. The usual starting dose is 0.1mgm to 0.3mgm subcutaneously per day. Injections are best given at night 5-7 days per week using a ¼ inch number 25 or 27 gauge needle perpendicular to midwaist pinched fatty tissue.

Side Effects and Adverse Events Profile

In general, the risks of GHRT are exceedingly low especially in studies where a low dose fixed regimen is used at bedtime or in divided daily doses.

In the clinical setting as promoted by the International Hormone Society and the A4M, adult GHRT employs doses that are 1/7th (one seventh) the pediatric dose schedule. For a seventy kg man the usual dose would be 0.05 mg to 0.56 mg per day.

When side effects do occur, they disappear with cessation of treatment. These include arthralgias, female breast fullness, mild hand numbness (carpal tunnel—like symptoms), mild fluid retention and transient elevation of blood sugar levels.

While adult GHRT may cause transient blood sugar elevation during the course of the first months of treatment, this does not go on to irreversible diabetes mellitus.

In small long-term GH treatment studies a decrease in glycosylated hemoglobin, a marker of diabetes, has been reported thanks to the increase in lean body mass and the decrease of body fat mass provided by GHRT. There is no study showing GHRT leads to a permanent diabetic state.

Promotion of cancer by GHRT has long been a concern of endocrinologists and the International Hormone Society and the A4M, however the following data refute this hypothesis:

1. Acromegaly patients do not have higher cancer rates than the general population
2. Pediatric GHD patients on long-term GHHRT have not shown an increased cancer incidence

3. As GH declines with age the rate of cancer increases
4. By stimulating improved immune function cancer rates should be reduced

In summary, GHRT is associated with negligible side effects when administered judiciously by a qualified physician.

Conclusions

The authors of this protocol do not endorse or condone the prescription or dispensation of controlled substances or any prescription drugs outside the scope of a bona fide physician-patient relationship. It is incumbent upon every practitioner to comply with the obligations imposed by federal and state laws and regulations in this area.

This protocol has presented the general guidelines and proposed expanded uses of GH for age-related adult GHD syndrome. A seventy-year-old patient may have an IGF-1 level 20 percent that of a twenty- to thirty-year-old patient. Physicians replace all other hormonal deficiencies (thyroid, sex hormones, adrenal hormones, etc.) with impunity and without the threat of criminal indictments but GH, because it was wrongly included in the Anabolic Steroids Control Act of 1990 and not the Controlled Substance Act, became a forbidden treatment for the natural and predictable stepwise decrease in quantity during the aging process. In March 2007, a bill was introduced into the U.S. Senate to amend the Controlled Substance Act (CSA) and to add HGH to schedule III. If we use the argument that hormonal decline is a natural part of aging then as doctors we must explain why we replace sex hormones during menopause and andropause and thyroid hormones in midlife.

The FDA has recognized that "off-label" prescribing is a legitimate part of the practice of medicine and that the practice of medicine is regulated by the state boards and not by the FDA. The pharmaceutical industry has recently reported that 50 percent of all general prescriptions are "off-label" and in Oncology it is 80 percent. It is the physicians' ethical responsibility to provide the best care for their patients.

This protocol is proposing an "on label" usage of HGH in age-related GHD to serve as a prevention for heart disease, cardiovascular disease, osteoarthritis, obesity and in general a healthier aging population. A more widespread usage of age-related GHD replacement therapy would also reduce health care costs and give patients the opportunity for higher quality of life during the aging process.

This protocol is submitted by James W. Forsythe, MD, HMD, as part of a settlement agreement with the United States prosecuting attorney's office, Reno, Nevada.

References:
Milder Forms of Growth Hormone Deficiency

Milder forms of growth hormone deficiency gradually appear with age in adults because of the gradual aging and thus age-related decline of the pituitary gland. Senescence is associated with lower GH and IGF-1 levels and increased somatostatin.

D. Rudman, M. H. Kutner, C. M. Rogers, M. F. Lubin, G. A. Fleming, R. P. Bain. "Impaired growth hormone secretion in the adult population: relation to age and adiposity," *Journal of Clinical Investigation* 67, no. 5 (May 1981): 1361–1369.

H. Bando, C. Zhang, Y. Takada, R. Yamasaki, S. Saito. "Impaired secretion of growth hormone-releasing hormone, growth hormone and IGF-1 in elderly men." *Acta Endocrinol* (Copenh) 124, no. 1 (Jan 1991): 31–33.

A. Iranmanesh, G. Lizarralde, J. D. Veldhuis. "Age and relative adiposity are specific negative determinants of the frequency and amplitude of growth hormone (GH) secretory bursts and the half-life of endogenous GH in healthy men," *Journal of Clinical Endocrinology Metabolism* 73, no. 5 (Nov 1991): 1081–1088.

D. Rudman, U.M.P. Rao. "The hypothalamic–growth hormone–somatomedin C axis: The effect of Aging," *Endocrinology & Metabolism in the Elderly*, J. C. Morley and S. O. Korenman, eds. (Boston, MA: Blackwell Science Publishers, 1992).

E. Rolandi, R. Franceschini, A. Marabini, V. Messina, A. Cataldi, M. Salvemini, and T. Barreca. "Twenty-four-hour beta-endorphin secretory pattern in the elderly," *Acta Endocrinol* (Copenh) 115, no. 4 (Aug 1987): 441–446.

Senescence is also associated with alterations in the circadian cycle of serum GH: a reduced amplitude and aphase advance.

G. Mazzoccoli, M. Correra, G. Bianco, A. De Cata, M. Balzanelli, A. Giuliani, R. Tarquini. "Age-related changes of neuro-endocrine-immune interactions in healthy humans," *Journal of Biological Regulators and Homeostatic Agents* 11, no. 4 (Oct–Dec 1997): 143–147.

Supporting Data on Growth Hormone's Beneficial Effects in Adults

Growth hormone is important for psychic well-being.

LOWER QUALITY OF LIFE AND FATIGUE
The Association with Lower GH and/or IGF-1 Levels

F. J. Gilchrist, R. D. Murray, S. M. Shalet. "The effect of long-term untreated growth hormone deficiency (GHD) and 9 years of GH replacement on the quality of life (QoL) of GH-deficient adults," in *Clinical Endocrinology* (Oxf) 57, no. 3 (Sep 2002): 363–370.

R. Abs, B. A. Bengtsson, E. Hernberg-Stahl, J. P. Monson , J. P. Tauber, P. Wilton, C. Wuster. "GH replacement in 1034 growth hormone deficient hypopituitary adults: demographic and clinical characteristics, dosing and safety," *Clinical Endocrinology* (Oxf) 50, no. 6 (Jun 1999): 703–713.

R. D. Murray, C. J. Skillicorn, S. J. Howell, C. A. Lissett, A. Rahim, S. M. Shalet. "Dose titration and patient selection increases the efficacy of GH replacement in severely GH deficient adults," *Clinical Endocrinology* (Oxf) 50, no. 6 (Jun 1999): 749–757.

The Effect of GH and/or IGF-1 Treatment

R. D. Murray, K. H. Darzy, H. K. Gleeson, S. M. Shalet. "GH-deficient survivors of childhood cancer: GH replacement during adult life," *Journal of Clinical Endocrinology Metabolism* 87, no. 1 (Jan 2002): 129–135.

R. D. Murray, C. J. Skillicorn, S. J. Howell, C. A. Lissett, A. Rahim, L. E. Smethurst, S. M. Shalet. "Influences on quality of life in GH deficient adults and their effect on response to treatment," *Clinical Endocrinology* (Oxf) 51, no. 5 (Nov 1999): 565–573.

A. M. Ahmad, M. T. Hopkins, J. Thomas, H. Ibrahim, W. D. Fraser, J. P. Vora. "Body composition and quality of life in adults with growth hormone deficiency; effects of low-dose growth hormone replacement," *Clinical Endocrinology* (Oxf) 54, no. 6 (Jun 2001): 709–717.

J. S. Davies, K. Obuobie, J. Smith, D. A. Rees, A. Furlong, N. Davies, L. M. Evans, M. F. Scanlon. "A therapeutic trial of growth hormone in hypopituitary adults and its influence upon continued prescription by general practitioners," *Clinical Endocrinology* (Oxf) 52, no. 3 (Mar 2000): 295–303.

G. A. McGauley. "Quality of life assessment before and after growth hormone treatment in adults with growth hormone deficiency," *Acta Paediatr Scand Suppl* 356 (1989): 70–72.

R. C. Cuneo, S. Judd, J. D. Wallace, D. Perry-Keene, H. Burger, S. Lim-Tio, B. Strauss, J. Stockigt, D. Topliss, F. Alford, L. Hew, H. Bode, A. Conway, D/ Handelsman, S. Dunn, S. Boyages, N. W. Cheung, D. Hurley. "The Australian Multicenter Trial of Growth Hormone (GH) Treatment in GH-Deficient Adults," *Journal of Clinical Endocrinology Metabolism* 83, no. 1 (Jan 1998): 107–116.

J. S. Li Voon Chong, S. Benbow, P. Foy, M. E. Wallymahmed, D. Wile, I. A. MacFarlane. "Elderly people with hypothalamic-pituitary disease and growth hormone deficiency: lipid profiles, body composition and quality of life compared with control subjects," *Clinical Endocrinology* (Oxf) 53, no. 5 (Nov 2000): 551–559.

G. Moorkens, J. Berwaerts, H. Wynants, R. Abs. "Characterization of pituitary function with emphasis on GH secretion in the chronic fatigue syndrome," *Clinical Endocrinology* (Oxf) 53, no. 1 (Jul 2000): 99–106.

M. E. Wallymahmed, G. A. Baker, G. Humphris, M. Dewey, I. A. MacFarlane. "The development, reliability, and validity of a disease specific quality of life model for adults with growth hormone deficiency,"

Clinical Endocrinology (Oxf) 44, no. 4 (Apr 1996 Apr): 403–411.

K. Lagrou, D. Xhrouet-Heinrichs, G. Massa, M. Vandeweghe, J. P. Bourguignon, J. De Schepper, F. de Zegher, C. Ernould, C. Heinrichs, P. Malvaux, M. Craen. "Quality of life and retrospective perception of the effect of growth hormone treatment in adult patients with childhood growth hormone deficiency," *Journal of Pediatric Endocrinology Metabolism* 14, supplement 5 (2001): 1249–1260.

B. Stabler. "Impact of growth hormone (GH) therapy on quality of life along the lifespan of GH-treated patients," Hormone Research 56, supplement 1 (2001): 55–58.

L. Wiren, G. Johannsson, B. A. Bengtsson. "A prospective investigation of quality of life and psychological well-being after the discontinuation of GH treatment in adolescent patients who had GH deficiency during childhood," *Journal of Clinical Endocrinology Metabolism* 86, no. 8 (Aug 2001): 3494–3498.

S. Bjork, B. Jonsson, O. Westphal, J. E. Levin. "Quality of life of adults with growth hormone deficiency: a controlled study," *Acta Paediatr Scand* 356, supplement (1989): 55–59; discussion 60, 73–74.

B. A. Bengtsson, R. Abs, H. Bennmarker, J. P. Monson, U. Feldt-Rasmussen, E. Hernberg-Stahl, B. Westberg, P. Wilton, C. Wuster. "The effects of treatment and the individual responsiveness to growth hormone (GH) replacement therapy in 665 GH-deficient adults. KIMS Study Group and the KIMS International Board," *Journal of Clinical Endocrinology Metabolism* 84, no. 11 (Nov 1999): 3929–3935.

Z. Laron. "Consequences of not treating children with Laron syndrome (primary growth hormone insensitivity)," *Journal of Pediatric Endocrinology Metabolism* 14, supplement 5 (2001): 1243–1248; discussion 1261–1262.

R. C. Page, M. S. Hammersley, C. W. Burke, J. A. Wass. "An account of the quality of life of patients after treatment for non-functioning pituitary tumours," *Clinical Endocrinology* (Oxf) 46, no. 4 (Apr 1997): 401–406.

The Improvement with GH Treatment

M. E. Wallymahmed, P. Foy, D. Shaw, R. Hutcheon, R. H. Edwards, I. A. MacFarlane. "Quality of life, body composition and muscle strength in adult growth hormone deficiency: the influence of growth hormone replacement therapy for up to 3 years," *Clinical Endocrinology* (Oxf) 47, no. 4 (Oct 1997): 439–446.

J. Kozakowski, M. Adamkiewicz, J. Krassowski, S. Zgliczynski. "The beneficial effects of growth hormone replacement therapy on elderly men," *Pol Merkuriusz Lek* 6, no. 33 (Mar 1999): 131–134.

D. Waters, J. Danska, K. Hardy, F. Koster, C. Qualls, D. Nickell, S. Nightingale, N. Gesundheit, D. Watson, D. Schade. "Recombinant human growth hormone, insulin-like growth factor 1, and combination therapy in AIDS-associated wasting. A randomized, double-blind, placebo-controlled trial," *Annals of Internal Medicine* 125, no. 11 (Dec 1, 1996): 865–872.

B. A. Bengtsson, R. Abs, H. Bennmarker, J. P. Monson, U. Feldt-Rasmussen, E. Hernberg-Stahl, B. Westberg, P. Wilton, C. Wuster C. "The effects of treatment and the individual responsiveness to growth hormone (GH) replacement therapy in 665 GH-deficient adults. KIMS Study Group and the KIMS International Board," *Journal of Clinical Endocrinology Metabolism* 84, no. 11 (Nov 1999): 3929–39235.

U. Feldt-Rasmussen, R. Abs, B. A. Bengtsson, H. Bennmarker H, Bramnert M, Hernberg-Stahl E, Monson JP, Westberg B, Wilton P, Wuster C; KIMS International Study Board on behalf of KIMS Study Group. "Growth hormone deficiency and replacement in hypopituitary patients previously treated for acromegaly or Cushing's disease." *European Journal of Endocrinology* 146, no. 1 (Jan 2002): 67–74.

E. Hernberg-Stahl, A. Luger, R. Abs, B. A. Bengtsson, U. Feldt-Rasmussen, P. Wilton, B. Westberg, J. P. Monson; KIMS International Board; KIMS Study Group. Pharmacia International Metabolic Database. "Healthcare consumption decreases in parallel with improvements in quality of life during GH replacement in hypopituitary adults with GH deficiency," *Journal of Clinical Endocrinology Metabolism* 86, no. 11 (Nov 2001): 5277–5281.

L. Wiren, B. A. Bengtsson, G. Johannsson. "Beneficial effects of long-term GH replacement therapy on quality of life in adults with GH deficiency," *Clinical Endocrinology* (Oxf) 48, no. 5 (May 1998): 613–620.

S. Fazio, D. Sabatini, B. Capaldo, C. Vigorito, A. Giordano, R. Guida, F. Pardo, B. Biondi, L. Sacca. "A preliminary study of growth hormone in the treatment of dilated cardiomyopathy," *New England Journal of Medicine* 334, no. 13 (Mar 1996): 809–814.

P. Burman, J. B. Deijen. "Quality of life and cognitive function in patients with pituitary insufficiency," *Psychotherapy and Psychosomatics* 67, no. 3 (1998): 154–167.

P. V. Carroll, R. Littlewood, A. J. Weissberger, P. Bogalho, G. McGauley, P. H. Sonksen, D. L. Russell-Jones. "The effects of two doses of replacement growth hormone on the biochemical, body composition and psychological profiles of growth hormone-deficient adults." *European Journal of Endocrinology* 137, no. 2 (Aug 1997): 14653.

P. Burman, J. E. Broman, J. Hetta, I. Wiklund, E. M. Erfurth, E. Hagg, F. A. Karlsson. "Quality of life in adults with growth hormone (GH) deficiency: response to treatment with recombinant human GH in a placebo-controlled 21-month trial," *Journal of Clinical Endocrinology and Metabolism* 80, no. 12 (Dec 1995): 3585–3590.

DEPRESSION
The Association with Lower GH and/or IGF-1 Levels

D. B. Jarrett, J. M. Miewald, D. J. Kupfer. "Recurrent depression is associated with a persistent reduction in sleep-related growth hormone secretion." *Archives of General Psychiatry* 47, no. 2 (Feb 1990): 113–118.

D. B. Jarrett, D. J. Kupfer, J. M. Miewald, V. J. Grochocinski, B. Frnz. "Sleep-related growth hormone secretion is persistently suppressed in women with recurrent depression: a preliminary longitudinal analysis," *Journal of Psychiatric Research* 28, no. 3 (May–Jun 1994): 211–223.

R. T. Rubin, R. E. Poland, I. M. Lesser. "Neuroendocrine aspects of primary endogenous depression. X: Serum growth hormone measures in patients and matched control subjects," *Biological Psychiatry* 27, no. 10 (May 1990): 1065–1082.

R. Schilkrut, O. Chandra, M. Osswald, E. Ruther, B. Baafusser, Matussek. "Growth hormone release during sleep and with thermal stimulation in depressed patients," *Neuropsychobiology* 1, no. 2 (1975): 70−79.

S. Barry, T. G. Dinan. "Neuroendocrine challenge tests in depression: a study of growth hormone, TRH and cortisol release," *Journal of Affective Disorders* 18, no. 4 (Apr 1990): 229−234.

T. G. Dinan, S. Barry. "Responses of growth hormone to desipramine in endogenous and non-endogenous depression," *British Journal of Psychiatry* 156 (May 1990): 680−684.

U. Voderholzer, G. Laakmann, R. Wittmann, C. Daffner-Bujia, A. Hinz, C. Haag, T. Baghai. "Profiles of spontaneous 24-hour and stimulated growth hormone secretion in male patients with endogenous depression," *Psychiatry Research* 47, no. 3 (Jun 1993): 215−227.

J. Harro, H. Rimm, M. Harro, M. Grauberg, K. Karelson, A. M. Viru. "Association of depressiveness with blunted growth hormone response to maximal physical exercise in young healthy men," *Psychoneuroendocrinology* 24, no. 5 (Jul 1999): 505−517.

J. F. Greden. "Biological markers of melancholia and reclassification of depressive disorders." *L'Encephale* 8, no. 2 (1982): 193−202.

C. V. McMillan, C. Bradley, J. Gibney, M. L. Healy, D. L. Russell-Jones, P. H. Sonksen. "Psychological effects of withdrawal of growth hormone therapy from adults with growth hormone deficiency," *Clinical Endocrinology* (Oxf) 59, no. 4 (Oct 2003): 467−475.

Improvement with GH Treatment

T. Mahajan, A. Crown, S. Checkley, A. Farmer, S. Lightman. "Atypical depression in growth hormone deficient adults, and the beneficial effects of growth hormone treatment on depression and quality of life," *European Journal of Endocrinology* 151, no. 3 (Sep 2004): 325−332.

J. O. Johansson, G. Larson, M. Andersson, A. Elmgren, L. Hynsjo, A. Lindahl, P. A. Lundberg, O. G. Isaksson, S. Lindstedt, B. A. Bengtsson. "Treatment of growth hormone-deficient adults with recombinant human growth hormone increases the concentration of growth hormone in the cerebrospinal fluid and affects neurotransmitters," *Neuroendocrinology* 61, no. 1 (Jan 1995): 57−66 *(GH increases endorphins and reduces dopamine).*

ANXIETY
The Association with Lower GH and/or IGF-1 Levels

M. E. Tancer, M. B. Stein, T. W. Uhde. "Growth hormone response to intravenous clonidine in social phobia: comparison to patients with panic disorder and healthy volunteers," *Biological Psychiatry* 34, no. 9 (Nov 1993): 591–595.

O. G. Cameron, J. L. Abelson, E. A. Young. "Anxious and depressive disorders and their comorbidity: effect on central nervous system noradrenergic function," *Biological Psychiatry* 56, no. 11 (Dec 2004): 875–883.

B. Stabler. "Impact of growth hormone (GH) therapy on quality of life along the lifespan of GH-treated patients," *Hormone Research* 56, supplement (2001): 55–58.

J. L. Abelson, D. Glitz, O. G. Cameron, M. A. Lee, M. Bronzo, G. C. Curtis. "Blunted growth hormone response to clonidine in patients with generalized anxiety disorder," *Archives of General Psychiatry* 48, no. 2 (Feb 1991): 157–162.

The Improvement with GH Treatment

L. I. Arwert, J. B. Deijen, M. Muller, M. L. Drent. "Long-term growth hormone treatment preserves GH-induced memory and mood improvements: a 10-year follow-up study in GH-deficient adult men," *Hormones and Behavior* 47, no. 3 (Mar 2005): 343–349.

L. Lasaite, R. Bunevicius, D. Lasiene, L. Lasas. "Psychological functioning after growth hormone therapy in adult growth hormone deficient patients: endocrine and body composition correlates," *Medicina* (Kaunas) 40, no. 8 (2004): 740–744.

MEMORY LOSS AND ALZHEIMER'S DISEASE
The Association with Lower GH and/or IGF-1 Levels

J. B. Deijen, H. de Boer, G. J. Blok, E. A. van der Veen. "Cognitive impairments and mood disturbances in growth hormone deficient men," *Psychoneuroendocrinology* 21, no. 3 (Apr 1996): 313–322.

A. Rollero, G. Murialdo, S. Fonzi, S. Garrone, M. V. Gianelli, E. Gazzerro, A. Barreca, A. Polleri. "Relationship between cognitive function, growth hormone and insulin-like growth factor I plasma levels in aged subjects," *Neuropsychobiology* 38, no. 2 (1998): 73–79.

P. S. van Dam, C. F. de Winter, R. de Vries, J. van der Grond, M. L. Drent, M. Lijffijt, J. L. Kenemans, A. Aleman, E. H. de Haan, H. P. Koppeschaar. "Childhood-onset growth hormone deficiency, cognitive function and brain N-acetylaspartate," *Psychoneuroendocrinology* 30, no. 4 (May 2005): 357–363.

T. Watanabe, S. Koba, M. Kawamura, M. Itokawa, T. Idei, Y. Nakagawa, T. Iguchi, T. Katagiri. "Small dense low-density lipoprotein and carotid atherosclerosis in relation to vascular dementia," *Metabolism* 53, no. 4 (Apr 2004): 476–482.

The Improvement with GH Treatment

J. B. Deijen, H. de Boer, E. A. van der Veen. "Cognitive changes during growth hormone replacement in adult men," *Psychoneuroendocrinology* 23, no. 1 (Jan 1998): 45–55.

H. P. Koppeschaar. "Growth hormone, insulin-like growth factor I and cognitive function in adults," *Growth Hormone IGF Research* 10, supplement B (Apr 2000: S69–73.

SLEEP DISORDERS
The Association with Lower GH and/or IGF-1 Levels

C. Astrom, J. Lindholm. "Growth hormone-deficient young adults have decreased deep sleep," *Neuroendocrinology* 51, no. 1 (Jan 1990): 82–84.

The Improvement with GH Treatment

C. Astrom, S. A. Pedersen, J. Lindholm. "The influence of growth hormone on sleep in adults with growth hormone deficiency," *Clinical Endocrinology* (Oxf) 33, no. 4 (Oct 1990): 495–500.

LOSS OF SEXUAL DRIVE, SENSITIVITY, AND/OR POTENCY
The Association with Lower GH and/or IGF-1 Levels

A. J. Becker, S. Uckert, C. G. Stief, F. Scheller, W. H. Knapp, U. Hartmann, G. Brabant, U. Jonas. "Serum levels of human growth hormone during different penile conditions in the cavernous and systemic blood of healthy men and patients with erectile dysfunction," *Urology* 59, no. 4 (Apr 2002): 609–614.

X. Huang, S. Li, L. Hu. "Growth hormone deficiency and age-related erectile dysfunction," *Zhonghua Nan Ke Xue* 10, no. 11 (Nov 2004): 867.

The Improvement with GH Treatment

A. J. Becker, S. Uckert, C. G. Stief, M. C. Truss, S. Machtens, F. Scheller, W. H. Knapp, U. Hartmann, U. Jonas. "Possible role of human growth hormone in penile erection," *Journal of Urology* 164, no. 6 (Dec 2000): 2138–2142.

X. S. Zhang, Y. X. Wang, Y. F. Han, Z. Li, Z. Q. Xiang, J. Leng, X. Y. Huang. "Effects of growth hormone supplementation on erectile function and expression of nNOS in aging rats," *Zhonghua Nan Ke Xue* 11, no. 5 (May 2005): 339–342.

G. W. Jung, E. M. Spencer, T. F. Lue. "Growth hormone enhances regeneration of nitric oxide synthase-containing penile nerves after cavernous nerve neurotomy in rats," *Journal of Urology* 160, no. 5 (Nov 1998): 1899–1904.

SARCOPENIA

The Association with Lower GH and/or IGF-1 Levels

A. Sartorio, M. V. Narici. "Growth hormone (GH) treatment in GH-deficient adults: effects on muscle size, strength, and neural activation," *Clinical Physiology* 14, no. 5 (Sep 1994): 527–537.

H. De Boer, G. J. Blok, H. J. Voerman, P. M. De Vries, E. A. van der Veen. "Body composition in adult growth hormone-deficient men, assessed by anthropometry and bioimpedance analysis," *Journal of Clinical Endocrinology and Metabolism* 75, no. 3 (Sep 1992): 833–837.

R. C. Cuneo, F. Salomon, C. M. Wiles, R. Hesp, P. H. Sonksen. "Growth hormone treatment in growth hormone-deficient adults: Effects on muscle mass and strength," *Journal of Applied Physiology* 70, no. 2 (Feb 1991): 688–694.

The Improvement with GH Treatment

N. Vahl, A. Juul, J. O. Jorgensen, H. Orskov, N. E. Skakkebaek, J. S. Christiansen. "Continuation of growth hormone (GH) replacement in GH-deficient patients during transition from childhood to adulthood: a two-year placebo-controlled study," *Journal of Clinical Endocrinology and Metabolism* 85, no. 5 (May 2000): 1874–1881.

G. E. Butterfield, R. Marcus, L. Holloway, G. Butterfield. "Clinical use of growth hormone in elderly people," *Journal of Reproduction and Fertility Supplement* 46, (1993): 115–118.

G. E. Butterfield, J. Thompson, M. J. Rennie, R. Marcus, R. L. Hintz, A. R. Hoffman. "Effect of rhGH and rhIGF-1 treatment on protein utilization in elderly women," *American Journal of Physiology* 272, no. 1 (pt. 1) (Jan 1997): E 94–99.

A. Sartorio, M. V. Narici. "Growth hormone (GH) treatment in GH-deficient adults: effects on muscle size, strength and neural activation," *Clinical Physiology* 14, no. 5 (Sep 1994): 527–537.

Y. J. Janssen, J. Doornbos, F. Roelfsema. "Changes in muscle volume, strength, and bioenergetics during recombinant human growth hormone (GH) therapy in adults with GH deficiency," *Journal of Clinical Endocrinology and Metabolism* 84, no. 1 (Jan 1999): 27984.

J. O. Jorgensen, S. A. Pedersen, L. Thuesen, J. Jorgensen, T. Ingemann-Hansen, N. E. Skakkebaek, J. S. Christiansen. "Beneficial effects of growth hormone treatment in GH-deficient adults," *Lancet* 1, no. 8649 (Jun 1989): 1221–1225.

J. C. ter Maaten, H. de Boer, O. Kamp, L. Stuurman, E. A. van der Veen. "Long-term effects of growth hormone (GH) replacement in men with childhood-onset GH deficiency," *Journal of Clinical Endocrinology and Metabolism* 84, no. 7 (Jul 1999): 2373–2380.

H. M. Whitehead, C. Boreham, E. M. McIlrath, B. Sheridan, L. Kennedy, A. B. Atkinson, D. R. Hadden. "Growth hormone treatment of adults with growth hormone deficiency: results of a 13-month placebo controlled cross-over study," *Clinical Endocrinology* (Oxf)36, no. 1 (Jan 1992): 45–52.

S. Y. Nam, K. R. Kim, B. S. Cha, Y. D. Song, S. K. Lim, H. C. Lee, K. B. Huh. "Low-dose growth hormone treatment combined with diet restriction decreases insulin resistance by reducing visceral fat and increasing muscle mass in obese type 2 diabetic patients," *International Journal of Obesity Related Metabolism Disorders* 25, no. 8 (Aug 2001): 1101–1107.

LEAN BODY MASS
The Association with Lower GH and/or IGF-1 Levels

H. De Boer, G. J. Blok, H. J. Voerman, P. M. De Vries, E. A. van der Veen. "Body composition in adult growth hormone-deficient men, assessed by anthropometry and bioimpedance analysis," *Journal of Clinical Endocrinology and Metabolism* 75, no. 3 (Sep 1992): 833–837.

The Improvement with GH Treatment

B. A. Bengtsson, S. Eden, L. Lonn, H. Kvist, A. Stokland, G. Lindstedt, I. Bosaeus, J. Tolli, L. Sjostrom, O. G. Isaksson. "Treatment of adults with growth hormone (GH) deficiency with recombinant human GH," *Journal of Clinical Endocrinology and Metabolism* 76, no. 2 (Feb 1993): 309–317.

G. Lombardi, A. Luger, J. Marek, D. Russell-Jones, P. Sonksen, A. F. Attanasio. "Short-term safety and efficacy of human GH replacement therapy in 595 adults with GH deficiency: a comparison of two dosage algorithms," *Journal of Clinical Endocrinology and Metabolism* 87, no. 5 (May 2002): 1974–1979.

N. Vahl, A. Juul, J. O. Jorgensen, H. Orskov, N. E. Skakkebaek, J. S. Christiansen. "Continuation of growth hormone (GH) replacement in GH-deficient patients during transition from childhood to adulthood: a two-year placebo-controlled study," *Journal of Clinical Endocrinology and Metabolism* 85, no. 5 (May 2000): 1874–1881.

D. Rudman, A. G. Feller, H. S. Nagraj, G. A. Gergans, P. Y. Lalitha, A. F. Goldberg, R. A. Schlenker, L. Cohn, I. W. Rudman, D. E. Mattson. "Effects of human growth hormone in men over 60 years old," *New England Journal of Medicine* 323, no. 1 (Jul 1990): 1–6.

J. S. Davies, K. Obuobie, J. Smith, D. A. Rees, A. Furlong, N. Davies, L. M. Evans, M. F. Scanlon. "A therapeutic trial of growth hormone in hypopituitary adults and its influence upon continued prescription by general practitioners," *Clinical Endocrinology* (Oxf) 52, no. 3 (Mar 2000): 295–303.

V. Olsovska, H. Siprova, M. Beranek, V. Soska. "The influence of long-term growth hormone replacement therapy on body composition, bone tissue and some metabolic parameters in adults with growth hormone deficiency," *Vnitr Lek* 51, no. 12 (Dec 2005): 1356–1364.

PHYSICAL APPEARANCE AND BODY MORPHOLOGY
Improvement with GH Treatment

T. Hertoghe. "Growth hormone therapy in aging adults," *Anti-Aging Medical Therapeutics*, no. 1 (1997): 10–28.

M. Zivicnjak, D. Franke, J. H. Ehrich, G. Filler. "Does growth hormone therapy harmonize distorted morphology and body composition in chronic renal failure?" *Pediatric Nephrology* 15, no. 3–4 (Dec 2000): 229–235.

U. Eiholzer, M. Schlumpf, Y. Nordmann, D. l'Allemand. "Early manifestations of Prader-Willi syndrome: influence of growth hormone," *Journal of Pediatric Endocrinology and Metabolism* 14, no. 6 supplement (2001): 1441–1444.

HYPERCHOLESTEROLEMIA
The Association with Lower GH and/or IGF-1 Levels

GH may protect—at least partially—against the appearance of age-related diseases.

T. A. Abdu, R. Neary, T. A. Elhadd, M. Akber, R. N. Clayton. "Coronary risk in growth hormone deficient hypopituitary adults: increased predicted risk is due largely to lipid profile abnormalities," *Clinical Endocrinology* (Oxf)55, no. 2 (Aug 2001): 209–216.

K. Landin-Wilhelmsen, L. Wilhelmsen, G. Lappas, T. Rosen, G. Lindstedt, P. A. Lundberg, B. A. Bengtsson. "Serum insulin-like growth factor I in a random population sample of men and women: relation to age, sex, smoking habits, coffee consumption and physical activity, blood pressure and concentrations of plasma lipids, fibrinogen, parathyroid hormone and osteocalcin," *Clinical Endocrinology* (Oxf) 41, no. 3 (Sep 1994): 351–357.

A. Sanmarti, A. Lucas, F. Hawkins, S. M. Webb, A. Ulied. "Observational study in adult hypopituitary patients with untreated growth hormone deficiency (ODA study). Socio-economic impact and health status. Collaborative ODA (Observational GH Deficiency in Adults) Group," *European Journal of Endocrinology* 141, no. 5 (Nov 1999): 481–489.

A. Colao, C. di Somma, R. Pivonello, A. Cuocolo, L. Spinelli, D. Bonaduce, M. Salvatore, G. Lombardi. "The cardiovascular risk of adult GH deficiency GHD improved after GH replacement and worsened in untreated GHD: a 12-month prospective study," *Journal of Clinical Endocrinology and Metabolism* 87, no. 3 (Mar 2002): 108893.

The Improvement with GH Treatment

B. Abrahamsen, T. L. Nielsen, J. Hangaard, G. Gregersen, N. Vahl, L. Korsholm, T. B. Hansen, M. Andersen, C. Hagen. "Dose-, IGF-I- and sex-dependent changes in lipid profile and body composition during GH replacement therapy in adult onset GH deficiency," *European Journal of Endocrinology* 150, no. 5 (May 2004): 671–679.

T. Elgzyri, J. Castenfors, E. Hagg, C. Backman, M. Thoren, M. Bramnert. "The effects of GH replacement therapy on cardiac morphology and function, exercise capacity and serum lipids in elderly patients with GH deficiency," *Clinical Endocrinology* (Oxf) 61, no. 1 (Jul 2004): 113–122.

R. S. Jallad, B. Liberman, C. B. Vianna, M. L. Vieira, J. A. Ramires, M. Knoepfelmacher. "Effects of growth hormone replacement therapy on metabolic and cardiac parameters, in adult patients with childhood-onset growth hormone deficiency," *Growth Hormone IGF Research* 13, no. 2–3 (Apr–Jun 2003): 81–88.

V. Olsovska, H. Siprova, M. Beranek, V. Soska. "The influence of long-term growth hormone replacement therapy on body composition, bone tissue and some metabolic parameters in adults with growth hormone deficiency," *Vnitr Lek* 51, no. 12 (Dec 2005): 1356–1364 (*"a decrease of total and LDL cholesterol occurred already after a half of the year of the treatment (p < 0.05), changes were significant also in further four years. HDL cholesterol levels have had a progressive tendency, but they were not statistically significant"*).

HOMOCYSTEINEMIA
The Improvement with GH Treatment

G. Sesmilo, B. M. Biller, J. Llevadot, D. Hayden, G. Hanson, N. Rifai Klibanski "Effects of growth hormone (GH) administration on homocyst(e)ine levels in men with GH deficiency: a randomized controlled trial," *Journal of Clinical Endocrinology and Metabolism* 86, no. 4 (Apr 2001): 1518–1524.

ATHEROSCLEROSIS
The Association with Lower GH and/or IGF-1 Levels

B. Capaldo, L. Patti, U. Oliviero, S. Longobardi, F. Pardo, F. Vitale, S. Fazio, F. Di Rella, B. Biondi, G. Lombardi, L. Sacca. "Increased arterial intima-media thickness in childhood-onset growth hormone deficiency," *Journal of Clinical Endocrinology and Metabolism* 82, no. 5 (May 1997): 1378–1381.

V. Markussis, S. A. Beshyah, C. Fisher, P. Sharp, A. N. Nicolaides, D. G. Johnston. "Detection of premature atherosclerosis by high-resolution ultrasonography in symptom-free hypopituitary adults," *Lancet* 34 (1992): 1188–1192.

M. Pfeifer, R. Verhovec, B. Zizek, J. Prezelj, P. Poredos, R. N. Clayton. "Growth hormone (GH) treatment reverses early atherosclerotic changes in GH-deficient adults," *Journal of Clinical Endocrinology and Metabolism* 84, no. 2 (Feb 1999): 453–457.

The Improvement with GH Treatment

M. Pfeifer, R. Verhovec, B. Zizek, J. Prezelj, P. Poredos, R. N. Clayton. "Growth hormone (GH) treatment reverses early atherosclerotic changes in GH-deficient adults," *Journal of Clinical Endocrinology and Metabolism* 84, no. 2 (Feb 1999): 453–457.

R. J. Irving, M. N. Carson, D. J. Webb, B. R. Walker. "Peripheral vascular structure and function in men with contrasting GH levels," *Journal of Clinical Endocrinology and Metabolism* 87, no. 7 (Jul 2002): 3309–3314.

F. Borson-Chazot, A. Serusclat, Y. Kalfallah, X. Ducottet, G. Sassolas, S. Bernard, F. Labrousse, J. Pastene, A. Sassolas, Y. Roux, F.

Berthezene. "Decrease in carotid intima-media thickness after one year growth hormone (GH) treatment in adults with GH deficiency," *Journal of Clinical Endocrinology and Metabolism* 84, no. 4 (Apr 1999): 132933.

D. V. Soares, L. D. Spina, R. R. de Lima Oliveira Brasil, E. M. da Silva, P. M. Lobo, E. Salles, C. M. Coeli, F. L. Conceicao, M. Vaisman. "Carotid artery intima-media thickness and lipid profile in adults with growth hormone deficiency after long-term growth hormone replacement," *Metabolism* 54, no. 3 (Mar 2005): 321.

ARTERIAL HYPERTENSION
The Association with Lower GH and/or IGF-1 Levels

K. Landin-Wilhelmsen, L. Wilhelmsen, G. Lappas, T. Rosen, G. Lundstedt, P. A. Lundberg, B. A. Bengtssopn. "Serum insulin-like growth factor 1 in a random population sample of men and women: relation to age, sex, smoking habits, coffee consumption and physical activity, blood pressure and concentrations of plasma lipids, fibrinogen, parathyroid hormone and osteocalcin," *Clinical Endocrinology* (Oxf) 41, no 3 (Sep 1994): 351–357.

The Improvement with GH Treatment

K. Caidahl, S. Eden, B. A. Bengtsson. "Cardiovascular and renal effects of growth hormone," *Clinical Endocrinology* (Oxf) 40, no. 3 (Mar 1994): 393–400.

CORONARY HEART DISEASE
The Association with Lower GH and/or IGF-1 Levels

E. Conti, F. Andreotti, A. Sciahbasi, P. Riccardi, G. Marra, E. Menini, G. Ghirlanda, A. Maseri. "Markedly reduced insulin-like growth factor-1 in the acute phase of myocardial infarction," *Journal of the American College of Cardiology* 38, no. 1 (Jul 2001): 26–32.

The Improvement with GH Treatment

H. E. Castagnino, N. Lago, J. M. Centrella, S. D. Calligaris, S. Farina, M. I. Sarchi, D. P. Cardinali. "Cytoprotection by melatonin and growth hormone in early rat myocardial infarction as revealed by Feulgen DNA staining," *Neuroendocrinology Letters* 23, nos. 5/6 (Oct–Dec 2002): 391–395.

STROKE AND OTHER CEREBROVASCULAR DISORDERS
The Association with GH and/or IGF-1 Levels

D. Rudman, H. S. Nagraj, D. E. Mattson, D. L. Jackson, I. W. Rudman, J. Boswell, D. C. Pucci. "Hyposomatomedinemia in the men of a Veterans Administration Nursing Home:prevalence and correlates," *Gerontology* 33, no. 5 (1987): 307–314.

OBESITY
The Association with Lower GH and/or IGF-1 Levels

S. A. Beshyah, C. Freemantle, E. Thomas, O. Rutherford, B. Page, M. Murphy, D. G. Johnston. "Abnormal body composition and reduced bone mass in growth hormone deficient hypopituitary adults," *Clinical Endocrinology* (Oxf) 42, no. 2 (Feb 1995): 179–189.

A. F. Attanasio, P. C. Bates, K. K. Ho, S. M. Webb, R. J. Ross, C. J. Strasburger, R. Bouillon, B. Crowe, K. Selander, D. Valle, S. W. Lamberts, Hypoptiuitary Control and Complications Study International Advisory Board. "Human growth hormone replacement in adult hypopituitary patients: long-term effects on body composition and lipid status—3-year results from the HypoCCS Database," *Journal of Clinical Endocrinology and Metabolism* 87, no. 4 (Apr 2002): 1600–1606.

P. J. Stouthart, C. M. de Ridder, L. T. Rekers-Mombarg, H. A. van der Waal. "Changes in body composition during 12 months after discontinuation of growth hormone therapy in young adults with growth hormone deficiency from childhood," *Journal of Pediatric Endocrinology and Metabolism* 12, supplement (Apr 1999): 335–358.

B. M. Biller, G. Sesmilo, H. B. Baum, D. Hayden, D. Schoenfeld, A. Klibanski. "Withdrawal of long-term physiological growth hormone (GH) administration: differential effects on bone density and body composition in men with adult onset GH deficiency," *Journal of Clinical Endocrinology and Metabolism* 85, no. 3 (Mar 2000): 970–976.

H. Kohno, N. Ueyama, S. Honda. "Unfavourable impact of growth hormone

(GH) discontinuation on body composition and cholesterol profiles after the completion of height growth in GH-deficient young adults," *Diabetes Obesity and Metabolism* 1, no. 5 (Sep 1999): 293–296.

R. Kuromaru, H. Kohno, N. Ueyama, H. M. Hassan, S. Honda, T. Hara. "Long-term prospective study of body composition and lipid profiles during and after growth hormone (GH) treatment in children with GH deficiency: gender-specific metabolic effects," *Journal of Clinical Endocrinology and Metabolism* 83, no. 11 (Nov 1998): 38906; and N. Vahl, A. Juul, J. O. Jorgensen, H. Orskov, N. E. Skakkebaek, J. S. Christiansen. "Continuation of growth hormone (GH) replacement in GH-deficient patients during transition from childhood to adulthood: a two-year placebo-controlled study," *Journal of Clinical Endocrinology and Metabolism* 85, no. 5 (May 2000): 1874–1881.

H. Norrelund, N. Vahl, A. Juul, N. Moller, K. G. Alberti, N. E. Skakkebaek, J. S. Christiansen, J. O. Jorgensen. "Continuation of growth hormone (GH) therapy in GH-deficient patients during transition from childhood to adulthood: impact on insulin sensitivity and substrate metabolism," *Journal of Clinical Endocrinology and Metabolism* 85, no. 5 (May 2000): 1912–1917.

G. Johannsson. "What happens when growth hormone is discontinued at completion of growth? Metabolic aspects," *Journal of Pediatric Endocrinology and Metabolism* 13, supplement 6 (2000): 1321–1326.

Improvement with GH Treatment

D. Rudman, A. G. Feller, H. S. Nagraj, G. A. Gergans, P. Y. Lalitha, A. F. Goldberg, R. A. Schlenker, L. Cohn, I. W. Rudman, D. E. Mattson. "Effects of human growth hormone in men over 60 years old," *New England Journal of Medicine* 323, no. 1 (Jul 1990): 1–6.

D. Rudman, A. G. Feller, L. Cohn, K. R. Shetty, I. W. Rudman, M. W. Draper. "Effects of human growth hormone on body composition in elderly men," *Hormone Research* 36, supplement 1 (1991): 73–81.

B. A. Bengtsson, S. Eden, L. Lonn, H. Kvist, A. Stokland, G. Lindstedt, I. Bosaeus, J. Tolli, L. Sjostrom, O. G. Isaksson. "Treatment of adults with growth hormone (GH) deficiency with recombinant human GH,"

Journal of Clinical Endocrinology and Metabolism 76, no. 2 (Feb 1993): 309–317.

T. Munzer, S. M. Harman, P. Hees, E. Shapiro, C. Christmas, M. F. Bellantoni, T. E. Stevens, K. G. O'Connor, K. M. Pabst, C. St. Clair, J. D. Sorkin, M. R. Blackman. "Effects of GH and/or sex steroid administration on abdominal subcutaneous and visceral fat in healthy aged women and men," *Journal of Clinical Endocrinology and Metabolism* 86, no. 8 (Aug 2001): 3604–3610.

J. Rodriguez-Arnao, A. Jabbar, K. Fulcher, G. M. Besser, R. J. Ross. "Effects of growth hormone replacement on physical performance and body composition in GH deficient adults," *Clinical Endocrinology* (Oxf) 51, no. 1 (Jul 1999): 53–60.

C. N. Soares, N. R. Musolino, M. Cunha Neto, M. A. Caires, M. C. Rosenthal, C. P. Camargo, M. D. Bronstein. "Impact of recombinant human growth hormone (RH-GH) treatment on psychiatric, neuropsychological and clinical profiles of GH deficient adults. A placebo-controlled trial," *Arq Neuropsiquiatr* 57, no. 2A (Jun 1999): 182–189.

R. Fernholm, M. Bramnert, E. Hagg, A. Hilding, D. J. Baylink, S. Mohan, M. Thoren. "Growth hormone replacement therapy improves body composition and increases bone metabolism in elderly patients with pituitary disease," *Journal of Clinical Endocrinology and Metabolism* 85, no. 11 (Nov 2000): 4104–4112.

A. F. Attanasio, S. W. Lamberts, A. M. Matranga, M. A. Birkett, P. C. Bates, N. K. Valk, J. Hilsted, B. A. Bengtsson, C. J. Strasburger. "Adult growth hormone (GH) deficient patients demonstrate heterogeneity between childhood onset and adult onset before and during human GH treatment," Adult Growth Hormone Deficiency Study Group. *Journal of Clinical Endocrinology and Metabolism* 82, no. 1 (Jan 1997): 82–88.

S. A. Beshyah, C. Freemantle, M. Shahi, V. Anyaoku, S. Merson, S. Lynch, E. Skinner, P. Sharp, R. Foale, D. G. Johnston. "Replacement treatment with biosynthetic human growth hormone in growth hormone-deficient hypopituitary adults," *Clinical Endocrinology* (Oxf) 42, no. 1 (Jan 1995): 73–84.

G. Moorkens, H. Wynants, R. Abs. "Effect of growth hormone treatment in patients with chronic fatigue syndrome: a preliminary study," *Growth Hormone IGF Research* 8, supplement B (Apr 1998): 131–133.

J. C. Lo, K. Mulligan, M. A. Noor, J. M. Schwarz, R. A. Halvorsen, C. Grunfeld, M. Schambelan. "The effects of recombinant human growth hormone on body composition and glucose metabolism in HIV-infected patients with fat accumulation," *Journal of Clinical Endocrinology and Metabolism* 86, no. 8 (Aug 2001): 3480–3487.

E. R. Christ, M. H. Cummings, E. Albany, A. M. Umpleby, P. J. Lumb, A. S. Wierzbicki, R. P. Naoumova, M. A. Boroujerdi, P. H. Sonksen, D. L. Russell-Jones. "Effects of growth hormone (GH) replacement therapy on very low density lipoprotein apolipoprotein B100 kinetics in patients with adult GH deficiency: a stable isotope study," *Journal of Clinical Endocrinology and Metabolism* 84, no. 1 (Jan 1999): 307–316.

C. M. Florkowski, G. R. Collier, P. Z. Zimmet, J. H. Livesey, E. A. Espiner, R. A. Donald. "Low-dose growth hormone replacement lowers plasma leptin and fat stores without affecting body mass index in adults with growth hormone deficiency," *Clinical Endocrinology* (Oxf) 45, no. 6 (Dec 1996): 769–773.

S. Ezzat, S. Fear, R. C. Gaillard, C. Gayle, H. Landy, S. Marcovitz, T. Mattioni, S. Nussey, A. Rees, E. Svanberg. "Gender-specific responses of lean body composition and non-gender-specific cardiac function improvement after GH replacement in GH-deficient adults," *Journal of Clinical Endocrinology and Metabolism* 87, no. 6 (Jun 2002): 2725–2733.

J. U. Weaver, J. P. Monson, K. Noonan, W. G. John, A. Edwards, K. A. Evans, J. Cunningham. "The effect of low dose recombinant human growth hormone replacement on regional fat distribution, insulin sensitivity, and cardiovascular risk factors in hypopituitary adults," *Journal of Clinical Endocrinology and Metabolism* 80, no. 1 (Jan 1995): 153–159.

N. Vahl, J. O. Jorgensen, T. B. Hansen, I. B. Klausen, A. G. Jurik, C. Hagen, J. S. Christiansen. "The favorable effects of growth hormone (GH) substitution on hypercholesterolaemia in GH-deficient adults are not associated with concomitant reductions in adiposity. A 12 month placebo-controlled study," *International Journal of Obesity Related Metabolism Disorders* 22, no. 6 (Jun 1998): 529–536.

T. B. Hansen, J. Gram, P. B. Jensen, J. H. Kristiansen, B. Ekelund, J. S. Christiansen, F. B. Pedersen. "Influence of growth hormone on whole body and regional soft tissue composition in adult patients on hemodialysis. A double-blind, randomized, placebo-controlled study," *Clinical Nephrology* 53, no. 2 (Feb 2000): 99107.

S. Fisker, N. Vahl, T. B. Hansen, J. O. Jorgensen, C. Hagen, H. Orskov, J. S. Christiansen. "Growth hormone (GH) substitution for one year normalizes elevated GH-binding protein levels in GH-deficient adults secondary to a reduction in body fat. A placebo-controlled trial," *Growth Hormone IGF Research* 8, no. 2 (Apr 1998): 105.

H. B. Baum, B. M. Biller, J. S. Finkelstein, K. B. Cannistraro, D. S. Oppenhein, D. A. Schoenfeld, T. H. Michel, H. Wittink, A. Klibanski. "Effects of physiologic growth hormone therapy on bone density and body composition in patients with adult-onset growth hormone deficiency. A randomized, placebo-controlled trial. *Annals of Internal Medicine*," 125, no. 11 (Dec 1996): 883–890.

P. Burman, A. G. Johansson, A. Siegbahn, B. Vessby, F. A. Karlsson. "Growth hormone (GH)-deficient men are more responsive to GH replacement therapy than women," *Journal of Clinical Endocrinology and Metabolism* 82, no. 2 (Feb 1997): 550–555.

M. Schambelan, K. Mulligan, C. Grunfeld, E. S. Daar, A. LaMarca, D. P. Kotler, J. Wang, S. A. Bozzette, J. B. Breitmeyer. "Recombinant human growth hormone in patients with HIV-associated wasting. A randomized, placebo-controlled trial. Serostim Study Group," *Annals of Internal Medicine* 125, no. 11 (Dec 1996): 873–882.

P. D. Lee, J. M. Pivarnik, J. G. Bukar, N. Muurahainen, P. S. Berry, P. R. Skolnik, J. L. Nerad, K. A. Kudsk, L. Jackson, K. J. Ellis, N. Gesundheit. "A randomized, placebo-controlled trial of combined insulin-like growth factor I and low dose growth hormone therapy for wasting associated with human immunodeficiency virus infection," *Journal of Clinical Endocrinology and Metabolism* 81, no. 8 (Aug 1996): 2968–2975.

A. A. Toogood, S. M. Shalet. "Growth hormone replacement therapy in the elderly with hypothalamic-pituitary disease: a dose-finding study," *Journal of Clinical Endocrinology and Metabolism* 84, no. 1 (Jan 1999): 131–136.

DIABETES
The Association with Lower GH and/or IGF-1 Levels

S. Y. Nam, K. R. Kim, B. S. Cha, Y. D. Song, S. K. Lim, H. C. Lee, K. B. Huh. "Low-dose growth hormone treatment combined with diet restriction decreases insulin resistance by reducing visceral fat and increasing muscle mass in obese type 2 diabetic patients," *International Journal of Obesity Related Metabolism Disorders* 25, no. 8 (Aug 2001): 1101–1107.

The Improvement with GH Treatment

G. Gotherstrom, J. Svensson, J. Koranyi, M. Alpsten, I. Bosaeus, B. Bengtsson, G. Johannsson. "A prospective study of five years of GH replacement therapy in GH-deficient adults: sustained effects on body composition, bone mass, and metabolic indices," *Journal of Clinical Endocrinology and Metabolism* 86, no. 10 (Oct 2001): 4657–4665.

J. Svensson, J. Fowelin, K. Landin, B. A. Bengtsson, J. O. Johansson. "Effects of seven years of GH-replacement therapy on insulin sensitivity in GH-deficient adults," *Journal of Clinical Endocrinology and Metabolism* 87, no. 5 (May 2002): 2121–2127.

K. L. Clayton, J. M. Holly, L. M. Carlsson, J. Jones, T. D. Cheetham, A. M. Taylor, D. B. Dunger. "Loss of the normal relationships between growth hormone, growth hormone-binding protein and insulin-like growth factor-I in adolescents with insulin-dependent diabetes mellitus," *Clinical Endocrinology* (Oxf) 41, no. 4 (Oct 1994): 517–524.

K. C. Yuen, J. Frystyk, D. K. White, T. B. Twickler, H. P. Koppeschaar, P. E. Harris, L. Fryklund, P. R. Murgatroyd, D. B. Dunger DB. "Improvement in insulin sensitivity without concomitant changes in body composition and cardiovascular risk markers following fixed administration of a very low growth hormone (GH) dose in adults with severe GH deficiency," *Clinical Endocrinology* (Oxf) 63, no. 4 (Oct 2005): 428–436.

RHEUMATISM
The Association with Lower GH and/or IGF-1 Levels

J. Neidel. "Changes in systemic levels of insulin-like growth factors and their binding proteins in patients with rheumatoid arthritis," *Clinical and Experimental Rheumatology* 19, no. 1 (Jan–Feb 2001): 81–84.

A. Leal-Cerro, J. Povedano, R. Astorga, M. Gonzalez, H. Silva, F. Garcia-Pesquera, F. F. Casanueva, C. Dieguez. "The growth hormone (GH)-releasing hormoneGH-insulin-like growth factor-1 axis in patients with fibromyalgia syndrome," *Journal of Clinical Endocrinology and Metabolism* 84, no. 9 (Sep 1999): 3378–3381.

E. Bagge, B. A. Bengtsson, L. Carlsson, J. Carlsson. "Low growth hormone secretion in patients with fibromyalgia—a preliminary report on 10 patients and 10 controls," *Journal of Rheumatology* 25, no. 1 (Jan 1998): 145–148.

The Improvement with GH Treatment

R. M. Bennett, S. C. Clark, J. Walczyk. "A randomized, double-blind, placebo-controlled study of growth hormone in the treatment of fibromyalgia," *American Journal of Medicine* 104, no. 3 (Mar 1998): 227–231.

R. Bennett. "Growth hormone in musculoskeletal pain states," *Current Pain and Headache Reports* 9, no. 5 (Oct 2005): 331–338.

OSTEOPOROSIS
The Association with Lower GH and/or IGF-1 Levels

J. Foldes, P. Lakatos, J. Zsadanyi, C. Horvath. "Decreased serum IGF-I and dehydroepiandrosterone sulphate may be risk factors for the development of reduced bone mass in postmenopausal women with endogenous subclinical hyperthyroidism," *European Journal of Endocrinology* 136, no. 3 (Mar 1997): 277–281.

J. P. Monson, R. Abs, B. A. Bengtsson, H. Bennmarker, U. Feldt-Rasmussen, E. Hernberg-Stahl, M. Thoren, B. Westberg, P. Wilton, C. Wuster. "Growth hormone deficiency and replacement in elderly hypopituitary adults. KIMS Study Group and the KIMS International Board. Pharmacia and Upjohn International Metabolic Database,"

Clinical Endocrinology (Oxf) 53, no. 3 (Sep 2000): 281–289.

S. Longobardi, F. Di Rella, R. Pivonello, C. Di Somma, M. Klain, L. Maurelli, R. Scarpa, A. Colao, B. Merola, G. Lombardi. "Effects of two years of growth hormone (GH) replacement therapy on bone metabolism and mineral density in childhood and adulthood onset GH deficient patients," *Journal of Endocrinological Investigation* 22, no. 5 (May 1999): 333–339.

V. Beckers, J. Milet, J. J. Legros. "Prolonged treatment with recombined growth hormone improves bone measures: study of body composition in 21 deficient adults on treatment," *Ann Endocrinol* (Paris) 62, no. 6 (Dec 2001): 507–515.

J. M. Gomez, N. Gomez, J. Fiter, J. Soler. "Effects of long-term treatment with GH in the bone mineral density of adults with hypopituitarism and GH deficiency and after discontinuation of GH replacement," *Hormone and Metabolic Research* 32, no. 2 (Feb 2000): 66–70.

J. M. Kaufman, P. Taelman, A. Vermeulen, M. Vandeweghe. "Bone mineral status in growth hormone-deficient males with isolated and multiple pituitary deficiencies of childhood onset," *Journal of Clinical Endocrinology and Metabolism* 74, no. 1 (Jan 1992): 11823.

L. Calo, R. Castrignano, P. A. Davis, G. Carraro, E. Pagnin, S. Giannini, A. Semplicini, A. D'Angelo. "Role of insulin-like growth factor-I in primary osteoporosis: a correlative study," *Journal of Endocrinological Investigation* 23, no. 4 (Apr 2000): 223–227.

A. Colao, C. Di Somma, R. Pivonello, S. Loche, G. Aimaretti, G. Cerbone, A. Faggiano, G. Corneli, E. Ghigo, G. Lombardi. "Bone loss is correlated to the severity of growth hormone deficiency in adult patients with hypopituitarism," *Journal of Clinical Endocrinology and Metabolism* 84, no. 6 (Jun 1999): 1919–1924.

D. Nakaoka, T. Sugimoto, H. Kaji, M. Kanzawa, S. Yano, M. Yamauchi, T. Sugishita, K. Chihara. "Determinants of bone mineral density and spinal fracture risk in postmenopausal Japanese women," *Osteoporosis International* 12, no. 7 (2001): 548–554.

H. Rico, A. Del Rio, T. Vila, R. Patino, F. Carrera, D. Espinos. "The role of growth hormone in the pathogenesis of postmenopausal osteoporosis," *Archives of Internal Medicine* 139, no. 11 (Nov 1979): 1263–1265.

S. Ljunghall, A. G. Johansson, P. Burman, O. Kampe, E. Lindh, F. A. Karlsson. "Low plasma levels of insulin-like growth factor 1 (IGF-1) in male patients with idiopathic osteoporosis," *Journal of Internal Medicine* 232, no. 1 (Jul 1992): 59–64.

The Improvement with GH Treatment

J. C. ter Maaten, H. de Boer, O. Kamp, L. Stuurman, E. A. van der Veen. "Long-term effects of growth hormone (GH) replacement in men with childhood-onset GH deficiency," *Journal of Clinical Endocrinology and Metabolism* 84, no. 7 (Jul 1999): 2373–2380.

J. M. Gomez, N. Gomez, J. Fiter, J. Soler. "Effects of long-term treatment with GH in the bone mineral density of adults with hypopituitarism and GH deficiency and after discontinuation of GH replacement," *Hormone and Metabolic Research* 32, no. 2 (Feb 2000): 66–70.

H. B. Baum, B. M. Biller, J. S. Finkelstein, K. B. Cannistraro, D. S. Oppenhein, D. A. Schoenfeld, T. H. Michel, H. Wittink, A. Klibanski. "Effects of physiologic growth hormone therapy on bone density and body composition in patients with adult-onset growth hormone deficiency. A randomized, placebo-controlled trial," *Annals of Internal Medicine* 125, no. 11 (Dec 1996): 883–890.

M. J. Valimaki, P. I. Salmela, J. Salmi, J. Viikari, M. Kataja, H. Turunen, E. Soppi. "Effects of 42 months of GH treatment on bone mineral density and bone turnover in GH-deficient adults," *European Journal of Endocrinology* 140, no 6 (Jun 1999): 545–554.

M. Vandeweghe, P. Taelman, J. M. Kaufman. "Short and long-term effects of growth hormone treatment on bone turnover and bone mineral content in adult growth hormone-deficient males," *Clinical Endocrinology* (Oxf) 39, no. 4 (Oct 1993): 409–415.

C. Clanget, T. Seck, V. Hinke, C. Wuster, R. Ziegler, J. Pfeilschifter. "Effects of 6 years of growth hormone (GH) treatment on bone mineral density in GH-deficient adults," *Clinical Endocrinology* (Oxf) 55, no. 1 (Jul 2001): 93–99.

S. A. Beshyah, E. Thomas, P. Kyd, P. Sharp, A. Fairney, D. G. Johnston. "The effect of growth hormone replacement therapy in hypopituitary adults on calcium and bone metabolism," *Clinical Endocrinology* (Oxf) 40, no 3 (Mar 1994): 383–391.

B. M. Biller, G. Sesmilo, H. B. Baum, D. Hayden, D. Schoenfeld, A. Klibanski. "Withdrawal of long-term physiological growth hormone (GH) administration: differential effects on bone density and body composition in men with adult-onset GH deficiency," *Journal of Clinical Endocrinology and Metabolism* 85, no. 3 (Mar 2000): 970–976.

C. A. Benbassat, M. Wass rman, Z. Laron. "Changes in bone mineral density after discontinuation and early reinstitution of growth hormone (GH) in patients with childhood-onset GH deficiency," *Growth Hormone IGF Research* 9, no. 5 (Oct 1999): 290–295.

A. Sartorio, S. Ortolani, E. Galbiati, G. Conte, V. Vangeli, M. Arosio, S. Porretti, and Faglia. "Effects of 12-month GH treatment on bone metabolism and bone mineral density in adults with adult-onset GH deficiency," *Journal of Endocrinological Investigation* 24, no. 4 (Apr 2001): 224–230.

G. Finkenstedt, R. W. Gasser, G. Hofle, C. Watfah, L. Fridrich. "Effects of growth hormone (GH) replacement on bone metabolism and mineral density in adult onset of GH deficiency: results of a double-blind placebo-controlled study with open follow-up," *European Journal of Endocrinology* 136, no. 3 (Mar 1997): 282–289.

R. J. Erdtsieck, H. A. Pols, N. K. Valk, O. B. M. Van, S. W. Lamberts, P. Mulder, J. C. Birkenhager. "Treatment of post-menopausal osteoporosis with a combination of growth hormone and pamidronate: a placebo controlled trial," *Clinical Endocrinology* (Oxf) 43 (1995): 557–565.

INFECTIONS AND LOWER IMMUNITY
The Association with Low Growth Hormone/IGF-1 Levels

R. Manfredi, F. Tumietto, L. Azzaroli, A. Zucchini, F. Chiodo, G. Manfredi. "Growth hormone (GH) and the immune system: impaired phagocytic function in children with idiopathic GH deficiency is corrected by treatment with biosynthetic GH," *Journal of Pediatric Endocrinology and Metabolism* 7, no. 3 (Jul–Sep 1994): 245–251.

D. C. Mynarcik, R. A. Frost, C. H. Lang, K. DeCristofaro, M. A. McNurlan, P. J. Garlick, R. T. Steigbigel, J. Fuhrer, S. Ahnn, M. C. Gelato. "Insulin-like growth factor system in patients with HIV infection: effect of exogenous growth hormone administration," *Journal of Acquired Immune Deficiency Syndrome* 22, no. 1 (Sep 1999): 49–55.

O. Panamonta, P. Kosalaraksa, B. Thinkhamrop, W. Kirdpon, C. Ingchanin, P. Lumbiganon. "Endocrine function in Thai children infected with human immunodeficiency virus," *Journal of Pediatric Endocrinology and Metabolism* 17, no. 1 (Jan 2004): 33–40.

K. L. Gupta, K. R. Shetty, J. C. Agre, M. C. Cuisinier, I. W. Rudman, D. Rudman. "Human growth hormone effect on serum IGF-I and muscle function in poliomyelitisn survivors," *Archives of Physical Medicine Rehabilitation* 75, no. 8 (Aug 1994): 889–894.

The Improvement with GH Treatment

A. Knyszynski, S. Adler-Kunin, A. Globerson. "Effects of growth hormone on thymocyte development from progenitor cells in the bone marrow," *Brain, Behavior, and Immunity* 6, no. 4 (Dec 1992): 327–340.

W. E. Beschorner, J. Divic, H. Pulido, X. Yao, P. Kenworthy, G. Bruce. "Enhancement of thymic recovery after cyclosporine by recombinant human growth hormone and insulin-like growth factor I," *Transplantation* 52, no. 5 (Nov 1991): 879–884.

W. J. Murphy, S. K. Durum, D. L. Longo. "Role of neuroendocrine hormones in murine T cell development. Growth hormone exerts thymopoietic effects in vivo," *Journal of Immunology* 149, no. 12 (Dec 1992): 3851–3857.

M. Kappel, M. B. Hansen, M. Diamant, J. O. Jorgensen, A. Gyhrs, B. K. Pedersen. "Effects of an acute bolus growth hormone infusion on the human immune system," *Hormone and Metabolic Research* 25, no. 11 (Nov 1993): 579–585.

K. A. Kudsk, C. Mowatt-Larssen, J. Bukar, T. Fabian, S. Oellerich, D. L. Dent, R. Brown. "Effect of recombinant human insulin-like growth factor I and early total parenteral nutrition on immune depression following severe head injury," *Archives of Surgery* 129, no. 1 (Jan 1994): 66–70.

R. Manfredi, F. Tumietto, L. Azzaroli, A. Zucchini, F. Chiodo, G. Manfredi. "Growth hormone (GH) and the immune system: impaired phagocytic function in children with idiopathic GH deficiency is corrected by treatment with biosynthetic GH," *Journal of Pediatric Endocrinology and Metabolism* 7, no. 3 (Jul–Sep 1994): 245–251.

P. Jardieu, R. Clark, D. Mortensen, K. Dorshkind. "In vivo administration of insulin-like growth factor-I stimulates primary B lymphopoiesis and enhances lymphocyte recovery after bone marrow transplantation," *Journal of Immunology* 152, no 9 (May 1994): 4320–4327.

R. Vara-Thorbeck, J. A. Guerrero, J. Rosell, E. Ruiz-Requena, J. M. Capitan. "Exogenous growth hormone: effects on the catabolic response to surgically produced acute stress and on postoperative immune function," *World Journal of Surgery* 17, no. 4 (Jul–Aug 1993): 530–537.

G. T. Peake, L. T. Mackinnon, W. L. Sibbitt Jr, J. C. Kraner. "Exogenous growth hormone treatment alters body composition and increases natural killer cell activity in women with impaired endogenous growth hormone secretion," *Metabolism* 36, no. 12 (Dec 1987): 1115–1117.

D. M. Crist, J. C. Kraner. "Supplemental growth hormone increases the tumor cytotoxic activity of natural killer cells in healthy adults with normal growth hormone secretion," *Metabolism* 39, no. 12 (Dec 1990): 1320–1324.

CANCER
The Association with Lower GH and/or IGF-1 Levels

K. Woodson, J. A. Tangrea, M. Pollak, T. D. Copeland, P. R. Taylor, J. Virtamo, D. Albanes. "Serum IGF-1: tumor marker or etiologic factor? A prospective study of prostate cancer among Finnish men," *Cancer Research* 63, no. 14 (Jul 2003): 3991–3994.

R. Baffa, K. Reiss, E. A. El-Gabry, J. Sedor, M. L. Moy, D. Shupp-Byrne, S. E. Strup, W. W. Hauck, R. Baserga, L. G. Gomella. "Low serum insulin-like growth factor 1 (IGF-1): a significant association with prostate cancer," *Tech Urol* 6, no. 3 (Sep 2000): 236–239.

Finne, A. Auvinen, H. Koistinen, W. M. Zhang, L. Maattanen, S. Rannikko, T. Tammela, M. Seppala, M. Hakama, U. H. Stenman. "Insulin-like growth factor I is not a useful marker of prostate cancer in men with elevated levels of prostate-specific antigen," *Journal of Clinical Endocrinology and Metabolism* 85, no. 8 (Aug 2000): 2744–2747.

A. P. Chokkalingam, M. Pollak, C. M. Fillmore, Y. T. Gao, F. Z. Stanczyk, J. Deng, I. A. Sesterhenn, F. K. Mostofi, T. R. Fears, M. P. Madigan, R. G. Ziegler, J. F. Fraumeni Jr, A. W. Hsing. "Insulin-like growth factors and prostate cancer: a population-based case-control study in China," *Cancer Epidemiology, Biomarkers, and Prevention* 10, no. 5 (May 2001): 421–427.

F. Colombo, F. Iannotta, A. Fachinetti, F. Giuliani, M. Cornaggia, G. Finzi, G. Mantero, F. Fraschini, A. Malesci, M. Bersani, et al. "Changes in hormonal and biochemical parameters in gastric adenocarcinoma," *Minerva Endocrinologica* 16, no. 3 (Jul–Sep 1991): 127–139.

Opposed by GH Treatment?

M. H. Torosian. "Growth hormone and prostate cancer growth and metastasis in tumor-bearing animals," *Journal of Pediatric Endocrinology and Metabolism* 6, no. 1 (Jan–Mar 1993): 93–97.

E. H. Ng, C. S. Rock, D. D. Lazarus, L. Stiaino-Coico, L. L. Moldawer, S. F. Lowry. "Insulin-like growth factor I preserves host lean tissue mass in cancer cachexia," *American Journal of Physiology* 262, no. 3 pt. 2 (Mar 1992): R426–431.

D. L. Bartlett, S. Charland, M. H. Torosian. "Growth hormone, insulin, and somatostatin therapy of cancer cachexia," *Cancer* 73, no. 5 (Mar 1994): 1499504.

LONGEVITY
The Association with GH and/or IGF-1 Levels

T. Rosen, B. A. Bengtsson. "Premature mortality due to cardiovascular disease in hypopituitarism," *Lancet* 336, no. 8710 (Aug 4, 1990): 285–288.

A. Besson, S. Salemi, S. Gallati, A. Jenal, R. Horn, P. S. Mullis, P. E. Mullis. "Reduced longevity in untreated patients with isolated growth hormone deficiency," *Journal of Clinical Endocrinology and Metabolism* 88, no. 8 (Aug 2003): 3664–3667.

A. S. Bates, W. Van't Hoff, P. J. Jones, R. N. Clayton. "The effect of hypopituitarism on life expectancy," *Journal of Clinical Endocrinology and Metabolism* 81, no. 3 (1996): 1169–1172.

The Improvement with GH Treatment

D. N. Khansari, T. Gustad. "Effects of long-term, low-dose growth hormone therapy on immune function and life expectancy of mice," *Mechanisms of Ageing and Development* 57, no. 1 (Jan 1991): 87–100.

W. E. Sonntag, C. S. Carter, Y. Ikeno, K. Ekenstedt, C. S. Carlson, R. F. Loeser, S. Chakrabarty, S. Lee, C. Bennett, R. Ingram, T. Moore, M. Ramsey. "Adult-onset growth hormone and insulin-like growth factor I deficiency reduces neoplastic disease, modifies age-related pathology, and increases life span," *Endocrinology* 146, no. 7 (2005): 2920–2932.

B. A. Bengtsson, H. P. Koppeschaar, R. Abs, H. Bennmarker, E. Hernberg-Stahl, B. Westberg, P. Wilton, J. P. Monson, U. Feldt-Rasmussen, C. Wuster. "Growth hormone replacement therapy is not associated with any increase in mortality. KIMS Study Group," *Journal of Clinical Endocrinology and Metabolism* 84, no. 11 (1999): 4291–4292.

ADVERSE SYMPTOMS OF PERSISTING, LOW GROWTH HORMONE LEVELS

R. C. Cuneo, F. Salomon, G. A. McGauley, P. H. Sonksen. "The growth hormone deficiency syndrome in adults," *Clinical Endocrinology* (Oxf) 37 (1992): 387–397.

E. R. Christ, P. V. Carroll, J. D. L. Russell, P. H. Sonksen. "The consequences of growth hormone deficiency in adulthood, and the effects of growth hormone replacement," *Schweiz Med Wochenschr* 127 (1997): 1440–1449.

E. K. Labram, T. J. Wilkin. "Growth hormone deficiency in adults and its response to growth hormone replacement," *QJM* 88 (1995): 391–399.

T. Rosen, G. Johannsson, J. O. Johansson, B. A. Bengtsson. "Consequences of growth hormone deficiency in adults and the benefits and risks of recombinant human growth hormone treatment," *Hormone Research*

43 (1995): 93—99.

J. O. Jorgensen, J. Muller, J. Moller, T. Wolthers, N. Vahl, A. Juul, N. E. Skakkebaek, J. S. Christiansen. "Adult growth hormone deficiency," *Hormone Research* 42 (1994): 235241.

S. A. Lieberman, A. R. Hoffman. "Growth hormone deficiency in adults: characteristics and response to growth hormone replacement," *Journal of Pediatrics* 128 (1996): S58-S60.

GROWTH HORMONE TREATMENT OF
PARTIAL GROWTH HORMONE DEFICIENCY

T. Hertoghe. "Growth hormone therapy in aging adults," *Anti-Aging Medical Therapeutics* eds. R. M. Klatz and R. Goldman, I (1997): 10—28.

GH TREATMENT: SAFETY, SIDE EFFECTS,
AND COMPLICATIONS

J. P. Monson. "Long-term experience with GH replacement therapy: efficacy and safety," *European Journal of Endocrinology* 148, supplement 2 (Apr 2003): S9—14.

L. Cohn, A. G. Feller, M. W. Draper, I. W. Rudman, D. Rudman. "Carpal tunnel syndrome and gynaecomastia during growth hormone treatment of elderly men with low circulating IGF-I concentrations," *Clinical Endocrinology* (Oxf.) 39 (1993): 417—425.

W. H. Daughaday. "The possible autocrine/paracrine and endocrine roles of insulin-like growth factors of human tumors," *Endocrinology* 127 (1990): 1—4

S. Ezzat, S. Melmed. "Clinical review 18: Are patients with acromegaly at increased risk for neoplasia?," *Journal of Clinical Endocrinology and Metabolism* 72 (1991): 245—249.

J. E. Brunner, C. C. Johnson, S. Zafar, E. L. Peterson, J. F. Brunner, R. C. Mellinger. "Colon cancer and polyps in acromegaly: increased risk associated with family history of colon cancer," *Clinical Endocrinology* (Oxf) 32 (1990): 65—71.

B. A. Bengtsson, S. Ed'en, I. Ernest, A. Od'en, B. Sjogren. "Epidemiology and long-term survival in acromegaly: a study of 166 cases diagnosed between 1955 and 1984," *Acta Med Scand* 223 (1988): 327–335.

G. Massa, M. Vanderschueren-Lodeweyckx, R. Bouillon. "Five-year follow-up of growth hormone antibodies in growth hormone deficient children treated with recombinant human growth hormone," *Clinical Endocrinology* 38 (1993): 13742.

S. L. Kaplan, G. P. August, S. L. Blethen, D. R. Brown, R. L. Hintz, A. Johansen, L. P. Plotnick, L. E. Underwood, J. J. Bell, R. M. Blizzard, T. P. Foley, N. J. Hopwood, R. T. Kirkland, R. G. Rosenfeld, J. J. Van Wyk. "Clinical studies with recombinantDNA-derived methionyl human growth hormone in growth hormone deficient children," *Lancet* I (1986): 697–700.

R. D. G. Milner, N. D. Barnes, J. M. H. Buckler, D. J. Carson, D. R. Hadden, I. A. Hughes, D. I. Johnston, J. M. Parkin, D. A. Price, P. H. Rayner, D. C. L. Savage, M. O. Savage, C. S. Smith, P. G. Swift, P. Pirazzoli, E. Cacciari, M. Mandini, A. Cicognani, S. Zucchini, T. Sganga, M. Capelli. "Follow-up anti-bodies to growth hormone in 210 growth hormone-deficient children treated with different commercial products," *Acta Paediatrics* 84 (1995): 1233–1236.

S. Malozowski, L. A. Tanner, D. Wysowski, G. A. Fleming. "Growth hormone, insulin-like growth factor I, and benign intracranial hypertension," *New England Journal of Medicine* 329 (1993): 665–666.

S. L. Blethen, D. B. Alien, D. Graves, G. August, T. Moshang, R. Rosenfeld. "Safety of recombinant deoxyribonucleic acid-derived growth hormone: The National Cooperative Growth Study experience," *Journal of Clinical Endocrinology and Metabolism* 81 (1996): 1704–1710.

Can Growth Hormone Treatment Cause Severe Discomfort and Side Effects?

Claim: GH treatment has substantial adverse effects such as edema, etc.
Fact: Substantial adverse effects appear only at overdoses such as is the case for any other medical treatment; it is sufficient to reduce the dose to avoid them.

C. Wuster, U. Melchinger, T. Eversmann, J. Hensen, P. Kann, A. von zur Muhlen, M. B. Ranke, H. Schmeil, H. Steinkamp, U. Tuschy. "Reduced incidence of side-effects of growth hormone substitution in 404 patients with hypophyseal insufficiency," Results of a multicenter indications Study. *Med Klin* 93, no. 10 (Oct 1998): 585–591.

G. Amato, G. Izzo, G. La Montagna, A. Bellastella. "Low dose recombinant human growth hormone normalizes bone metabolism and cortical bone density and improves trabecular bone density in growth hormone deficient adults without causing adverse effects," *Clinical Endocrinology* (Oxf) 45, no. 1 (Jul 1996): 27–32 *(no adverse effects with doses of 10µg/kg/day or a mean of 500 to 800 µg /day).*

K. Chihara, E. Koledova, A. Shimatsu, Y. Kato, H. Kohno, T. Tanaka, A. Teramoto, P. C. Bates, A. F. Attanasio. "An individualized GH dose regimen for long-term GH treatment in Japanese patients with adult GH deficiency," *European Journal of Endocrinology* 153, no. 1 (Jul 2005): 57–65 *("The incidence of edema and cases with high IGF-1 level were less frequent under the IGF-1 controlled regimen compared with those during the fixed-dose titration method").*

Can Growth Hormone Treatment Cause or Aggravate Diabetes?

Suspicion: Can GH at physiological doses cause diabetes?

Facts: GH's role is to prevent hypoglycaemia by elevating the low serum glucose levels of GH deficient subjects back to normal. It does not at physiological doses cause diabetes.

ARGUMENTS AGAINST GH USE

GH is a hyperglycemic hormone:

P. S. Ward, D. C. Savage. "Growth hormone responses to sleep, insulin hypoglycaemia and arginine infusion," *Hormone Research* 22, nos. 1–2 (1985): 7–11.

Treatment of GH-deficient children and the higher incidence of diabetes:

W. S. Cutfield, P. Wilton, H. Bennmarker, K. Albertsson-Wikland, P. Chatelain, M. B. Ranke, D. A. Price. "Incidence of diabetes mellitus and impaired glucose tolerance in children and adolescents receiving growth-hormone treatment," *Lancet* 355, no 9204 (Feb 19, 2000): 610–613 *("GH treatment did not affect the incidence of type 1 diabetes mellitus in any age group . . . the higher than expected incidence of type 2 diabetes mellitus with GH treatment may be an acceleration of the disorder in predisposed individuals. Type 2 diabetes did not resolve after GH therapy was stopped; critics say very high GH doses are used in children; no increased incidence of type 2 diabetes has been seen in adults taking GH).*

Serum GH levels are higher in diabetes patients:

Critics say, yes, two times higher serum GH, but 50 percent lower serum IGF-1, which reflects GH activity; insulin treatment of diabetes significantly increases serum IGF-1 and lower GH).

P. I. Shishko, R. E. Sadykova, P. A. Kovalev, B. V. Goncharov. "Insulin-like growth factor I in patients with newly detected insulin-dependent diabetes mellitus," *Probl Endokrinol* (Mosk) 38, no. 1 (Jan–Feb 1992): 17–19.

Acromegaly is associated with an increased incidence of diabetes:

M. Mercado, A. L. Espinosa de los Monteros, E. Sosa, S. Cheng, V. Mendoza, I. Hernandez, C. Sandoval, G. Guinto, M. Molina. "Clinical-biochemical correlations in acromegaly at diagnosis and the real prevalence of biochemically discordant disease," *Hormone Research* 62, no. 6 (2004): 293–299.

A. Mestron, S. M. Webb, R. Astorga, P. Benito, M. Catala, S. Gaztambide, J. M. Gomez, I. Halperin, T. Lucas-Morante, B. Moreno, G. Obiols, P. de Pablos, C. Paramo, A. Pico, E. Torres, C. Varela, J. A. Vazquez, J. Zamora, M. Albareda, M. Gilabert. "Epidemiology, clinical characteristics, outcome, morbidity and mortality in acromegaly based on the Spanish Acromegaly Registry (Registro Espanol de Acromegalia, REA)," *European Journal of Endocrinology* 151, no. 4 (Oct 2004): 439–446.

I. Fukuda, N. Hizuka, Y. Murakami, E. Itoh, K. Yasumoto, A. Sata, K. Takano. "Clinical features and therapeutic outcomes of 65 patients with acromegaly at Tokyo Women's Medical University," *Internal Medicine* 40, no. 10 (Oct 2001): 987–992.

ARGUMENTS FOR GH USE

The tonic secretion of insulin from the beta-cells depends on IGF-1:

R. N. Kulkarni, M. Holzenberger, D. Q. Shih, U. Ozcan, M. Stoffel, M. A. Magnuson, C. R. Kahn. "Beta-cell-specific deletion of the Igf1 receptor leads to hyperinsulinemia and glucose intolerance but does not alter beta-cell mass," *Natural Genetics* 31, no. 1 (May 2002): 111–115.

GH is an anti-hypoglycemic hormone. It neutralizes hypoglycemia.

P. S. Ward, D. C. Savage. "Growth hormone responses to sleep, insulin hypoglycaemia and arginine infusion," *Hormone Research* 22, nos. 1–2 (1985): 7–11.

T. E. West, P. H. Sonksen. "Is the growth-hormone response to insulin due to hypoglycaemia, hyperinsulinaemia or a fall in plasma free fatty acids?" *Clinical Endocrinology* (Oxf) 7, no. 4 (Oct 1977): 283–288 *(Hypoglycemia per se was the important stimulus to GH secretion and not hyperinsulinemia or a lowering of plasma-free fatty acids).*

A. Khaleeli, M. Perumainar, A. V. Spedding, J. D. Teale, V. Marks. "Treatment of tumor-induced hypoglycaemia with human growth hormone," *Journal of the Royal Society of Medicine* 85, no. 5 (May 1992): 303.

IGF-1 therapy has insulin-like effects. It reduces glycemia and serum insulin in controls and type 2 diabetic patients:

A. C. Moses, S. C. Young, L. A. Morrow, M. O'Brien, D. R. Clemmons. "Recombinant human insulin-like growth factor I increases insulin sensitivity and improves glycemic control in type II diabetes," *Diabetes* 45, no. 1 (Jan 1996): 91–100.

The association with lower GH and/or IGF-1 levels in diabetes:

S. Y. Nam, K. R. Kim, B. S. Cha, Y. D. Song, S. K. Lim, H. C. Lee, K. B. Huh. "Low-dose growth hormone treatment combined with diet restriction decreases insulin resistance by reducing visceral fat and increasing muscle mass in obese type 2 diabetic patients," *International Journal of Obesity Related Metabolism Disorders* 25, no. 8 (Aug 2001): 1101–1107.

Diabetes patients have high GH, but low IGF-1, marker of GH meta-bolic activity: *a lower IGF-1 in insulin-dependent diabetes pubers is associated with a higher serum glycosylated hemoglobine HbA1C).*

K. L. Clayton, J. M. Holly, L. M. Carlsson, J. Jones, T. D. Cheetham, A. M. Taylor, D. B. Dunger. "Loss of the normal relationships between growth hormone, growth hormone-binding protein and insulin-like growth factor-I in adolescents with insulin-dependent diabetes mellitus," *Clinical Endocrinology* (Oxf) 41, no. 4 (Oct 1994): 517−524.

In acromegaly, GH production is ten to one hundred times the normal production; ten to three hundred times the doses used in GH therapy. The pituitary GH-secreting tumor in the sella turcica crushes down the production of other pituitary hormones such as ACTH, LH, FSH, and TSH, creating a polyhormonal deficit: hypothyroidism, hypogonadism, hypocorticism—endocrine conditions that increase the risk of glucose intolerance and diabetes. These conditions are not found in corrective GH treatment of GH deficiency.

G. van den Berg, M. Frolich, J. D. Veldhuis, F. Roelfsema. "Growth hormone secretion in recently operated acromegalic patients," *Journal of Clinical Endocrinology and Metabolism* 79, no. 6 (Dec 1994): 1706−1715 ("*Patients with active acromegaly . . . secretion rate per twenty-four hours was twenty-five times greater in female acromegalics and one hundred times greater in male acromegalics than that in the controls.*")

R. P. Lamberton, I. M. Jackson. "Investigation of hypothalamic-pituitary disease," *Journal of Clinical Endocrinology and Metabolism* 12, no. 3 (Nov 1983): 509−534. ("*The possibility of deficiencies of the other pituitary hormones should then be addressed in patients with secretory tumors. In patients with large macroadenomas pituitary hormone deficiencies are al-most invariable with GH and FSH/LH being the most commonly affected, followed by TSH and ACTH in that order. Basal thyroid function tests, serum oestradiol or testosterone, and basal gonodotrophins should be rou-tinely obtained in patients with macroadenomas. Additionally, the integrity of the pituitary axis should be determined and an overnight water depri-vation test for assessment of neurohypophyseal function is also recom-mended.*")

P. J. Snyder, H. Bigdeli, D. F. Gardner, V. Mihailovic, R. S. Rudenstein, F. H. Sterling, R. D. Utiger. "Gonadal function in fifty men with untreated pituitary adenomas," *Journal of Clinical Endocrinology and Metabolism* 48, no. 2 (Feb 1979): 309–314.

L. J. Valenta, R. D. Sostrin, H. Eisenberg, J. A. Tamkin, A. N. Elias. "Diagnosis of pituitary tumors by hormone assays and computerized tomography," *American Journal of Medicine* 72, no. 6 (Jun 1982): 861–873.

GH therapy increases the glycemia during the first months, then reduces it when given to HIV-infected patients with fat accumulation:

J. C. Lo, K. Mulligan, M. A. Noor, J. M. Schwarz, R. A. Halvorsen, C. Grunfeld, M. Schambelan. "The effects of recombinant human growth hormone on body composition and glucose metabolism in HIV-infected patients with fat accumulation," *Journal of Clinical Endocrinology and Metabolism* 86, no. 4 (Aug 2001): 3480–3487.

GH therapy at physiological doses to type 1 diabetics has no effect on glycemia:

G. M. Bright, R. W. Melton, A. D. Rogol, W. L. Clarke. "The effect of exogenous growth hormone on insulin requirements during closed loop insulin delivery in insulin-dependent diabetes mellitus," *Hormone and Metabolic Research* 16, no. 6 (Jun 1984): 2869.

GH therapy to type 1 diabetics has increased insulin requirements, but improved control of hypoglycemic attacks:

E. R. Christ, H. L. Simpson, L. Breen, P. H. Sonksen, D. L. Russell-Jones, E. M. Kohner. "The effect of growth hormone (GH) replacement therapy in adult patients with type 1 diabetes mellitus and GH deficiency," *Clinical Endocrinology* (Oxf) 58, no. 3 (Mar 2003): 309–315.

Low dose GH therapy (0.10 mg/day) improves insulin sensitivity in young, healthy adults:

K. C. Yuen, J. Frystyk, D. K. White, T. B. Twickler, H. P. Koppeschaar, P. E. Harris, L. Fryklund, P. R. Murgatroyd, D. B. Dunger. "Improvement in insulin sensitivity without concomitant changes in body composition and cardiovascular risk markers following fixed administration of a very low growth hormone (GH) dose in adults with severe GH deficiency," *Clinical Endocrinology* (Oxf) 63, no. 4 (Oct 2005): 428–436.

*("The low GH dose [0.10 mg/day] decreased fasting glucose levels [p <
0.01] and enhanced insulin sensitivity [p < 0.02], the standard GH [mean
dose 0.48 mg/day] did not modify insulin sensitivity.")*

Diabetes

The improvement with GH treatment:

G. Gotherstrom, J. Svensson, J. Koranyi, M. Alpsten, I. Bosaeus, B. Bengtsson, G. Johannsson. "A prospective study of 5 years of GH replacement
therapy in GH-deficient adults: sustained effects on body composition, bone mass, and metabolic indices," *Journal of Clinical Endocrinology and Metabolism* 86, no. 10 (Oct 2001): 4657–4665.

J. Svensson, J. Fowelin, K. Landin, B. A. Bengtsson, J. O. Johansson. "Effects
of seven years of GH-replacement therapy on insulin sensitivity in
GH-deficient adults," *Journal of Clinical Endocrinology and Metabolism*
87, no. 5 (May 2002): 2121–2127.

K. L. Clayton, J. M. Holly, L. M. Carlsson, J. Jones, T. D. Cheetham, A. M.
Taylor, D. B. Dunger. "Loss of the normal relationships between growth
hormone, growth hormone-binding protein and insulin-like growth
factor-I in adolescents with insulin-dependent diabetes mellitus,"
Clinical Endocrinology (Oxf) 41, no. 4 (Oct 1994): 517–524.

K. C. Yuen, J. Frystyk, D. K. White, T. B. Twickler, H. P. Koppeschaar, P. E.
Harris, L. Fryklund, P. R. Murgatroyd, D. B. Dunger. "Improvement in
insulin sensitivity without concomitant changes in body composition
and cardiovascular risk markers following fixed administration of a
very low growth hormone (GH) dose in adults with severe GH deficiency," *Clinical Endocrinology* (Oxf) 63, no. 4 (Oct 2005): 428–436.

Can Growth Hormone Treatment Cause or Facilitate Cancer?

Claim: GH increases the risk of cancer
Facts: The epidemiological studies, which indicate an association between
serum IGF-I and cancer risk, have not established causality. An increased
cancer risk with GH therapy has not been proven in humans.

ARGUMENTS AGAINST GH USE IN
RELATION TO CANCER

Studies with positive associations between higher serum GH and/or IGF-1 levels and an increased risk of prostate or breast cancer:

Studies where a higher serum IGF-1 and/or high IGF-I to IGFBP-3 molar ratio was found associated with an increased risk of prostate cancer *(Critics say the increased IGF-1 may be due to local production of IGF-1 by the tumor and may thus be a marker, and not a cause of cancer, or a bias due to nutritional factors).*

L. Peng, S. Tang, J. Xie, T. Luo, B. Dai. "Quantitative analysis of IGF-1 and its application in the diagnosis of prostate cancer," *Hua Xi Yi Ke Da Xue Xue Bao* 33, no. 1 (Jan 2002): 137.

L. Li, H. Yu, F. Schumacher, G. Casey, J. S. Witte. "Relation of serum insulin-like growth factor-I (IGF-I) and IGF binding protein-3 to risk of prostate cancer (United States)," *Cancer Causes Control* 14, no. 8 (Oct 2003): 721–726.

A. P. Chokkalingam, M. Pollak, C. M. Fillmore, Y. T. Gao, F. Z. Stanczyk, J. Deng, I. A. Sesterhenn, F. K. Mostofi, T. R. Fears, M. P. Madigan, R. G. Ziegler, J. F. Fraumeni Jr, A. W. Hsing. "Insulin-like growth factors and prostate cancer: a population-based case-control study in China," *Cancer Epidemiology Biomarkers and Prevention* 10, no. 5 (May 2001): 421–427.

S. M. Harman, E. J. Metter, M. R. Blackman, P. K. Landis, H. B. Carter. "Baltimore Longitudinal Study on Aging. Serum levels of IGF-I, IGF-II, IGF-BP-3, and PSA as predictors of clinical prostate cancer," *Journal of Clinical Endocrinology and Metabolism* 85, no. 11 (Nov 2000): 4258–4265.

Higher serum GH was found associated with an increased risk of breast cancer:

This is based on the measurement of the daytime serum GH level, which is not representative of GH twenty-four-hour secretion).

J. T. Emerman, M. Leahy, P. W. Gout, N. Bruchovsky. "Elevated growth hormone levels in sera from breast cancer patients," *Hormone and Metabolic Research* 17, no. 8 (Aug 1985): 421–424.

Higher serum IGF-1 or IGF-1/IGF-BP-3 ratio is found associated with an increased risk of breast cancer:

H. Yu, B. D. Li, M. Smith, R. Shi, H. J. Berkel, I. Kato. "Polymorphic CA repeats in the IGF-I gene and breast cancer," *Breast Cancer Research and Treatment* 70, no. 2 (Nov 2001): 117−122.

J. V. Vadgama, Y. Wu, G. Datta, H. Khan, R. Chillar. "Plasma insulin-like growth factor-I and serum IGF-binding protein 3 can be associated with the progression of breast cancer, and predict the risk of recurrence and the probability of survival in African-American and Hispanic women," *Oncology* 57, no. 4 (Nov 1999): 330−340. *(There is up to seven times greater breast cancer incidence in women in the highest quintile of serum IGF-1: serum IGFBP-3 ratio compared to women in the lowest quintile.)*

Lower serum IGF-BP-3 was found in breast cancer patients:

P. F. Bruning, J. Van Doorn, J. M. Bonfrer, P. A. Van Noord, C. M. Korse, T. C. Linders, A. A. Hart. "Insulin-like growth-factor-binding protein 3 is decreased in early-stage operable pre-menopausal breast cancer," *International Journal of Cancer* 62, no. 3 (Jul 1995): 266−270.

Higher serum IGF-1 / IGF-BP-3 was found associated with an increased colon cancer risk:

The colon cancer risk was four times increased only for subjects in the upper tertile of IGF-1 and lower tertile of IGF-BP-3; for other tertiles or a combination of tertiles there was no significant association.

J. Ma, M. N. Pollak, E. Giovannucci, J. M. Chan, Y. Tao, C. H. Hennekens, M. J. Stampfer. "Prospective study of colorectal cancer risk in men and plasma levels of IGF-1 and IGF-BP-3," *Journal of the National Cancer Institute* 91 (1999): 620−625.

In acromegaly, the incidence of and/or mortality from digestive cancer is increased:

E. Ron, G. Gridley, Z. Hrubec, W. Page, S. Arora, J. F. Fraumeni Jr. "Acromegaly and gastrointestinal cancer," *Cancer* 68, no. 8 (Oct 1991): 1673−1677 *(but no increase in overall cancer incidence).*

S. M. Orme, R. J. McNally, R. A. Cartwright, P. E. Belchetz. "Mortality and cancer incidence in acromegaly: a retrospective cohort study. United

Kingdom Acromegaly Study Group," *Journal of Clinical Endocrinology and Metabolism* 83, no. 8 (Aug 1998): 2730–2734 *(but decreased overall incidence of cancer in acromegaly, and no increased overall cancer mortality).*

G. van den Berg, M. Frolich, J. D. Veldhuis, F. Roelfsema. "Growth hormone secretion in recently operated acromegalic patients," *Journal of Clinical Endocrinology and Metabolism* 79, no. 6 (Dec 1994): 1706–1715. *("Patients with active acromegaly . . . secretion rate per twenty-four hours was twenty-five times greater in female acromegalics and one hundred times greater in male acromegalics than that in the controls.")*

R. P. Lamberton, I. M. Jackson. "Investigation of hypothalamic-pituitary disease," *Clinical Endocrinology and Metabolism* 12, no. 3 (Nov 1983): 509–534. *("In patients with large macroadenomas pituitary hormone deficiencies are almost invariable with GH and FSH/LH being the most commonly affected, followed by TSH and ACTH in that order .")*

P. J. Snyder, H. Bigdeli, D. F. Gardner, V. Mihailovic, R. S. Rudenstein, F. H. Sterling, R. D. Utiger. "Gonadal function in fifty men with untreated pituitary adenomas," *Journal of Clinical Endocrinology and Metabolism* 48, no. 2 (Feb 1979): 309–314.

L. J. Valenta, R. D. Sostrin, H. Eisenberg, J. A. Tamkin, A. N. Elias. "Diagnosis of pituitary tumors by hormone assays and computerized tomography," *American Journal of Medicine* 72, no. 6 (Jun 1982): 861–873.

Growth Hormone Treatment with Human Pituitary GH Hormone

A study where the use of human pituitary GH as therapy to GH-deficient patients treated during childhood and early adulthood up to 1985 was associated with an increased risk of colon cancer and overall cancer mortality. *Critics claim the data are based on patients having taken GH extracted from human cadavers; now only biosynthetic growth hormone is used; moreover, the doses used in childhood are extremely high—at least seven times those used in treatment of GH-deficiency in adults.*

A. J. Swerdlow, C. D. Higgins, P. Adlard, M. A. Preece. "Risk of cancer in patients treated with human pituitary growth hormone in the UK, 1959–1985: a cohort study," *Lancet* 360, no. 9329 (Jul 27, 2002): 273–277.

Neutral Information and Alternative Explanations

of a Possible GH and Cancer Relation

It is possible that there is bias in the studies that discuss increased prostate and breast cancer risk:

Bias 1: The diagnosis of cancer may be more rapidly made in patients with high IGF-1 because they may undergo more intensive scrutiny: *As raised IGF-1 may cause tissue hyperplasia, including increase in size of prostate and breast tissue, the existence of these bigger tissues and possibly of the symptoms they may cause, may lead to more intensive scrutiny, from increased rate of PSA, CEA, or C1.25 measurements, to ultrasound and RX examinations, prostate, or breast biopsies, and thus an increased rate of detection of very slow, asymptomatic prostate or breast cancers that would have remained undiagnosed or diagnosed much later in patients with low IGF-1. Such higher rate of cancer detection may be particularly the case for prostate cancer, where the number of detected prostate cancer cases is very low compared to the total number of cases found at autopsy, and premenopausal breast cancer patients who were diagnosed within the two years after the first blood sample.*

P. Cohen, D. R. Clemmons, R. G. Rosenfeld. "Does the GH-IGF axis play a role in cancer pathogenesis?" *Growth Hormone IGF Research* 10, no. 6 (Dec 2000): 297–305.

Higher Levels of IGF-1 or GH or Acromegaly Have Been Associated with Benign Prostatic Hyperplasia, but Not Necessarily with Prostate Cancer:

A. P. Chokkalingam, Y. T. Gao, J. Deng, F. Z. Stanczyk, I. A. Sesterhenn, F. K. Mostofi, J. F. Fraumeni Jr, A. W. Hsing. "Insulin-like growth factors and risk of benign prostatic hyperplasia," *Prostate* 52, no. 2 (Jul 2002): 98–105.

A. Colao, P. Marzullo, D. Ferone, S. Spiezia, G. Cerbone, V. Marino, A. Di Sarno, B. Merola, G. Lombardi. "Prostatic hyperplasia: an unknown feature of acromegaly," *Journal of Clinical Endocrinology and Metabolism* 83, no. 3 (Mar 1998): 775–779.

GH and IGF-1 treatment of primates can increase breast hyperplasia, not specifically breast cancer:

S. T. Ng, J. Zhou, O. O. Adesanya, J. Wang, D. LeRoith, C. A. Bondy.

"Growth hormone treatment induces mammary gland hyperplasia in aging primates," *Natural Medicine* 3, no. 10 (Oct 1997): 1141–1144.

Bias 2: After adjustment for prostate volume, no longer significant associations between serum IGF-I and prostate cancer risk may persist: *(serum IGF-1 is not useful for diagnosis of prostate cancer, but a marker of benign prostatic hyperplasia and enlargement).*

P. Finne, A. Auvinen, H. Koistinen, W. M. Zhang, L. Maattanen, S. Rannikko, T. Tammela, M. Seppala, M. Hakama, U. H. Stenman. "Insulin-like growth factor I is not a useful marker of prostate cancer in men with elevated levels of prostate-specific antigen," *Journal of Clinical Endocrinology and Metabolism* 85, no. 8 (Aug 2000): 2744–2777.

Bias 3: Serum IGF-1 may actually be a surrogate marker of nutritional factors *that may increase the cancer risk such as meat and milk intake (persons who eat a lot of protein, especially red meat, have higher IGF-1 levels and an increased cancer risk).*

Q. Dai, Xiao-ou Shu, Fan Jin, Yu-Tang Gao, Zhi-Xian Ruan, W. Zheng. "Consumption of Animal Foods, Cooking Methods, and Risk of Breast Cancer," *Cancer, Epidemiology, Biomarkers, and Prevention* 11 (2002): 801–808. (**Link between meat, milk and/or protein intake, and prostate or breast cancer.**)

W. Zheng, A. C. Deitz, D. R. Campbell, W. Q. Wen, J. R. Cerhan, T. A. Sellers, A. R. Folsom, D. W. Hein. "N-acetyltransferase 1 genetic polymorphism, cigarette smoking, well-done meat intake, and breast cancer risk," *Cancer, Epidemiology, Biomarkers, and Prevention* 8, no. 3 (Mar 1999): 233–239.

A. E. Norrish, Lynnette R. Ferguson, Mark G. Knize, James S. Felton, Susan J. Sharpe, R. T. Jackson. "Heterocyclic Amine Content of Cooked Meat and Risk of Prostate Cancer," *Journal of the National Cancer Institute* 91, no. 23 (1999): 2038–2044.

R. Sinha, W. H. Chow, M. Kulldorff, J. Denobile, J. Butler, M. Garcia-Closas, R. Weil, R. N. Hoover, N. Rothman. "Well-done, grilled red meat increases the risk of colorectal adenomas," *Cancer Research* 59, no. 17 (1999): 4320–4324.

L. M. Butler, R. Sinha, R. C. Millikan, C. F. Martin, B. Newman, M. D.

Gammon, A. S. Ammerman, R. S. Sandler. "Heterocyclic amines, meat intake, and association with colon cancer in a population-based study," *American Journal of Epidemiology* 157, no. 5 (2003): 434–445.

A. Wolk. "Diet, lifestyle, and risk of prostate cancer," *Acta Oncologica* 44, no. 3 (2005): 27781.

W. B. Grant. "An ecologic study of dietary links to prostate cancer," *Alternative Medicine Review* 4, no. 3 (1999): 162–169.

E. Cho, D. Spiegelman, D. J. Hunter, W. Y. Chen, M. J. Stampfer, G. A. Colditz, W. C. Willett. "Premenopausal fat intake and risk of breast cancer," *Journal of the National Cancer Institute* 95, no. 14 (Jul 16, 2003): 1079–1085.

Red meat and milk intake is correlated with high IGF-1:

V. G. Kaklamani, A. Linos, E. Kaklamani, I. Markaki, Y. Koumantaki, C. S. Mantzoros. "Dietary fat and carbohydrates are independently associated with circulating insulin-like growth factor 1 and insulin-like growth factor-binding protein 3 concentrations in healthy adults," *Journal of Clinical Oncology* 17, no. 10 (Oct 1999): 3291–3298 .

S. C. Larsson, K. Wolk, K. Brismar, A. Wolk. "Association of diet with serum insulin-like growth factor I in middle-aged and elderly men," *American Journal of Clinical Nutrition* 81, no. 5 (May 2005): 1163–1167.

N. E. Allen, P. N. Appleby, G. K. Davey, R. Kaaks, S. Rinaldi, T. J. Key. "The associations of diet with serum insulin-like growth factor I and its main binding proteins in 292 women meat-eaters, vegetarians, and vegans," *Cancer, Epidemiology, Biomarkers, and Prevention* 11, no. 11 (Nov 2002): 1441–1448.

C. Hoppe, C. Molgaard, A. Juul, K. F. Michaelsen. "High intakes of skimmed milk, but not meat, increase serum IGF-I and IGFBP-3 in eight-year-old boys," *European Journal of Clinical Nutrition* 58, no. 9 (Sep 2004): 1211–1216.

Bias 4: The increases of serum IGF-1 may be produced by the malignant tumor and constitute a consequence, and not a cause, as suggested in some animal studies.

J. DiGiovanni, K. Kiguchi, A. Frijhoff, E. Wilker, D. K. Bol, L. Beltran, S. Moats, A. Ramirez, J. Jorcano, C. Conti. "Deregulated expression of insulin-like growth factor 1 in prostate epithelium leads to neoplasia in transgenic mice," *Proceedings of the National Academy of Science* (U.S.) 97, no. 7 (Mar 28, 2000): 3455–3460.

P. J. Kaplan, S. Mohan, P. Cohen, B. A. Foster, N. M. Greenberg. "The insulin-like growth factor axis and prostate cancer: lessons from the transgenic adenocarcinoma of mouse prostate (TRAMP) model," *Cancer Research* 59, no. 9 (May 1, 1999): 2203–2209.

Bias 5: The variability of serum IGF-1 makes that if two weeks after the initial blood test another measurement of IGF-1 was done, the results of the studies would have been different (about 40 percent of participants of the study would have switched from one quartile to the other).

D. Milani, J. D. Carmichael, J. Welkowitz, S. Ferris, R. E. Reitz, A. Danoff, D. L. Kleinberg. "Variability and reliability of single serum IGF-I measurements: impact on determining predictability of risk ratios in disease development," *Journal of Clinical Endocrinology and Metabolism* 89, no. 5 (May 2004): 2271–2274. (*"If fasting serum IGF-1 is measured twice, two weeks apart, individual differences range from -36.25 to +38.24 percent, while the mean value for the group of eighty-four shows high correlation between the two IGF-Is (r=0.922; p<0.0001) and varies much less (mean 120 at first visit) versus 115; p=0.03) in normal volunteers between the ages of fifty and ninety years. When considered in quartiles, IGF-1 changed from one quartile to another in 34/84 (40.5 percent) of the volunteers. When the group was divided in halves, thirds, quarters, or fifths, there was an increasing number of subjects who changed from one subdivision to another as the number of gradations increased. These results suggest that the predictive outcomes of earlier studies that used single IGF-1 samples for analysis of risk ratios according to thirds, quarters, or fifths could have been different if a second IGF-1 was used to establish the risk ratio."*)

There are no significant associations of serum levels with prostate cancer risk, and there is no difference in plasma GH or IGF-1 between prostate cancer patients and control groups.

H. Yu, M. R. Nicar, R. Shi, H. J. Berkel, R. Nam, J. Trachtenberg, E. P. Diamandis. "Levels of IGF-I and IGF BP- 2 and -3 in serial postoperative serum samples and risk of prostate cancer recurrence," *Urology* 57, no. 3 (Mar 2001): 471–475.

M. Hill, R. Bilek, L. Safarik, L. Starka. "Analysis of relations between serum levels of epitestosterone, estradiol, testosterone, IGF-1 and prostatic specific antigen in men with benign prostatic hyperplasia and carcinoma of the prostate," *Physiological Research* 49, supplement 1 (2000): S113–118.

R. Kurek, U. W. Tunn, O. Eckart, G. Aumuller, J. Wong, H. Renneberg. "The significance of serum levels of insulin-like growth factor-1 in patients with prostate cancer," *British Journal of Urology International* 85, no. 1 (Jan 2000): 125–129.

C. W. Cutting, C. Hunt, J. A. Nisbet, J. M. Bland, A. G. Dalgleish, R. S. Kirby. "Serum insulin-like growth factor-1 is not a useful marker of prostate cancer," *British Journal of Urology International* 83, no. 9 (Jun 1999): 996–999.

H. A. Ismail, M. Pollak, H. Behlouli, S. Tanguay, L. R. Begin, A. G. Aprikian. "Serum insulin-like growth factor (IGF)-1 and IGF-binding protein-3 do not correlate with Gleason score or quantity of prostate cancer in biopsy samples," *British Journal of Urology International* 92, no. 7 (Nov 2003): 699–702.

K. Woodson, J. A. Tangrea, M. Pollak, T. D. Copeland, P. R. Taylor, J. Virtamo, D. Albanes. "Serum insulin-like growth factor I: tumor marker or etiologic factor? A prospective study of prostate cancer among Finnish men," *Cancer Research* 63, no. 14 (Jul 15, 2003): 3991–3994.

A. H. Ismail, M. Pollak, H. Behlouli, S. Tanguay, L. R. Begin, A. G. Aprikian. "Insulin-like growth factor-1 and insulin-like growth factor binding protein-3 for prostate cancer detection in patients undergoing prostate biopsy," *Journal of Urology* 168, no. 6 (Dec 2002): 2426–2430.

G. J. Bubley, S. P. Balk, M. M. Regan, S. Duggan, M. E. Morrissey, W. C. Dewolf, E. Salgami, C. Mantzoros. "Serum levels of insulin-like growth factor-1 and insulin-like growth factor-1 binding proteins after radical prostatectomy," *Journal of Urology* 168, no. 5 (Nov 2002): 2249–2252.

K. DeLellis, S. Rinaldi, R. J. Kaaks, L. N. Kolonel, B. Henderson, L. Le

Marchand. "Dietary and lifestyle correlates of plasma insulin-like growth factor-I (IGF-I) and IGF binding protein-3 (IGFBP-3): the multiethnic cohort," *Cancer, Epidemiology, Biomarkers, and Prevention* 13, no. 9 (Sep 2004): 1444—1451.

In acromegaly, the incidence of cancer, other than possibly colon cancer, does not appear to be significantly increased; *in one study it was even significantly reduced by -14 percent. Overall mortality is normal for patients with low post-treatment GH, but increased for patients with high post-treatment GH.*

J. Svensson, B.-Å. Bengtsson, T. Rosén, A. Odén, G. Johannsson. "Malignant Disease and Cardiovascular Morbidity in Hypopituitary Adults with or without GH Replacement Therapy," *Journal of Clinical Endocrinology and Metabolism* 89, no. 7 (Jul 2004): 330612.

S. M. Orme, R. J. McNally, R. A. Cartwright, P. E. Belchetz. "Mortality and cancer incidence in acromegaly: a retrospective cohort study," United Kingdom Acromegaly Study Group. *Journal of Clinical Endocrinology and Metabolism* 83, no. 8 (Aug 1998): 2730—2734. *("The overall cancer incidence rate was 24 percent lower than that in the general population of the United Kingdom; the overall cancer mortality rate was not increased, but the colon cancer mortality rate was increased.")*

There is no difference in serum IGF-1 between breast cancer patients and control groups.

B. D. Li, M. J. Khosravi, H. J. Berkel, A. Diamandi, M. A. Dayton, M. Smith, H. Yu. "Free insulin-like growth factor-I and breast cancer risk," *International Journal of Cancer* 91, no. 5 (Mar 1, 2001): 736—739.

K. DeLellis, S. Rinaldi, R. J. Kaaks, L. N. Kolonel, B. Henderson, L. Le Marchand. "Dietary and lifestyle correlates of plasma insulin-like growth factor-I (IGF-I) and IGF binding protein-3 (IGFBP-3): the multiethnic cohort," *Cancer, Epidemiology, Biomarkers, and Prevention* 13, no. 9 (Sep 2004): 1444—1451.

GH transgenic mice with high serum IGF-1 do not develop breast, prostate, or colonic malignancies.

H. Wennbo, M. Gebre-Medhin, A. Gritli-Linde, C. Ohlsson, O. G. Isaksson, J. Tornell. "Activation of the prolactin receptor but not the growth hormone receptor is important for induction of mammary tumors in transgenic mice," *Journal of Clinical Investigation* 100, no. 11 (Dec 1, 1997): 2744–2751.

H. Wennbo, J. Tornell. "The role of prolactin and GH in breast cancer," *Octogene* 19 (2000): 1072–1076.

ARGUMENTS FOR GH USE IN RELATION TO CANCER

Inverse (protective) associations of serum GH/IGF-1 levels and overall cancer risk. Untreated, GH-deficient patients have an increased overall cancer incidence (two times the normal incidence) and cancer mortality (four times the normal incidence).

J. Svensson, B. Å. Bengtsson, T. Rosén, A. Odén, G. Johannsson. "Malignant disease and cardiovascular morbidity in hypopituitary adults with or without growth hormone replacement therapy," *Journal of Clinical Endocrinology and Metabolism* 89, no. 7 (Jul 2004): 3306–3312.

A high serum IGF-1 is found associated with a lower risk of prostate cancer:

P. Finne, A. Auvinen, H. Koistinen, W. M. Zhang, L. Maattanen, S. Rannikko, T. Tammela, M. Seppala, M. Hakama, U. H. Stenman. "Insulin-like growth factor I is not a useful marker of prostate cancer in men with elevated levels of prostate-specific antigen," *Journal of Clinical Endocrinology and Metabolism* 85, no. 8 (Aug 2000): 2744–2747.

K. Woodson, J. A. Tangrea, M. Pollak, T. D. Copeland, P. R. Taylor, J. Virtamo, D. Albanes. "Serum IGF-1: tumor marker or etiologic factor? A prospective study of prostate cancer among Finnish men," *Cancer Research* 63, no. 14 (2003): 3991–3994 (*-48 percent for men in the highest quartile of serum IGF-1*).

R. Baffa, K. Reiss, E. A. El-Gabry, J. Sedor, M. L. Moy, D. Shupp-Byrne, S. E. Strup, W. W. Hauck, R. Baserga, L. G. Gomella. "Low serum insulin-like growth factor 1 (IGF-1): A significant association with prostate cancer," *Tech Urol* 6, no. 3 (Sep 2000): 236–239.

There is no significant association between serum IGF-1 and prostate cancer. GH therapy increases serum IGF-BP-3, *which may protect against cancer: IGFBP-3 causes apoptosis of cancer cells and inhibits IGF action on cancer cells in vitro => Serum IGFBP-3 is in general negatively correlated with the cancer risk cancer: the higher IGF-BP-3, the lower the cancer risk.*

H. A. Wollmann, E. Schonau, W. F. Blum, F. Meyer, K. Kruse, M. B. Ranke. "Dose-dependent responses in insulin-like growth factors, insulin-like growth factor-binding protein-3 and parameters of bone metabolism to growth hormone therapy in young adults with growth hormone deficiency," *Hormone Research* 43, no. 6 (1995): 249–256.

A. Grimberg, P. Cohen. "GH and prostate cancer: guilty by association?" *Journal of Endocrinological Investigation* 22, no. 5 supplement (1999): 64–73.

A high serum IGF-BP-3 is associated with a reduced prostate cancer risk (-30 percent), and/or prostate cancer recurrence.

S. M. Harman, E. J. Metter, M. R. Blackman, P. K. Landis, H. B. Carter. "Baltimore Longitudinal Study on Aging. Serum levels of IGF-I, IGF-II, IGF-BP-3, and PSA as predictors of clinical prostate cancer," *Journal of Clinical Endocrinology and Metabolism* 85, no. 11 (Nov 2000): 4258–4265.

Studies where GH therapy given to cancer patients reduced the cancer recurrence, and reduces the cancer mortality or increases survival time:

A. J. Swerdlow, R. E. Reddingius, C. D. Higgins, H. A. Spoudeas, K. Phipps, Z. Qiao, W. D. Ryder, M. Brada, R. D. Hayward, C. G. Brook, P. C. Hindmarsh, S. M. Shalet. "Growth hormone treatment of children with brain tumors and risk of tumor recurrence," *Journal of Clinical Endocrinology and Metabolism* 85, no. 12 (Dec 2000): 4444–4449.

J. Tacke, U. Bolder, A. Herrmann, G. Berger, K. W. Jauch. "Long-term risk of gastrointestinal tumor recurrence after postoperative treatment with recombinant human growth hormone," *Journal of Parenter Enteral Nutrition* 24, no. 3 (May–Jun 2000): 140–144.

Long-term GH replacement (sixty months) reduced the increased cancer risk and mortality of GH deficient patients by half:

J. Svensson, B. Å. Bengtsson, T. Rosén, A. Odén, G. Johannsson. "Malignant disease and cardiovascular morbidity in hypopituitary adults with or without growth hormone replacement therapy," *Journal of Clinical Endocrinology and Metabolism* 89, no. 7 (Jul 2004): 3306–3312.

GH or IGF-1 Therapy to Animals with Cancer

Growth hormone may reduce the tumor incidence and/or progression. Combined GH- insulin therapy reduced the development of mammary carcinoma in female rats:

D. L. Bartlett, S. Charland, M. H. Torosian. "Growth hormone, insulin, and somatostatin therapy of cancer cachexia," *Cancer* 73, no. 5 (Mar 1994): 1499504.

GH-therapy reduced the development of lung metastases in rats with prostate cancer:

M. H. Torosian. "Growth hormone and prostate cancer growth and metastasis in tumor-bearing animals," *Journal of Pediatric Endocrinology and Metabolism* 6, no. 1 (Jan–Mar 1993): 93–97.

A Lower Serum GH Level Is Found in Gastric Cancer Patients

F. Colombo, F. Iannotta, A. Fachinetti, F. Giuliani, M. Cornaggia, G. Finzi, G. Mantero, F. Fraschini, A. Malesci, M. Bersani, et al. "Changes in hormonal and biochemical parameters in gastric adenocarcinoma," *Minerva Endocrinologica* 16, no. 3 (Jul–Sep 1991): 127–139.

GH-therapy inhibits the development of liver cancer due to carcinogens (aflatoxin B1 or N-OH-acetyl- aminofluoren) in male rats:

D. Liao, I. Porsch-Hallstrom, J. A. Gustafsson, A. Blanck. "Sex differences at the initiation stage of rat liver carcinogenesis—influence of growth hormone," *Carcinogenesis* 14, no. 10 (Oct 1993): 2045–2049.

IGF-1-therapy preserved lean mass in rats with sarcoma and cachexia:

E. H. Ng, C. S. Rock, D. D. Lazarus, L. Stiaino-Coico, L. L. Moldawer, S. F. Lowry. "Insulin-like growth factor I preserves host lean tissue mass in cancer cachexia," *American Journal of Physiology* 262, no. 3 pt. 2 (Mar 1992): R426–431.

Conclusion on the Cancer Studies and GH

- GH therapy raises both the levels of IGF-1 and IGFBP-3. IGF-BP-3 is a potent inhibitor of IGF action in breast and prostate tissues.
- Autocrine production of IGFs and GH have been identified in cancer cells and tissues. Thus, serum IGF-I may actually be a confounding variable, serving as a marker for local prostatic IGF-I production.
- Since GH-deficient patients often have a subnormal IGF-1 serum level, which normalizes on therapy the cancer risk on GH therapy does probably not substantially increase above that of the normal population. On the contrary, the evidence points to a normalization of the risk.
- It seems prudent that when we treat adult GH deficiency, we should aim to maintain serum IGF-1 in the normal range.

Can Growth Hormone Treatment Reduce Lifespan?

Claim: GH may have adverse effects on lifespan

Facts: GH treatment appears to reduce mortality, except for special mice species and humans put in extreme conditions.

ARGUMENTS AGAINST GH USE
Studies where higher GH and/or IGF-1 levels were found associated with premature death

A high serum GH was associated with premature death in humans. *Critics claim an old-fashioned technique, which lacked assay precision, was used to measure GH; the daytime serum GH were measured, which is not accurate except for acromegaly patients; serum GH does not reflect GH activity, serum IGF-1 does it, but up to a certain degree; an increased serum GH may possibly reflect increased binding of GH to increased serum GHBP and thus inactivation of GH, but the serum GHBP level was not checked in the study.* P. Maison, B. Balkau, D. Simon, P. Chanson, G. Rosselin, E. Eschwege.

"Growth hormone as a risk for premature mortality in healthy subjects: data from the Paris prospective study," *British Medical Journal* 316, no. 7138 (Apr 11, 1998): 1132–1133.

Acromegaly adults have premature death only when they keep high posttreatment GH *and thus a probably continuing active growth hormone-secreting tumor that crushes down all the other pituitary cells; overall mortality is normal for patients with low posttreatment GH.*

S. M. Orme, R. J. McNally, R. A. Cartwright, P. E. Belchetz. "Mortality and cancer incidence in acromegaly: a retrospective cohort study," United Kingdom Acromegaly Study Group. *Journal of Clinical Endocrinology and Metabolism* 83, no. 8 (Aug 1998): 27304.

Mice models of genetic pituitary failure with multiple hormone deficiency (Ames and Snell mice) and GH receptor knockout mice (primary IGF-1-deficiency) may have a significant higher longevity. *Critics claim the heterozygous IGF-1 receptor knockout mutants are special mice species, as are Ames and Snell mice. They react in a completely different way to GH than normal mice species. They have a 50 percent decrease in IGF-1 receptors, but a 32 percent higher serum IGF-1; they have more glucose intolerance; are slightly smaller; the lifespan was only significantly longer in female mice (+33 percent), not in male mice (+16 percent); the results based on a short-living species (mice) may not be necessarily true for species with a long life such as humans.*

H. Liang, E. J. Masoro, J. F. Nelson, R. Strong, C. A. McMahan, A. Richardson. "Genetic mouse models of extended lifespan," *Experimental Gerontology* 38, nos. 11–12 (Nov–Dec 2003): 1353–1364.

M. Holzenberger. "The GH/IGF-I axis and longevity," *European Journal of Endocrinology* 151, supplement 1 (Aug 2004): S23–27.

R. N. Kulkarni, M. Holzenberger, D. Q. Shih, U. Ozcan, M. Stoffel, M. A. Magnuson, C. R. Kahn. "Beta-cell-specific deletion of the IGF-1 receptor leads to hyper-insulinemia and glucose intolerance but does not alter beta-cell mass," *Nature Genetics* 31, no. 1 (May 2002): 111–115 *(lack IGF-1 receptors on beta-cells =› glucose interance and less beta-cells).*

S. J. Hauck, J. M. Aaron, C. Wright, J. J. Kopchick, A. Bartke. "Antioxidant enzymes, free-radical damage, and response to paraquat in liver and kidney of long-living growth hormone receptor/binding protein gene-disrupted mice," *Hormone and Metabolic Research* 34, no. 9 (Sep 2002): 481–486.

Can GH Therapy Increase Mortality?

GH therapy to critically ill patients:
doubles the mortality rate

J. Takala, E. Ruokonen, N. R. Webster, M. S. Nielsen, D. F. Zandstra, G. Vundelinckx, C. J. Hinds. "Increased mortality associated with growth hormone treatment in critically ill adults," *New England Journal of Medicine* 341, no. 11 (Sep 9, 1999): 785–792. (*Critics on the study: the doses used were too high: ten to seventy times the normal dose in very weak persons; the control group had an abnormally lower mortality rate than predicted; combined to the high mortality rates of the treatment group, the average mortality rate was very similar to that of a historical cohort; GH treatment lowers cortisol levels, which are crucial to critically ill patients*).

B. D. Freeman, R. L. Danner, S. M. Banks, C. Natanson. "Safeguarding patients in clinical trials with high mortality rates," *American Journal of Respiratory and Critical Care Medicine* 164, no. 2 (Jul 15, 2001): 190–192.

Studies where GH therapy lowered the levels of cortisol and its metabolites by 20 to 40 percent, which is dangerous for critically ill patients who desperately need cortisol for their survival.

H. Vierhapper, P. Nowotny, W. Waldhausl. "Treatment with growth hormone suppresses cortisol production in man," *Metabolism* 47, no 11 (Nov 1998): 1376–1378.

J. Rodriguez-Arnao, L. Perry, G. M. Besser, R. J. Ross. "Growth hormone treatment in hypopituitary GH deficient adults reduces circulating cortisol levels during hydrocortisone replacement therapy," *Clinical Endocrinology* (Oxf) 45, no. 1 (Jul 1996): 33–37.

J. U. Weaver, L. Thaventhiran, K. Noonan, J. M. Burrin, N. F. Taylor, M. R. Norman, J. P. Monson. "The effect of growth hormone replacement on cortisol metabolism and glucocorticoid sensitivity in hypopituitary adults," *Clinical Endocrinology* (Oxf) 41, no. 5 (Nov 1994): 639–648.

. . . and a study where patients who have poor responsive adrenals (poorly able to increase their cortisol production) and are in septic shock, die easier:

P. M. Rothwell, Z. F. Udwadia, P. G. Lawler. "Cortisol response to corti-
cotropin and survival in septic shock," *Lancet* 337, no 8741 (Mar 9, 1991): 582–583.

. . . and studies where glucocorticoid treatments considerably increased survival of critically ill patients and survival of HIV patient from pneumonia:

S. Gagnon, A. M. Boota, M. A. Fischl, H. Baier, O. W. Kirksey, L. La Voie.
"Corticosteroids as adjunctive therapy for severe Pneumocystis carinii pneumonia in the acquired immunodeficiency syndrome. A double-
blind, placebo-controlled trial," *New England Journal of Medicine* 323, no. 21 (Nov 22, 1990): 1444–1450.

Survival from typhus:

S. L. Hoffman, N. H. Punjabi, S. Kumala, M. A. Moechtar, S. P. Pulungsih, A. R. Rivai, R. C. Rockhill, T. E. Woodward, A. A. Loedin. "Reduction of mortality in chloramphenicol-treated severe typhoid fever by high-
dose dexamethasone," *New England Journal of Medicine* 310, no. 2 (Jan 12, 1984): 82–88.

Neutral Information on GH and Longevity

No increased mortality in acromegaly if levels of GH are less than 2.5 ng/ml.

Orme SM, McNally RJ, Cartwright RA, Belchetz PE. "Mortality and cancer incidence in acromegaly: a retrospective cohort study. United Kingdom Acromegaly Study Group." *Journal of Clinical Endocrinology and Metabolism.* 1998 Aug;83(8):27304.

ARGUMENTS FOR GH USE GH/IGF-1 Levels

Higher serum GH and IGF-1 levels are associated with a higher survival. Persistent GH deficiency (without GH therapy) in humans is associated with a shorter life expectancy: increased overall and cardiovascular mortality.

T. Rosen, B. A. Bengtsson. "Premature mortality due to cardiovascular disease in hypopituitarism," *Lancet* 336, no. 8710 (Aug 4, 1990): 285– 288.

A. S. Bates, W. Van't Hoff, P. J. Jones, R. N. Clayton. "The effect of hypopituitarism on life expectancy," *Journal of Clinical Endocrinology and Metabolism* 81, no. 3 (Mar 1996): 1169–1172.

Higher Mortality in GH Deficient Women

J. Svensson, B. Å. Bengtsson, T. Rosén, A. Odén, G. Johannsson. "Malignant disease and cardiovascular morbidity in hypopituitary adults with or without growth hormone replacement therapy," *Journal of Clinical Endocrinology and Metabolism* 89, no. 7 (Jul 2004): 3306–3312.

Higher mortality in 11 GH deficient adults suffering from a genetic defect (6.7 kb spanning deletion of genomic DNA of the GH-1 gene) that causes isolated GH deficiency (hereditary dwarfism), *untreated men lost twenty-one years of life (-25 percent compared to the unaffected brothers) and women thirty-four years less (-44 percent versus unaffected sisters).*

A. Besson, S. Salemi, S. Gallati, A. Jenal, R. Horn, P. S. Mullis, P. E. Mullis. "Reduced longevity in untreated patients with isolated growth hormone deficiency," *Journal of Clinical Endocrinology and Metabolism* 88, no. 8 (2003): 3664–3667.

Patients with hypopituitarism have increased overall and cardiovascular mortality; **the increased mortality from cerebrovascular disease (esp. in women) was the main contributor to the increased cardiovascular mortality.**

B. Bulow, L. Hagmar, Z. Mikoczy, C. H. Nordstrom, E. M. Erfurth. "Increased cerebrovascular mortality in patients with hypopituitarism," *Clinical Endocrinology* (Oxf) 46, no. 1 (Jan 1997): 75–81.

B. A. Bengtsson, H. P. Koppeschaar, R. Abs, H. Bennmarker, E. Hernberg-Stahl, B. Westberg, P. Wilton, J. P. Monson, U. Feldt-Rasmussen, C. Wuster. "Growth hormone replacement therapy is not associated with any increase in mortality," KIMS Study Group. *Journal of Clinical Endocrinology and Metabolism* 84, no. 11 (Nov 1999): 4291–4292.

GH Treatment

Corrective GH hormone treatment increases survival. GH replacement therapy of GH deficient adults lowers the excessive mortality back to normal.

B. A. Bengtsson, H. P. Koppeschaar, R. Abs, H. Bennmarker, E. Hernberg-Stahl, B. Westberg, P. Wilton, J. P. Monson, U. Feldt-Rasmussen, C. Wuster. "Growth hormone replacement therapy is not associated with any increase in mortality," KIMS Study Group. *Journal of Clinical Endocrinology and Metabolism* 84, no. 11 (Nov 1999): 4291–4292.

J. Svensson, B. Å. Bengtsson, T. Rosén, A. Odén, G. Johannsson. "Malignant disease and cardiovascular morbidity in hypopituitary adults with or without growth hormone replacement therapy," *Journal of Clinical Endocrinology and Metabolism* 89, no. 7 (Jul 2004): 3306–3312.

GH treatment of normal, elderly mice extended the mean and maximal lifespan:

D. N. Khansari, T. Gustad. "Effects of long-term, low-dose growth hormone therapy on immune function and life expectancy of mice," *Mechanisms of Ageing and Development* 57, no. 1 (Jan 1991): 87–100.

GH treatment of GH-deficient mice extended lifespan, *but lifespan of (non-GH-treated) mice was similar to that of normal mice:*

W. E. Sonntag, C. S. Carter, Y. Ikeno, K. Ekenstedt, C. S. Carlson, R. F. Loeser, S. Chakrabarty, S. Lee, C. Bennett, R. Ingram, T. Moore, M. Ramsey. "Adult-onset growth hormone and insulin-like growth factor I deficiency reduces neoplastic disease modifies age-related pathology, and increases life span," *Endocrinology* 146, no. 7 (Jul 2005): 2920–2932.

Conclusion

Persistent growth hormone deficiency reduces the life expectancy, while growth hormone treatment of GH-deficient patients improves it. Caution should be applied when using GH treatment in critically ill patients.

Appendix B

Physician Referral Resources

THE FOLLOWING REPRESENTS AN INCOMPLETE LIST OF MORE THAN AN estimated twenty thousand physicians who regularly prescribe human growth hormone for the purpose of age-related growth hormone deficiency (GHD) syndrome.

Many of these "cutting edge" physicians prefer to remain "under the radar," despite the fact that the "not guilty verdict" of James W. Forsythe, MD, HMD, now gives them legal precedent to practice good medicine. For the reader's convenience, these physicians are listed by geographical region.

LISTED STATES	REGION
Arizona	Southwestern United States
California	West Coast
Colorado	Mountain States
Connecticut	Mid-Atlantic United States
Florida	Southeastern United States
Georgia	Southeastern United States
Idaho	Great Basin Region
Illinois	Midwestern United States
Indiana	Midwestern United States

Maryland...............Mid-Atlantic United States

Massachusetts.......Northeastern United States

Michigan ....Midwestern United States

Minnesota ....Midwestern United States

Nevada ....Great Basin Region

New York...............Northeastern United States

New Jersey.............Mid-Atlantic United States

North Carolina.......Southeastern United States

Pennsylvania..........Mid-Atlantic United States

Tennessee..............Midwestern United States

Texas.....................Southwestern United States

Utah......................Mountain States

Vermont ....Northeastern United States

Virginia ....Mid-Atlantic United States

Washington...........Great Basin Region

Wisconsin ....Midwestern United States

Great Basin Region

IDAHO

POST FALLS
Paul Brillhart, MD
(208)773-1311
www.drpaulbrillhart.com

NEVADA

CARSON CITY
Frank Shallenberger, M.D,
HMD
(775) 884-3990

LAS VEGAS
Julie Garcia, MD
(702) 870-0058

Robert Milne, MD
(702) 385-1393

Fuller Royal, MD
(702) 732-1400

RENO
James W. Forsythe, MD HMD,
and
Earlene M. Forsythe, APN
(775) 827-0707
www.drforsythe.com

WASHINGTON

BELLINGHAM
Andrew Pauli, MD
(360) 527-9785

Mid-Atlantic United States

CONNECTICUT

MANCHESTER
Stephen Sinatra, MD
(860) 643-5101

MARYLAND

BALTIMORE
Dean Kane, MD
(410) 602-3322

B. Rothstein, DO
(410) 484-2121

NEW JERSEY

CHERRY HILL
Allan Magaziner, MD
(856) 424-8222,
www.drmagaziner.com

Vijay Vijh, MD
(856) 489-0505

SHREWSBURY
Neil Rosen, MD
(732) 219-0895

TRENTON
Initiaz Ahmad, MD
(609) 890-2966

PENNSYLVANIA

PITTSBURGH
Brenda McMahon, MD
(412) 487-8638

VIRGINIA

ARLINGTON
Denise Bruner, MD
(703) 558-4949

VIRGINIA BEACH
Jennifer Krup, MD
(757) 306-4300

Midwestern United States

ILLINOIS

CHICAGO
Paul Savage, MD
(866) 535-2563,
www.bodylogicmd.com

John Zaborowski, MD
(847) 291-4148

LIBERTYVILLE
Craig Dean, MD
(847) 367-6347

INDIANA

GOSHEN
Tammy Born, MD
www.bornclinic.com

INDIANAPOLIS
Linda Spencer, MD
(317) 298-3850
www.complementaryfamily
medicalcare.com

LAFAYETTE
Charles Turner, MD
(765) 471-1100
www.charlesturnermd.com

MICHIGAN

CANTON
Pamela Smith, MD
(734) 398-7522

DETROIT
Cynthia Shelby-Lane, MD
(800) 436-9777

GRAND RAPIDS
Tammy Born, MD
(616) 656-3700,
www.bornclinic.com

SOUTHFIELD
Edward Lichten, MD
(248) 358-3433

WEST BLOOMFIELD
David Brownstein, MD
(248) 851-1600

MINNESOTA

EDINA
Khalid Mahmud, MD
(952) 943-1529

TENNESSEE

BRISTOL
David Marden, DO
(423) 844-4925

WISCONSIN

WAUKESHA
James Nagel, MD
(262) 542-0860

Mountain States

COLORADO

DENVER
Peter Hanson, MD
(303) 733-2521
www.peterhansonmd.com

UTAH

ST. GEORGE
Gordon Reynolds, MD
(435) 628-8060

Northeastern United States

MASSACHUSETTS

BROOKLINE
Alan Altman, MD
(617) 232-0262

NEW YORK

NEW YORK CITY
Eric Braverman, MD
(212) 213-6188

Rashmi Gulati
(212) 794-4466
www.patientsmedical.com

Ronald Hoffman, MD
(212) 779-1744
www.drhoffman.com

Alexander Kulice, MD
(212) 838-8265
www.ostrow.medem.com

Richard Linchitz, MD
(212) 252-1942
www.metropolitanwellness.com

Jeffrey Morrison, MD
(212) 989-9828
www.themorrisoncenter.com

John Salerno, MD
(212) 582-1700
www.salernocenter.com

Erika Schwartz, MD
(212) 873-3420

PORT WASHINGTON
Thomas Lodi, MD
(516) 883-6771

RHINEBECK
Steven Bock, MD
(845) 876-7082
www.rhinebeckhealth.com

VERMONT
NEW CHAPTER
Paul Schulick, MD
(802) 257-9345
www.new-chapter.info

Southeastern United States

FLORIDA
BOCA RATON
Gary Brandwein, DO
(954) 396-3908

LAUDERHILL
Herbert Slavin, MD
(954) 748-4991

SARASOTA
Robert Carlson, MD
(941) 955-1815
www.preventaging.org

GEORGIA
ALPHARETTA
Daniela Paunesky, MD
(770) 777-7707

STOCKBRIDGE
Frank McCafferty, MD
(770) 506-0087

NORTH CAROLINA
GREENSBORO
Larry Webster, MD
(336) 272-2030
www.lwebster.com

Southwestern United States

ARIZONA
TUCSON
Dharma Khalsa, MD
(520) 749-8374

Daniel Mihalyi, MD
(520) 742-1585

SUN CITY
Alan Miles, MD
(623) 974-2226

TEXAS
BULVERDE
Donna Becker, DO

DALLAS
Clark Ridley, MD
(214) 303-1888
www.lifespanmedicine.com

HOUSTON

Gurney Pearsall, MD
(713) 522-4037

Theodore Piliszek, MD
(281) 469-4156

THE WOODLANDS

Garth Denyer, MD
(281) 367-1414

WEATHERFORD

Ronald McDaniel, DO
(817) 599-4301

WIMBERLY

Lane Sebring, MD
(512) 847-5618

West Coast

CALIFORNIA

BEVERLY HILLS

Jennifer Berman, MD
(310) 432-6644

Cathie Lippman, MD
(310) 289-8430

Gary London, MD
(310) 207-4500

Prabin Mishra, MD
(310) 247-8577

Uzzi Reiss, MD
(310) 474-1945

BISHOP

David Greene, MD
(760) 873-8982

BURLINGAME

Tedde Rinker, DO
(650) 259-9500

ENCINO

Mark Gordon, MD
(818) 990-1166

FRESNO

Narges Mazj, MD
(559) 433-9170

LOS ANGELES

Michael Galitzer, MD
(800) 392-2623

Hans Gruenn, MD
(310) 966-9194

Ann Pretre, MD
(310) 839-1510

Joseph Sciabbarrasi, MD
(310) 268-8466

Michael P. Wai Lam, MD
(213) 383-0105

LOS GATOS

Phillip Lee Miller, MD
(408) 358-8855

NEWPORT BEACH

Catherine Arvantely, MD
(949) 660-1399

ORANGE

Gary Ruelas, MD
(714) 771-2880

PASADENA

Maria Sulindro, MD
(626) 403-6200

REDDING

Robert Greene, MD
(530) 244-9052

SAN DIEGO

Joseph Filbeck, MD
(848) 457-5700

Ron Rothenberg, MD
(800) 943-3331

SANTA BARBARA

Robert Mathis, MD
(805) 569-7100

Julie Taguchi, MD
(805) 681-7500

Duncan Turner, MD
(805) 682-6340

SANTA MONICA

David Allen, MD
(310) 966-9194

Prudence Hall, MD
(310) 458-7979

SANTEE

Stephen Center, MD
(858) 273-5757

UPLAND

Wendy Miller Rashidi, MD
(909) 982-4000

WOODLAND HILLS

Jerel Tilton, MD
(818) 704-5500

Authors' contact information

James W. Forsythe, MD HMD
Century Wellness Clinic
& Cancer Screening & Treatment Center of Nevada
Toll Free: 877-789-0707
521 Hammill Lane, Reno, NV 89511
www.drforsythe.com
Voice, 775-827-0707; Fax, 775-827-1006

Stay Informed About the Latest Anti-Aging Developments

You can have access to the most up-to-date information on the latest anti-aging discoveries and products by subscribing to Dr. James Forsythe's monthly newsletter, *Fountain Of Youth,* which provides practical advice on how you can apply cutting-edge medical science research on aging and the health problems usually associated with aging. Go to www.get fountainofyouth.com and subscribe now!

Index

About the Author

James W. Forsythe, MD, HMD has long been considered one of the most respected physicians in the United States, particularly for his treatment of cancer and the legal use of human growth hormone.

In the early 1960s, Dr. Forsythe earned his MD from the University of California, San Francisco, before spending two years residency in Pathology at Tripler Army Hospital in Honolulu. After a tour of Vietnam, he returned to San Francisco and completed an internal medicine residency and an oncology fellowship.

Today in Reno, Nevada, Dr. Forsythe maintains a conventional medical clinic, the Cancer Screening and Treatment Center, and a homeopathic practice, Century Wellness Clinic. A former associate professor of medicine at the University of Nevada School of Medicine, Dr. Forsythe has conducted numerous original and clinical outcome-based studies on many natural substances. For more than twenty years, he has been interested in integrating alternative and conventional medicine.